The Failure and the Future of Accounting

To my family

The Failure and the Future of Accounting

Strategy, Stakeholders, and Business Value

DAVID HATHERLY

GOWER

Gower Applied Business Research
Our programme provides leaders, practitioners, scholars and researchers with thought provoking, cutting edge books that combine conceptual insights, interdisciplinary rigour and practical relevance in key areas of business and management.

Published by
Gower Publishing Limited
Wey Court East
Union Road
Farnham
Surrey, GU9 7PT
England

Ashgate Publishing Company
110 Cherry Street
Suite 3-1
Burlington,
VT 05401-3818
USA

www.gowerpublishing.com

British Library Cataloguing in Publication Data
Hatherly, David J.
 The failure and the future of accounting : strategy,
 stakeholders, and business value.
 1. Accounting--Standards. 2. Corporations--Auditing--
 Standards. 3. Disclosure in accounting. 4. Corporations--
 Valuation. 5. Intangible property--Accounting.
 6. Misleading financial statements.
 I. Title
 657-dc23

 ISBN: 978-1-4094-5354-3 (hbk)
 ISBN: 978-1-4094-5355-0 (ebk – PDF)
 ISBN: 978-1-4094-6249-1 (ebk – ePUB)

Library of Congress Cataloging-in-Publication Data
Hatherly, David J.
 The failure and the future of accounting : strategy, stakeholders, and business value / by
 David Hatherly.
  p. cm.
 Includes bibliographical references and index.
 ISBN 978-1-4094-5354-3 (hardback) -- ISBN 978-1-4094-5355-0 (ebook) 1. Accounting. I.
 Title.
 HF5636.H38 2013
 657--dc23

2012032131

Printed and bound in Great Britain by the
MPG Books Group, UK

Contents

List of Figures

List of Tables

List of Abbreviations

AOE	Abnormal operating earnings
AP	Accounting profit
Capex	Capital expenditure
CCP	Currently consumable product
CDO	Collateralised debt obligation
CEO	Chief Executive Officer
CI	Comprehensive income
CUVI	Current use value of intangibles
ESTA	Equity stake in traditional assets
FA	Fixed assets
GDP	Gross domestic product
GOV	Growth and opportunity value
IT	Information technology
LEADERS	Leverage, engage, align, develop, reshape
LTRP	Long-term reward plan
M & A	Mergers and acquisitions
MC	Market capitalisation
MVA	Market value added
NBV	Net book value
NVP	Net value of promises
NHS	National Health Service
NICE	National Institute for Health and Clinical Excellence
OCI	Other comprehensive income
PBI	Profit before interest
R and D	Research and development
RI	Residual income
ROCE	Return on capital employed
ROE	Return on equity
ROTA	Return on total assets
RRSP	Risk and revenue sharing partner

SGA	Selling general and administrative (costs)
SKN	Stakeholder Knowledge Network
SMD	Systems maximise delivery (teaching case)
SPE	Special purpose entity
UK	United Kingdom
US	United States
WACC	Weighted average cost of capital
WC	Working capital
WE	Weekend experience (teaching case)
WLEC	World's largest energy company
WMM	We make markets
4S	4 slices (of equity)

About the Author

David Hatherly was born in Bradford but grew up in Chelmsford, Essex, where he attended the local grammar school. He holds an economics degree from Cardiff University and a Masters in Accounting from the University of Glasgow. He qualified as an accountant with Peat Marwick Mitchell in London. He was, for 20 years, a Professor of Accounting at the University of Edinburgh where he held various positions, including Head of Accounting and Finance and Director of The University of Edinburgh Management School. He had previously served as Director of Accounting and Auditing Research at the Institute of Chartered Accountants of Scotland. He is now an Emeritus Professor, contactable at D.Hatherly@ed.ac.uk.

Preface

Some 16 years ago after the part-time MBA class, one of my students, Robin McLean, came up to me and said 'I would like you to meet my father'. Robin's late father, Ralph, and his four sons ran the family business providing electronic point-of-sale equipment (cash tills) and the accompanying software to chains of public houses in the UK. There was a much smaller operation in Florida supporting bars and restaurants. Ralph had been a pub owner himself and knew what was needed by way of management information to protect and enhance revenue. He had started experimenting with management systems on his own personal computer before approaching a specialist to develop a commercial software product. I met Ralph and Robin a number of times in the pub round the corner from their offices in Edinburgh's New Town. After a few meetings they invited me to come and join the Board as a non-executive. The pub meetings were not formal interviews – everything about the company was informal – but they would ask me questions. For instance, Ralph explained that the company had just developed software for one of their biggest customers. The customer had introduced the 'happy hour' (actually a happy two hours) and needed the prices in all of its 600 pubs to halve at five o'clock and go back again, spot on, at seven o'clock. The developed software did this automatically across the whole pub estate thus preventing any sales at the lower prices except between the appropriate times. Ralph was keen to roll out the new software to the rest of his customer base but the original customer was not keen for this to happen. How would I handle this?

There were many such issues pertaining to the management of a network of customers who for the most part were happy to pool software development costs but on occasion, when they felt competitive advantage was at stake, were not. The customer network was a case of what is termed 'co-opetition', a sometimes delicate balance of cooperation and competition. I found that my understanding of Zonal, the till company I had joined, depended in significant measure upon my understanding of the customer and other stakeholder networks. An important issue was how those networks handled the development and dissemination of knowledge. It took a little while for me to gain a good understanding of the company and thus to be able to deliver what Ralph and Robin wanted, namely help with the analysis of the financial numbers and to lead discussions of strategy. The reason for retelling some of my experience with the till company is that it was the first time I thought of the stakeholder network as an intermediary to connect strategy and the accounting numbers, and this book owes much to those Zonal experiences. In more formal terms, the book aims to provide a new understanding of accounting based upon an understanding of business that comes from the coordination of three different representations of business – business as strategy, business as a stakeholder network and business as value.

Discussions of strategy at Zonal could be robust and did not follow any text book. On one occasion two directors returned from Taiwan sporting a touch screen till which could host our software and was substantially less cost than the tills we assembled ourselves in a small facility just outside Edinburgh. Most of the Board wanted to pull out of till assembly and buy the till from Taiwan, but Ralph was having none of it. He was proud of the fact that the company was manufacturing in Britain and pronounced that our own tills must be redesigned to match the Taiwanese on cost. He had no idea whether this could be done, but it was done. Someone recommended a hardware designer who redesigned our till to meet the cost specification. We were very impressed. Of course we could have taken the new design to Taiwan for production but no-one was going to raise that possibility! I realised that Ralph's view was right for our workers and in a small way it was right for Britain's balance of payments. Ralph's instincts were not so much that we were giving up profit, but that somehow profit did not give the right answer. For my part, I began to wonder about the relationship, or rather a lack of relationship, between accounting and the needs of the macro economy and this concern is a feature of the book and of my search for a new accounting.

Zonal had been founded with one dominant Edinburgh-based customer, Scottish and Newcastle, and, when following a dispute that customer went elsewhere for its new tills, Zonal was struggling. What kept the company going at that time were the maintenance contracts to keep the old tills running in Scottish and Newcastle's pub estate. Consequently, Robin and Ralph had a reverence for the maintenance side of the business. However, it struck me as odd that the maintenance of the tills should be steady business whilst the sale of the very same tills which gave the customer service over their useful lives was not regarded as steady business since sales tended to be unpredictable. I felt this volatility was an artefact of accounting rather than the reality of the business. I wondered if the sale of the till was really deferred income and should be released to profit over the till's useful life to match its consumption (depreciation) by the customer and its maintenance. To my mind, precautionary cash should be held back to cover the deferred income. Of course we did not change our accounting to accommodate these thoughts, and these specific thoughts have not been carried forward in this book since in any case the information to make the adjustments is not readily available from published accounts. However, the till experience once again illustrated the difficult relationship between the macro economy, with its need to match production with consumption, and on the other hand, accounting. Around the same time, I was doing consultancy work for what was then Her Majesty's Customs and Excise, helping with their trader visit strategy to check value added tax payments. It always seemed neat that the tax followed the creation of value through the economy so that in principle at least, value added by the individual traders summed to the value added in the economy as the tax base. No such neatness or discipline seems to exist in corporate reporting or in respect of taxes based upon reported profits.

The book therefore has one major theme, being the coordination of strategy, stakeholder networks and accounting, with an important secondary theme being the coordination of accounting with the need of the macro economy to match production and consumption. The book will demonstrate how the two themes are interconnected.

The imbalance between production and consumption came to the fore as a consequence of the 2008 financial crisis. Of course, there are potentially two sides to the matching of consumption and production. One is when speculation gains are used to fuel consumption rather than productive investment and the other is when gains from production are reinvested or saved rather than used to support consumption. In the light of the financial crisis and its association in the United Kingdom (UK) and other deficit nations with consumption in excess of production, the book focuses on the former and in particular the role of accounting in the chain of speculation which is largely the province of the financial industry. Less attention is paid to the role of accounting as a performance measure in the circumstances where production exceeds consumption as would be the case in surplus nations. The book also pays little attention to the role of accounting in the public services supply chain and the public sector deficit. The relevance of a new accounting to the public sector remains another issue for further thought and development, but as in the private sector, the public sector has the stakeholder (knowledge) network as the key intermediary between strategy and value.

The notion of understanding as being the coordination of different representative media follows the 'cognitivist' approach. I was introduced to Hutchins's work on distributed cognition along with Latour and Callon and their work on networks by my colleague in the Sociology School at Edinburgh, Donald MacKenzie. I am grateful to Donald for his help with these authors, as well as other works on the sociology of knowledge. The process of coordination is not neutral and in our case impacts upon each of the three representations of business. It is the impact upon the representation of business as (equity) value which generates the new accounting.

I call the new accounting 4S (four slice) accounting as it is based upon the analysis of market capitalisation into four funds or slices of equity. My grateful thanks to my many MBA students, and in particular Yuhsin Tang, who have given me feedback on 4S accounting over the years. For similar reasons I am grateful to colleagues in the Centre for Accountability, Governance and Sustainability at the University of South Australia and in The New Thinking Group at the University of Edinburgh Business School. Gavin Kretzschmar, who is now in Barcelona, worked with me on financialisation and we 'chewed the cud' on our many ascents of Arthur's Seat. Jonathan Hayward of Independent Audit gave me a lot of time in the early stages. Finally, I would like to thank my son Andrew for reading chapters and making helpful and encouraging comment. Andrew is an accountant in commerce and it meant a lot to be able to convince him!

My hope for the book is that it will lead to a new accounting that primarily coordinates strategy, stakeholders and value within the business model, but also has the potential to coordinate the macroeconomic model with the business models of the wealth creating sector. I believe that an appropriate (4S) accounting could be the missing ingredient in motivating the economy to respond to the challenge of the financial crisis and the opportunities for growth provided by the subsequent economic stimulus measures introduced by government. If our economy needs one thing but our performance measures in the wealth creating sector motivate something different, then we shouldn't be surprised if our economic performance is disappointing.

David Hatherly
Edinburgh 2012

1

The Internal and External Failure of Accounting

This book aims to provide a new understanding of accounting based upon an understanding of business that comes from the coordination of three different representations of business – business as strategy, business as a stakeholder network and business as value (Figure 1.1). The notion of understanding as being the coordination of different representative media comes from Hutchins's (1995) work on distributed cognition. Commenting upon Hutchins's work, Latour (1995: 4) supports the idea that cognition comes from the propagation and coordination of representations expressed through different media. He states

> Cognition has nothing to do with minds or individuals but with <u>the propagation of representations through various media which are co-ordinated by a very lightly equipped human subject working in a group, inside a culture, with many artefacts and who might have internalized some parts of the process</u>. [underlining in the original]

The process of coordination of representations coming through various media is not neutral and in this case impacts upon each of the three representations of business. It is the impact upon the representation of business as (equity) value which generates the new accounting. Equity value is the value of the shareholders' stake in the business.

To achieve coordination between strategy and the stakeholder network, strategy needs to be represented in terms of the stakeholder network. Hence strategy is described in terms of the leverage, engagement, alignment and development of the network, itself represented as a set of stakeholder propositions. In order to coordinate the stakeholder network with business value, the stakeholder propositions are in turn coordinated with equity

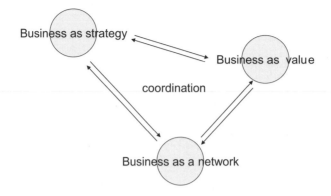

Figure 1.1   Coordinating three representations of business

represented by four funds (or slices) of equity value. The four slices of equity provide a new comprehensive balance sheet whilst movements within and between the four slices give the new comprehensive income. The evaluation of the business provided by the 'new' accounting does not sit outside the business model but is integral to it and leads to the reshaping of the stakeholder network and possibly the strategy itself. The point is that it is important for any business model to know how it will react to its own success or failure. Overall, the business model, being the articulation of how business is carried out, is represented by the mnemonic LEADERS. LEADERS stands for *Leverage*, *Engage*, *Align*, *Develop* (the strategic dimensions of the model), *Evaluate* (the accounting dimension of the model) and, on the basis of the evaluation, (*Re*) *Shape* the stakeholder network. For accounting to play its feedback role within this business model effectively, it must coordinate with both strategy and the stakeholder network.

Much of this book is concerned with the internal failure of accounting. The internal failure of accounting is its failure to coordinate with (the rest of) the business model. Through coordination, accounting should not merely measure economic success; it should explain how that success (or failure) has been achieved and thereby identify the nature of the value created. Accounting should not stand outside the business but should be integral to the business and play a crucial role in its learning dynamics. To meet this challenge, the business model and the accounting model must be 'co-developed', a process that gives insights on both accounting and on business. The then incoming President of the English Institute of Chartered Accountants, Martin Hagen, was reported in *Accountancy* (Beattie 2009: 39) as being adamant that auditors are not to blame

for the 2008 credit crisis. He is quoted as saying, 'Let's be clear –'
has been turmoil in the markets is that businesses had inappr/
models for the circumstances'. But if inappropriate business
revealed by the reporting arrangements of which accounting ...
a central part, what is the use of financial reporting? We need an accounting
which reveals any deficiencies in how business is carried out.

Coordinating with the Stakeholder Network

To understand the performance of the business we need to know not just *how
much* value is created, but *how* value is created, *who* it is created for, *what kind*
of value is created and *how* it is measured. We need an accounting model that
covers each of these questions.

First of all business gets done and *value is created* through the capabilities
of a network of stakeholders – customers, suppliers, employees, investors,
government, management and of course the company itself which contributes
capability in the form of fixed assets and intangibles such as patents. The
company as a legal entity creates the network by contracting with other
stakeholders but it is also a stakeholder in its own network. The idea that
action takes place through networks of human and non-human actors is well
established in the sociology of knowledge (see, for example, Callon 2008).
Callon makes the point that actions (upon which business depends), such as
piloting a plane or a shopper choosing between products in a supermarket,
are possible because of distributed action and cognition around a network of
'actors'. For business actions, knowledge is distributed around the stakeholder
network and accessed through stakeholder relationships. This focus on access
challenges traditional entity concepts for accounting based upon ownership
and/or control. Control influences the risks attaching to access and ownership
influences control, but access is the key intangible that in particular drives the
new economy. The stakeholder network represents the distributed nature of
modern business where knowledge/capability, reward, risk and value are all
distributed.

WHO IS THE VALUE FOR?

The business creates value for all the stakeholders but if we are accounting to
the company's investors then they are primarily concerned with the value that
the network creates for them as investors. Thus we should be accounting for the

value of equity, rather than the value of the network or the value of the entity as a legal construct. Consequently, we need an accounting which analyses the movement in total equity value, taken to be market capitalisation, whilst relating this movement to the business model. It may indeed be possible to apply the concept of coordinating (strategic) direction, a stakeholder network and stakeholder values in other arenas such as the public sector and non-listed companies but these applications are not directly the focus of this book which is primarily concerned with accounting for equity in listed companies.

WHAT KIND OF VALUE?

The book introduces a six-dimensional stakeholder proposition in which the selection, engagement and alignment of stakeholders depends upon: (1) the specification of the product to be provided; (2) the price and volume; (3) the stakeholder knowledge and capabilities required (4) the nature of the relationship with the stakeholder; (5) the contractual promises made to the stakeholder; and (6) prospects for the entity and its business model (based upon non-contractual expectations). These are the six dimensions of the proposition that the company in effect makes to each stakeholder.

These dimensions are followed through to both returns and risk in order to identify how and where the network creates value. It is shown that equity value can reside in four distinct funds – the four slices of equity – being: (1) the traditional assets of tangibles and working capital; (2) intangibles; (3) promises; and (4) prospects.

HOW IS VALUE MEASURED?

Each of the four funds corresponds to both a different kind of value and a different kind of measurement. The 'value' of the *traditional assets* (net of loans) is taken to be the same as currently given in the reported financial statements. *Intangibles* are taken as the capitalised value of the current residual profit; residual profit being what is left after providing an appropriate return on the traditional assets. Thus the value of both traditional assets and intangibles is underpinned by the profitability of current production and together they form the 'productive equity capital'. *Promises*, which can include pensions, warranties, deferred tax, derivatives and fixed price contracts, are taken at fair value net of any precautionary assets set aside. *Prospects* are valued as market capitalisation adjusted for the values of the other three funds and it is the credibility of this valuation which becomes the focus of attention for the investor. Promises and prospects both derive their value from expectations rather than current production and hence form the 'speculative equity capital'.

Coordinating with Strategy

Currently accounting is most suited to an 'old economy' company in which strategy is designed to maximise returns on the traditional assets. However, the better option for many companies, particularly those primarily based in a developed (high cost, high technology) nation, is to compete for ideas in the new economy rather than to compete on cost and volume in the old. A 'new economy' business strategy is one which builds and exploits (leverages) the strengths of the stakeholder network, particularly those network intangibles connected with leading-edge knowledge and innovative propositions to customers and other stakeholders. Leverage in the new economy comes not only through increasing volumes but also increasing margins to reflect the leading-edge nature of the product. For services in the new economy the margin often flows from the ability to adapt the product to the specific needs of the customer. Investment in intangibles is higher risk and potentially higher reward than investment in fixed assets for the production of established products. Indeed a strategy to exploit intangibles drives the company into riskier business activities and consequently seeks to share or reposition the risks and rewards across the stakeholder network (Miller, Kurunmaki and O'Leary 2008). For this purpose, there may be risk and reward sharing agreements between the company and its suppliers, customers, employees, directors and financial institutions in addition to the traditional arrangements with shareholders. Moreover, risk and reward sharing is intended to help bind the stakeholder network together by engaging stakeholders and aligning them with the objectives of the company. The knowledge and capability of the stakeholder network leverages the capabilities of the company itself.

Risk and reward sharing agreements facilitate the implementation of any new economy business strategy. However, they are contractual promises and they leave a legacy for the future since the value of the contracts will move, at times unpredictably, as part of a changing environment and changing expectations. If not properly managed, this legacy itself can be a substantial source of risk for the company. The company should hold liquid 'precautionary' assets to cover this risk as well as 'opportunity' cash necessary to invest quickly in, and take early advantage of, any new ideas and knowledge 'breakthroughs'.

It follows from this brief discussion of strategy that a new accounting should: (1) focus upon the performance and leverage of intangibles; (2) be responsive to the impact of risk in any strategy of leveraging intangibles; and (3) recognise separately the legacy value of promises made to reposition risk and reward around the network. There is a fourth requirement which is discussed in the next section: it is to distinguish the gains from productive activity and the gains from speculation.

Production and Speculation

Following the 2008 crisis, a lesson that should be learnt is the need to distinguish the results of production and speculation. Profits from 'production' occur when an activity produces outputs which are the subject of current consumption. The value of the outputs is matched with the corresponding inputs to give what might be termed phase one (productive) profit. The flow of future 'phase one' profits can be capitalised to give their capital value and this securitisation/monetisation gives rise to an increase in assets and 'phase two' profits. Subsequent changes in this capital value give 'phase three' profits. 'Phase four' profits come from commissions, fees and other charges that are associated with the initial capitalisation or with the management, trading or repackaging of existing capital. They are not associated with current production and are thus, like phase two and three, speculative. If speculative gains/profits lead to excessive salaries, bonuses, dividends and taxation which are spent on consumption, then, from a macroeconomic viewpoint, the economy becomes unbalanced insofar as there is no matching production. An economy is regarded as unbalanced when consumption runs ahead of production.

This book will argue that distributions, whether in the form of dividends, excessive salaries, bonuses or taxation, should be restricted to the yield on productive capital. Realised gains on speculative capital should be reinvested in productive capital and not distributed as these represent either wealth transfers or changed expectations as to the future and do not relate to current production. Distribution of speculative gains has been a particular problem in relation to financial institutions, notably banks. A bank's productive capital exists in respect of banking activities when the activity, such as a business loan, is an input to a business conducting productive activity. Apart from this, most banking activity can be identified as speculative activity by the bank or its clients, or as lending to individuals to support consumption. Lending for consumption has played its part in unbalancing the economy and profits from this activity can be termed 'phase five'. The problem is that when the economy needs more production and less consumption and speculation, rewarding on the basis of profits other than phase one profit motivates resources and talent toward non-productive activity.

An Unbalanced Economy

The macroeconomic indicators associated with an unbalanced economy (high on consumption and speculation, low on production) are well known and include excessive borrowing, an unconstrained financial sector, the sale of assets (notably infrastructure) to overseas buyers, unfunded and inadequately funded pension promises and, above all, persistent trading imbalances. The UK for instance has not had a significant trade surplus since the early 1980s and even then there was a substantial reliance upon North Sea oil and gas. Unlike say Kazakhstan, the UK did not create a sovereign wealth fund to try and sustain, albeit in a different form, the nation's capital inherited in the form of natural resources. Conversely, there are other unbalanced economies which are low on consumption, high on production and with 'excessive' savings. Market mechanisms have either failed, or not been allowed, to deal with these imbalances. It is the imbalance between consumption and production which, colliding with financial innovation (Turner 2009), took us into the financial crisis of 2008 and it is these imbalances which make it difficult to grow out of the crisis. There is a popular view that deficit nations should go for growth and sort out the imbalances after the economy has been kick-started through stimulus policies. This, however, assumes that how to sort out the imbalances is understood. The problem is that for any already badly unbalanced economy with inadequate productive capability, supporting consumption through low interest rates or increased government spending tends to suck in imports and the economic imbalance between production and consumption is liable to continue or even deteriorate. Persistent trading imbalances will ultimately challenge the viability of globalisation and open markets. Stimulus should therefore be accompanied by incentives to rebalance the economy, and accounting has an important role to play here.

In particular, the accounting for banks and other financial institutions is crucial. It is argued that the banks should only be permitted to distribute gains from lending to businesses for productive investment and that all other gains, once realised, should not be distributed but should be invested in productive activity. It follows that banks need to report both the sources of profit (whether phase one, two, three, four or five) and the destination of realised gains. Arguably the financial reporting by banks does not currently do this with clarity. Consequently, the accounts of the banks provide little help for the management of the economy. Moreover, given that the fortunes of the banks and those of the economy are intimately linked, it seems reasonable to assert that the banks' accounts provide little help either for those charged with governance of the banks. A one way accounting 'valve' in which speculative gains can be invested in production but not vice versa serves to meet the UK government's concern that UK taxpayers should be insulated from the downside of speculative activity and the concern that banks are not sufficiently incentivised to support non-financial business.

The proximate cause of the 2008 financial crisis was irresponsible lending in the United States (US) housing market. Because the mortgages could not be repaid, capital was being lost but this was not recognised in good time by the accounting. This was a serious business failure and an accounting failure but, as has been argued, there is a deeper problem with accounting for financial activities than the timing of bad debts and impairments. The deeper issue is that much financial sector activity has the potential to imbalance the economy by converting capital in the form of speculative gains into consumption without, at present, this being recognised at all in the accounting for the financial institution. This is because the accounting for the financial institution is concerned with the maintenance of the institution's financial capital and not with the maintenance of the productive economy as a whole. Speculative gains boost a financial institution's financial capital but add nothing to the current production of the economy. And so the charge against accounting is that it reports the 'capital into consumption' activities of the financial sector as good news (increased profits and balance sheets) when in fact, from a wider perspective, it may not be. This charge uses the classic externality argument used to criticise accounting for its failure to recognise pollution from manufacturing, except this is the 'pollution' of the economy by the financial sector. The circumstances where the profits and balance sheets of the financial sector expand much faster than those of the productive sector that financial services are there to support is termed financialisation (see for example Elliott and Atkinson 2008: 17). With financialisation the financial sector absorbs an inappropriate level of capital, talent and consumption, and the productive economy struggles. There is both underinvestment (in production) and misdirected investment (toward the financial sector).

Accounting has an important job to do. It is to help direct financial capital (plus human talent and other resources) to the most productive sites in the economy by signposting both the size and *nature* of current economic success. Gains from productive activity must be distinguished from speculative gains. This is not to say that speculative gains are necessarily a bad thing. It is part of good management to improve the company's positioning for the future and it is this improvement which is reflected in speculative gain embedded in the equity value as 'promises' and 'growth and opportunity'. However, the future has yet to be delivered and such gains should not be distributed but should be invested in productive capability. Accounting has a second important job to do by signalling how much we can distribute for consumption without unbalancing the economy. When applied to an economy, Hick's famous maxim (Hicks 1946: 172) that 'A man's income is the maximum value which he can consume during a week, and still expect to be as well off at the end of the week as he was at the beginning' implies that consumption should not run ahead of production.

Thus the external failure of accounting is the failure to look beyond capital maintenance in the entity to the impact of the entity's activities on (productive) capital maintenance in the economy as a whole. It is important to recognise that just as accounting has an important job to do for the economy by directing resources, so the managers of the economy have an important responsibility to support accounting. For instance, accounting's roles, and those of taxation and regulation which depend upon accounting, can be undermined by inflation and/or the artificial pricing of interest which distorts interest expense and thus asset and liability prices.

So What Should the New Financial Reporting Look Like?

Comprehensive accounts should be divided into four sections showing movements within and between the four slices of equity. Impairments should be charged through the 'prospects' section and movements in derivatives and other promises through the 'promises' section. The business review should connect the four funds to both strategy and the stakeholder network. Traditional 'one fund' performance measures such as return on capital and earnings per share are irrelevant. It will be shown that accounting for leases and, in particular, business combinations should be considerably simplified. The user needs to see how much of the change in each of the four funds has been purchased as a result of the acquisition. Upon an acquisition the price paid should be distributed across the four funds acquired and these funds proportionally consolidated with the existing equivalent funds of the acquirer. There is no goodwill, no impairment testing of goodwill and no minority interest. Leases are not capitalised since there is no equity funding of leased assets and the need is to account for the equity stake in the network. Leases like loans and long-term fixed price commitments are an important part of the analysis of risk in the business review. The current cash flow statement should be revised. Management hold cash as liquidity for each of the four funds. The cash flow presentation should track cash changes within and between the funds whilst the business review explains management's view of these. The impact on accounting is considerable whilst the business review is given a new sense of direction.

The proposed accounting model – four slice (4S) accounting – allows managers and shareholders to analyse the effectiveness of the business model and therefore for management to be held to account. The proposal prevents the misreporting of speculative gains as distributable income and therefore allows capital to be better allocated towards productive enterprise. Financial crises such as that in 2008 become less likely and recovery from the financial crisis more doable since the balance and generation of equity value between production and speculation is clearly signalled.

The book proceeds as follows: Chapter 2 gives a brief introduction to the basics of traditional accounting sufficient to enable the reader to follow the arguments of the book. Traditional accounting is explained as a 'one fund' model. It also contains a critique of traditional performance measures such as return on capital, and has a brief but important discussion on the role of accounting-based performance measures in the economy. Chapter 2 provides an introduction to the case used in Chapter 12 to illustrate 4S accounts and the 4S business review. Chapter 3 covers the Enron case as an exemplar of the feedback failures of current accounting and a harbinger of the 2008 financial crisis. Five years before the credit crunch, with Enron's demise, the profession received its first warning of the future. Enron adopted the techniques of Wall Street to transform an old economy company based upon fixed assets into a new economy company based upon knowledge of markets and risk. Enron's demise was a harbinger of bigger things to come on Wall Street itself and a clear expression of the inadequacy of the existing financial reporting model to reflect and to capture the effects and risks of the (new economy) business model.

Chapters 4 and 5 introduce the Stakeholder Knowledge Network (SKN) as an example of distributed knowledge and its central role in the LEADERS business model. Chapter 4 deals with the structural development of the SKN. Chapter 5 deals with the SKN as a framework for analysing a company's valuation taken to be its market capitalisation. This analysis is given in the 4S balance sheet that divides market capitalisation into the four slices of equity (four funds). Risk and reward are both integral to the analysis and Chapter 6 'understands' these concepts in the context of the coordination of business risk as: (1) strategy risk; (2) stakeholder risk (the SKN is considered as a risk matrix); and (3) risks to business value. Chapter 7 discusses 4S accounting for intangibles over a period before and after the 2008 crisis with Halma, the health and safety products manufacturer, and DMGT, the media company, as case studies. The two companies have different types of intangible assets. Chapter 8 covers the 4S accounting for promises and it includes the takeover of engineering company FKI by Melrose and Rolls Royce's treatment of foreign exchange derivatives during the 2008 financial crisis as cases. The first case focuses upon the 'implied promise' of sustaining production capability. The second focuses on the 'promise' of derivative contracts.

Chapter 9 studies the relationship between 4S accounting and strategic choice. It is the relationship between 4S accounting and the SKN together with the relationship between the SKN and strategy which help provide insight on accounting's relationship with strategy. In this sense, accounting and strategy are 'coordinated' through the stakeholder knowledge network. Chapter 9 draws on a number of well-known companies to demonstrate the issues. These include the issue of reporting for acquisitions, since acquisitions are an important strategic choice for growth and development. The chapter uses the case of Croda International's acquisition of Uniqema. Chapter 10 discusses the relationship between 4S accounting and 'financialisation', demonstrating the relevance of 4S as a response to both the internal and external failures of current accounting. This chapter is based upon joint work with Gavin Kretzschmar, published in the academic journal *Accounting Forum* (Hatherly and Kretzschmar 2011). Chapter 11 discusses the significance of 4S accounting for today's accounting and business reporting. It suggests some radical changes to current reporting notably in the reporting of comprehensive income, the reporting of acquisitions, the reporting of cash management and the reporting by banks. Chapter 12 provides an illustration of how 4S accounts build from traditional accounts to provide a frame for the 4S business review which expresses a coordination of strategy, stakeholders and business value, the emphasis being on the coordination of strategy and the 4S accounts.

Chapter 13 is a concluding summary demonstrating the new 'landscape' for the future of accounting, and its relevance to the management of companies, investments and the wider economy.

2

The Inadequacy of Traditional Accounting

The financial accounting that we use today has its origins in an 'old' economy, where companies produce physical products from machines located in factories. It is an economy where *financial* capital in the form of shares and loans is used to pay for the *physical* capital of machines and factories and to provide cash as *'working* capital', needed because employees and creditors are generally paid before the cash comes in from customers. The accountant's traditional model of business pays little attention to networks even though an old economy company needs a network of stakeholders. To accounting, the old economy is one where business creates a balance sheet by issuing shares and taking on liabilities to enable investment in tangible assets, and then conducts business transactions so as to strengthen its balance sheet. The difference between the opening and closing balance sheets, allowing for capital payments and dividends during the year, is profit. Two principal performance measures are the return on equity and the return on assets (capital) employed. The return on assets is the multiple of the asset turnover (sales/assets) and margins (profit/ sales). In the old economy there are usually several companies producing very similar products, margins are low and costs must be a focus of management in order to maintain margins. It is also important to maximise the use of the fixed assets (maximise asset turnover).

The accounting profession's response to the increased importance of intangibles and to the greater risk and risk sharing that comes with the new economy has been one of trying to fit intangibles and risk sharing contracts into the traditional old economy model and/or to supplement the model with information on intangibles and risk. For example, the advent of risk shifting contracts such as derivatives has pushed the profession towards the inclusion of fair values on the balance sheet, but in the absence of a strong conceptual basis for financial reporting this is done somewhat piecemeal. Movements in the value of derivatives can be taken to profit or to other changes in equity, depending upon the circumstances. The rationale for these different treatments remains unclear. Similarly, the profession has included intangibles on the balance sheet when they are purchased from a third party, perhaps as part of a company acquisition, but intangibles internally generated, for example through research and development, are excluded. Accounting does not yet have a coherent approach to the new economy.

This chapter takes a simple hypothetical company – Systems Maximise Delivery (SMD plc) – to explain the traditional financial statements and performance measures. It hopefully provides a level of understanding of current accounting that helps the reader who is not a trained accountant follow most of the rest of the book. For the trained accountant, the chapter provides familiarity with the SMD case which is, in Chapter 12, used to illustrate the 4S accounts and (4S) business review. The closing section examines briefly the relationship between traditional performance measures based on returns and the difficulties in managing the (UK) economy. This is an important discussion. In Chapter 12, SMD is used to illustrate how 4S accounting both builds from, and takes a more coherent approach than, the traditional accounts. To illustrate both accountings, SMD has been used because, like many companies, both the old and new economy ideas are relevant. It has substantial investment in its fixed assets of vehicles, storage facilities and sales sites. At the same time it invests in research and development (R and D) to promote its leading edge technology in logistics and pricing models. It is also highly dependent upon its network of suppliers and customers as well as the loyalty and experience of its employees.

With the exception of the term 'equity', this chapter mostly uses traditional British accounting terminology and Table 2.1 is designed to help those readers who are more familiar with the equivalent US terms. Many of the US terms are also used in the UK.

Table 2.1   UK versus US terms

UK only	US and UK
shareholder funds	equity
shares	stock
loans	debt
stocks	inventory
creditors	accounts payable
debtors	accounts receivable
profit	income, earnings
sales turnover	sales revenue
loss	negative income

SMD: The Traditional Accounts

SMD is a supplier to builders' merchants. At the end of year 1 the market capitalisation (number of shares times share price) is £119.58 m and at the end of year 2 it is £133.52 m. Its conventional balance sheets at the beginning and end of the year are as shown in Table 2.2.

Table 2.2   SMD balance sheet

	Year (X+)1 £m	Year (X+)2 £m
Fixed assets at cost	60	70
Provision for depreciation	(30)	(34)
Intangible	12	10
Cash	25	33.94
Other current assets (net)	18	20
Loans	(20)	(25)
Employee long-term reward plan	(16)	(22)
Equity (book value)	49	52.94

The balance sheet gives not the value of the equity stake in the company, which may be taken to be the market capitalisation of £133.52 m at the end of year 2, but the 'book' value of equity of £52.94 m. The balance sheet shows the composition of a different construct – book equity. Book equity comprises assets (the positive numbers in Table 2.2) less liabilities and provisions (the negative numbers shown in brackets). In SMD's accounts, the assets and most of the liabilities/provisions are shown at the value of the originating transaction. Fixed assets and loans can be taken to illustrate this.

FIXED ASSETS AND LOANS

The balance sheet at the end of year 2 shows that the fixed assets were originally purchased for £70 m. The provision for depreciation at the end of year 2 (£34 m in Table 2.2) is also based upon the cost of £70 m. Depreciation reflects the consumption or wearing out of the asset through usage. The ratio of 34 / 70 (0.486) shows that the fixed assets are on average 48.6 per cent through their expected useful life. They are getting on average very slightly younger since the previous year they were 50 per cent (30 / 60) of the way through their expected life. There is a significant amount of judgment in accounting and the expected useful life of the fixed assets is one of the biggest judgments. In many published balance sheets it is the net fixed assets, being cost less depreciation provision, which is shown on the face of the balance sheet and the individual details of cost and depreciation are given in a note. The net figure is known as the net book value of the fixed assets. However Table 2.2 shows both cost and the depreciation provision. The balance sheet item 'fixed assets at cost' is increased by the cost of the assets when new fixed assets are purchased and reduced by the original cost of the fixed assets when they are scrapped or sold. The balance sheet item 'provision for depreciation', also known as cumulative depreciation, is increased (a larger negative number) as the cumulative asset usage increases, but is reduced by the accumulated depreciation on any asset that is scrapped or sold. The movement of fixed assets during year 2 is shown in Table 2.3.

It should be noted from the footnote to Table 2.7 that the company made a profit of £7 m on disposal of fixed assets. As shown by Table 2.3 these disposed assets had an original cost of £5 m and cumulative depreciation of £2 m. This net book value of £3 m is compared to the sale proceeds of £10 m to give a 'one off' profit on disposal of £7 m. The sale proceeds appear in the cash flow (Table 2.6) and profit on sale appears in the profit statement (Table 2.7). These statements will be discussed shortly.

Table 2.3   Movement of fixed assets

	Year 2 £m
Opening balance (cost)	60
Opening balance (cumulative depreciation)	(30)
Opening net book value	30
Fixed asset purchases	15
Depreciation charge for year	(6)
Cost of disposal	(5)
Cumulative depreciation on disposal	2
Closing balance (cost)	70
Closing balance (cumulative depreciation)	(34)
Closing net book value	36

Loans are also generally shown in the balance sheet at a value taken from the amount of the originating transaction. The balance sheet (Table 2.2) shows that at the end of year 2 SMD had borrowed a total of £25 m. The average interest rate paid on the loans during the year is £1.75 m (interest taken from Table 2.7), over the average loans outstanding of £22.5 m (Table 2.2). This gives 7.78 per cent. If the loans are fixed rate loans and interest rates in the economy suddenly increase then the fixed rate loans are valuable to SMD, whereas if rates fall they are a burden. These changes in the value of the loans are not generally recognised in the balance sheet or profit statement, at least not in a non-financial company. The balance sheet item 'loans' is reduced when loans are repaid and increased when new loans are taken out. During year 2 SMD has borrowed, net of any repayments, a further £5 m. This is slightly less than the increase in the net book value of the fixed assets from £30 m to £36 m, indicating that some, though a small part, of the expansion has been funded from internal resources.

INTANGIBLES

Intangibles and their accounting treatment are discussed in greater detail in Chapter 7 (Accounting for Intangibles). SMD has acquired its intangibles as a result of acquiring a smaller regional competitor some years ago. It paid £30 m cash for the competitor's share capital and consequently acquired fixed assets then valued at £15 m and a working capital of £3 m. In the SMD accounts at the time of the acquisition, the amounts of £15 m and £3 m were added to SMD's own fixed assets and working capital respectively and £30 m subtracted from cash. The other £12 m of the acquisition price not represented by fixed assets or working capital was paid for intangibles not on the competitor's balance sheet. Most of the intangibles related to the competitor's customer base which at the time was profitable. Accordingly, the intangible was included in the SMD balance sheet and subjected to annual impairment testing. Impairment testing means that each year the future cash flows of the acquired branches are considered in order to assess whether they continue to justify the value of the intangible on the SMD balance sheet. The acquired company's branches are in a depressed area which has been hit by recession and are likely to continue to struggle for some time. Accordingly, it has been decided that the value of the goodwill should be reduced to £10 m corresponding to the discounted value of the relevant expected future cash flows. Table 2.2 shows the intangible of £12 m at the beginning of year 2 reducing to £10 m at the end of the year. This is due to the impairment charge of £2 m.

WORKING CAPITAL

Working capital consists of cash plus items soon to be turned into cash such as stock and debtors less items such as creditors, which are about to be a charge upon cash. In Table 2.2 working capital items other than cash are lumped together as 'other (net) current assets'. The working capital being cash plus other current assets is £53.94 m, up from £43 m the year before. It is generally healthy for working capital to be a positive number as it is for SMD. However, some retailers such as the big supermarkets manage their business so that they take cash from their customers before they pay their suppliers for the goods sold. In this reversal of normal payment timings it is plausible to operate the business with negative or very low working capital. It becomes the suppliers rather than equity (or loans) that provide the working capital. This is a business model dependent upon a certain set of propositions to suppliers and customers. SMD is sensitive to the cash flow needs of its customers and operates with a significant positive working capital.

Non-cash working capital is increased by increases in stock and debtors and reduced by increases in creditors. The movement in non-cash working capital items is given in Table 2.4. As a simplification, Table 2.4 assumes that purchases, depreciation and the value of this year's promises made under the long-term reward plan (LTRP) are charged to stock as being costs of production. Purchases do not appear in Table 2.4 since they increase both stock

Table 2.4   Movement in non-cash working capital

	Movement £m
Opening balance	18
Sales (increasing debtors)	230
Received from debtors	(220.69)
Depreciation charged to stock	6
LTRP promises charged to stock	4
Cost of sales (reducing stock)	(180)
Paid to creditors	162.69
Closing balance	20

and creditors by the same amount and therefore have no net impact upon non-cash working capital. Working capital is also increased by increases in cash. The movement in cash is examined in a financial statement of its own, being the cash flow statement (Table 2.6), and this is examined later. It is not always the case that all of the cash held by a company is necessary or intended to meet routine payments such as purchases and wages. In the case of SMD we shall see that a substantial portion of the cash held is (voluntarily) ring-fenced by the company to support a long-term reward plan for the employees. Cash held for such precautionary purposes should be considered separately from cash held as working capital. This is considered in more detail in the 4S accounts. As a simplification, the example of SMD assumes that no interest is received on the cash balances.

EMPLOYEE LONG-TERM REWARD PLAN (LTRP)

SMD recognises the importance of its experienced employees and offers them a proposition designed to encourage them to stay. After each five years of service an SMD employee admitted to the plan receives a bonus calculated on the basis of the company's performance over the five years. Table 2.5 sets out the financial consequences of the plan. The service cost during year 2 was calculated as £4 m and increases the liability of the company in respect of the LTRP promise (Table 2.5). This is SMD management's assessment of the value of the rewards earned under the scheme in respect of employment during the year by those eligible. These rewards are charged to stock in year 2 (Table 2.4) since it is an employment expense and assumed for simplification to relate to productive workers. In addition, the company's liability for previous service accumulated under the plan was revalued upwards by £4 m due to a lowering of expectations of staff turnover and increasing expectations regarding the company's performance. This revaluation of previous years' service due to changed expectations increases the liability of the company as per Table 2.5, and as will be shown later (Table 2.7) it is treated by SMD as a charge to equity that does not go through profit. Payments under the plan during the year were £2 m. These reduce the company's liability under the scheme and reduce cash. Table 2.5 shows that the year end obligations under the plan increased during year 2 by £6 m, from £16 m to £22 m. As will be revealed in Chapter 12 by the 4S accounts, the company holds £11 m of ring-fenced cash on behalf of the employees in respect of this LTRP promise. The movement in the (value of) promises made under the long-term reward plan is shown in Table 2.5. The opening and closing balances cross-check to Table 2.2.

Table 2.5   Movement in the promises made under the LTRP

	Year 2 £m
Opening balance	(16)
Promises met by payment	2
New promises charged to cost of sales	(4)
Upward revaluation of legacy promises	(4)
Closing balance	(22)

CASH FLOW

The movement in cash during year 2 is shown in Table 2.6. The opening and closing cash balances check with the balance sheets of Table 2.2. Cash is received from debtors (customers) and paid to creditors and to production employees in respect of wages. As per Table 2.5 there is a payment of £2 m made to employees in respect of the LTRP. Interest and dividends are paid to a total of £9.75 m. Cash has been received from loans and disposals to a total of £15 m whilst the sum of £15 m has also been spent on new fixed assets (Table 2.3).The sum of £7m has been spent on research and development.

Table 2.6   **The cash flow statement**

	£ m
Opening cash	25
Cash received from debtors	220.69
Cash paid to creditors and employees	(162.69)
Cash paid for administration and tax	(30.31)
Cash paid in respect of LTRP	(2)
Cash paid for interest and dividends	(9.75)
Cash received from new loans (net)	5
Cash paid for new fixed assets	(15)
Cash received from disposal of fixed asset	10
Cash paid for R and D	(7)
Closing cash	33.94

MOVEMENTS IN EQUITY

The movement in equity is shown in Table 2.7. This shows the movement has two component parts. Of the total movement of £3.94 m (from £49 m to £52.94 m), £7.94 m is accounted for by the retained profit for the year, whilst a reduction of £4 m is accounted for by the revaluation of the company's liability (promise) under the LTRP (Table 2.5). The retained profit is derived from the net profit for the year after tax (£15.94 m) less dividends (£8 m).

Profit for the year comprises sustainable profits plus 'one offs'. Sustainable profits are sales, being the value of outputs delivered to customers, less the value of the matching inputs (expenses) incurred in order to make the sales. These profits are sustainable over time assuming existing business conditions remain. Expenses include the purchase and production costs of the items sold, administration, interest expense and research and development (R and D). The purchase and production costs of items which remain unsold at the end of the year are included in the balance sheet as stock (part of current assets). Research and development expenditure may not match with current sales since it is concerned with developing products for the future. Nevertheless, it is normally written off (charged) against current profits in case it is unsuccessful and no new products are forthcoming. The immediate expensing of R and D is not too much of a distortion of the matching principle provided the R and D expenditures of today are comparable with the R and D expenditures of the past, made in order to create today's products.

Table 2.7   **The profit statement and movement in equity**

	Year 1 £m	Year 2 £m
Sales	200	230
Cost of sales	(160)	(180)
Administration	(20)	(25)
Interest	(1.4)	(1.75)
One offs*		5
Research and development	(4)	(7)
Profit before tax	14.6	21.25
Tax (25%)	3.65	5.31
Net profit	10.95	15.94
Dividends	5	8
To equity	5.95	7.94
Opening equity		49
Retained profit for year		7.94
Revaluation of promises		(4)
Closing equity		52.94

* profit on disposal of £7 m less impairment of intangibles of £2 m.

The 'one offs' for SMD shown as £5 m in Table 2.7 are the profit (£7 m) on disposal of the fixed asset less the impairment of intangibles (£2 m). The profit on disposal implies that the fixed asset was not wearing out as fast as the depreciation charge assumed or that new (and hence disposal) fixed asset prices have risen significantly. Assuming it is the result of a misjudgement of depreciation, then this profit on disposal really belongs in past years rather than current profits. Earlier years have been charged with too much depreciation. However, in the case of SMD it is the rising value of the sites that have been disposed that leads to the profit on disposal. Again this profit has accrued over the years during which the sites have been owned rather than the year of disposal. Once again the profit on disposal really belongs in past years. The impairment charge, on the other hand, arises through a forward look at cash flows which are not found sufficient to justify the full carrying value of the intangible concerned. The write down is anticipating future losses and accelerating them so as to recognise future losses in the current year. Thus the impairment really belongs as losses in future years rather than the current year. The profit on disposal and the impairment are not so much 'one offs' as items credited/charged in the wrong year because they do not match this year's sales. There will be other impairments and disposals in other years. It will be seen that one of the qualities of 4S accounting is a clearer demarcation between the productivity of the present, the legacy of the past and the opportunity of the future.

The Difference Between Cash Flow and Profit

A reconciliation of profit, taken as the net profit before interest (£17.69 m) and cash flow (£8.94 m), is shown in Table 2.8. In terms of Table 2.7 the net profit before interest is the net profit (£15.94 m) plus interest (£1.75 m). The reconciliation presented by Table 2.8 starts with net profit before interest and then takes into account all items where either: (a) the charge to profit differs from the cash paid; or (b) the credit to profit differs from the cash received. In the first case the charge is added to the net profit and replaced by the cash paid. In the second case the credit is subtracted from net profit and replaced by the cash received. Thus, as per Table 2.8, the charge for depreciation (£6 m) is added to net profit and replaced by the cash paid for the purchase of new fixed assets (£15 m). Similarly the charge for the LTRP promise (£4 m) is added to net profit and replaced by the cash paid out under the scheme (£2 m). For the fixed asset disposal, the credit to profit (£7 m) is subtracted from net profit and replaced by the cash proceeds (£10 m).

Adjustments also need to be made when there is a credit or a charge to profit but no equivalent receipt or payment of cash. In the reconciliation, credits with no equivalent cash received are subtracted from net profit and charges without equivalent cash payments are added to net profit. The increase of (other) net current assets (£2 m) shows that profits have, to the amount of £2 m, not flowed through to cash but have been held up (tied up) in current assets such as debtors or stock. In Table 2.8 net profit therefore is reduced by £2 m to adjust for this profit that has no equivalent cash flow. The impairments charge to profit (£2 m) has no cash equivalent and is added to net profit.

Finally, adjustments need to be made for cash payments and receipts that have no equivalent credit or charge to profit. The increase in loans (£5 m) increases cash but has no profit equivalent. The adjustment is an addition to net profit. The payments in respect of dividends and interest (£9.75 m) have no profit equivalent in Table 2.8 since the starting profit of £17.69 m is taken before interest and dividends are charged. The adjustment for these payments is a reduction to net profit.

Table 2.8   The reconciliation of profit and cash flow

	£m
Net profit for year before interest	17.69
Depreciation charged	6
Profit on disposal	(7)
Cash from disposal	10
Movements in other current assets	(2)
Promises charged this year	4
Promises paid this year	(2)
Impairments charged on intangibles	2
Cash from operations	28.69
Additions to fixed assets (investing activity)	(15)
Increase in loans	5
Dividends and interest (financing activity)	(9.75)
Increase in cash (cash flow)	8.94

Traditional Performance Measures

The traditional balance sheet shows equity as a single fund which consists of assets less liabilities and provisions (Table 2.2). This equity fund is increased by profit (less dividends) and reduced by the revaluation of the LTRP promise (Table 2.7). The traditional performance measures, having their origins in the old economy, are the return on equity (ROE) and the return on assets/capital employed (ROCE). In the first measure, the return is to shareholders and is taken after interest and tax have been deducted but before dividends. Thus the return comes either as retained profit, invested in the business on behalf of the shareholders, or as a dividend distribution. The denominator is the (book) equity stake made to earn this return and will normally be the average of the opening and closing equity funds since the profit is earned over the year as a whole. For SMD the return on equity for year 2 is 15.94 / 50.97 which gives a very healthy return of 31.27 per cent. It should be noticed that the revaluation of the LTRP reduces equity but does not reduce profit and therefore tends to distort the rate of return upwards. It is difficult for the ROE to deal with changes in equity that do not flow through the profit statement. With the increasing use of promises in the new economy in order to reposition risk and reward around the stakeholder network, the use of the ROE becomes increasingly problematic.

A second problem with ROE is the treatment of intangibles in the traditional accounting model. The equity fund includes purchased intangibles as a consequence of past acquisitions but it does not include intangibles that are generated internally such as knowledge developed through research and development or stakeholder networks developed through business transacted. The equity fund in traditional accounting therefore understates the shareholders' true equity stake in the business since the true equity stake includes unrecorded intangibles. Moreover, as discussed previously, the profit is charged with current R and D costs and with impairments, both of which can distort this year's profit. The ROE calculation therefore is liable to use a distorted profit and an understated equity. Once again it is unsuitable to the new economy where intangibles (unrecorded equity) play a crucial role.

The second common performance measure is return on capital employed (ROCE). In this measure the return is the return on all long-term capital employed whether from shareholders (equity) or from loan holders. The return therefore is the sum of the return used in the ROE calculation plus interest on the loans. In the case of SMD, the return is £15.94 m plus interest of £1.75 m, giving £17.69 m. The average equity plus average loans is £73.47 m being (£49 m + £20 m + £52.94 m + £25 m) / 2. This gives a ROCE for year 2 of 17.69 / 73.47 = 24.08 per cent, still a healthy return but noticeably less than the ROE of 31.27 per cent. Since this calculation includes both equity and the return on equity, it suffers from the same deficiencies as ROE in respect of the new economy. In addition, it becomes unclear whether the promises (LTRP) liability in the balance sheet (an average of £19 m being (16 + 22) / 2) should be treated as a loan for purposes of the ROCE calculation. This promise is a significant source of funds for SMD which has in effect borrowed from the promises fund to invest in assets to the extent, at the end of year 2, of £22 m less the ring-fenced cash for the LTRP of £11 m. ROCE's introduction of loans and interest into the performance measure comes from a feeling that management should be held responsible for all funds invested in the company and not just the equity fund. It is a step towards recognising the contribution of other stakeholders and so the funding provided by the employees through the LTRP deficit should probably be treated as a loan. The LTRP deficit is in effect a 'free' source of funds for the business. If the LTRP 'loan' is included in capital employed then the next question is whether it should be included 'gross' or net of ring-fenced cash. Assuming it is included at its average 'gross' amount of £19 m then ROCE falls to 19.13 per cent being 17.69 / 92.47 where £92.47 m is the average capital employed during the year and equals the average total assets employed being fixed assets, intangibles, non-cash working capital and all cash. Thus ROCE equals the return on total assets (ROTA).

The previous paragraph demonstrates that the treatment of promises, in this case the liability represented by the LTRP, in the traditional ROCE is somewhat uncertain. Arguably ROCE was designed for the old economy where such promises did not play a significant part in the affairs of the business and/ or were not recognised in the traditional accounts for the part they played.

THE DUPONT FORMULA

The 'Dupont' formula, so named since it was first used by the Dupont company, a major 'old economy' bulk chemicals manufacturer, states that:

$$\text{ROCE (ROTA)} = (P + I) / TA = [S / TA] \text{ times } [(P + I) / S]$$

where P is net profit, I is interest, TA is total assets and S is sales.

Thus ROCE is the product of the asset turnover (S / TA) and the margins ((P + I) / S). For SMD the ROCE is 19.13 per cent = 2.487 times 7.69. In this calculation, 7.69 per cent being 17.69 / 230 is the margin and 2.487 times being 230 / 92.47 is the asset turnover. The margin reflects the efficiency of the company in using resources. The consumption of resources is measured by expenses and the higher the margin, the greater the uplift achieved on those resources when turning those resources into product. Asset turnover is increased by sales reflecting the company's ability to leverage its efficiency through product sales. In the old economy the focus is upon the leverage of recorded assets (and the equivalent recorded capital). In the new economy it will be seen that the focus is upon the leverage of intangibles, which, as a general rule, remain unrecorded in the balance sheet. This leverage may also be achieved either through increasing volumes or increasing margins. The maximization of return on capital employed through increasing margins and asset turnover is important insofar as it leads to increases in the value of productive capital. As will be discussed in the forthcoming section on performance measures and the economy, the ultimate goal is to build productive capital.

In order to ascertain the returns for shareholders (ROE), it is necessary to understand the relationship between ROE and ROCE. Financial gearing, also known as financial leverage, is the key to understanding the relationship between ROE and ROCE. Gearing (G) is the proportion of loan finance (D for debt) in relation to equity funding (E). Loan finance enhances ROE if ROCE is greater than the interest rate paid on the loans. Alternatively, loan finance decreases ROE if the ROCE is lower than the interest rate paid on the loans. This is demonstrated in Figure 2.1. The illustration given in Figure 2.1 assumes that SMD promises are treated as a loan and ROE (0.3127), ROCE (0.1913), the gearing (0.8142) and the effective interest rate (r = 0.04217)) are calculated on this basis.

To summarise the discussion of traditional performance measures, an 'old economy' business strategy is one which builds the fixed asset base and exploits (leverages) it through volumes and margins. Its performance is measured by traditional financial analysis based upon (recorded) asset turnover and margins as the drivers of the return on recorded assets and recorded equity. The performance of the business in terms of the returns for shareholders can be magnified by financial gearing. However, since many intangibles are not recorded in the balance sheet, consequently understating assets and equity, a financial analysis based upon recorded assets and recorded equity is not workable in the new economy. A new financial analysis is required. In spite of this, traditional measures such as return on assets (or capital employed) and return on equity remain popular with analysts and for directors' and senior employee pay plans. For example, it is reported (Hall 2011) that Tesco plc is 'simplifying' its performance plan for rewards to use just two performance measures – return on capital employed and earnings per share. The former may

P is net profit, E is equity, D is debt, I is interest expense, r is the interest rate and G is gearing, then
- ROCE = (I + P)/(E + D) --------------(1)
- ROE = P/E -------------------------(2)
- G = D/E and I = r*D
- From (1)   I+P = ROCE*(E + D) and
- P = (ROCE*(E + D)) – I
- Substituting in (2) for P and since I = r*D and G = D/E, (2) gives
- ROE =   ROCE*(1 + G) - r*G
- ROE = ROCE + G (ROCE - r)
- Thus if ROCE>r, a higher G gives a higher ROE
- If ROCE<r, a higher G gives a lower ROE
- For SMD, taking the promise as a loan, ROE is 0.3127, ROCE is 0.1913, G is 0.8142, r is 0.04217
- Checks out since 0.3127 = 0.1913 + 0.8142 (0.1913 – 0.04217)

Figure 2.1   The gearing effect

not be appropriate for a company like Tesco that has much of its assets tied up in intangibles such as market position, its network of suppliers, its reputation with customers and its management skills.

Performance Measures and the Economy

Suppose there are two investment opportunities, both of which give sales of £100 m and expenses, including required returns on fixed assets, of £70 m. Both opportunities therefore translate resources of £70 m into resources of £100 m and in that sense they make identical contributions to the economy. Suppose the first opportunity requires an investment in fixed assets of £100 m but the second only requires £30 m of fixed assets. An economy dominated by the need to maximise return on capital/asset measures will take up the second opportunity but not the first since it would dilute the return. The first opportunity might be off-shored to another economy that focused on absolute profit rather than returns. The return maximising economy would move towards service since this does not require so much capital whilst the other economy would move towards physical production. A problem for the return maximising economy arises insofar as service is not as exportable as physical production and consequently trading imbalances develop. In principle, though politics and capital flows can interfere, exchange rates move to close any trading imbalances by reducing cost differentials. Exchange rate adjustment is important; however, in this stylised illustration the cause of the imbalance is not cost differential but rather differences in the performance measures used by the two economies. What you measure is what you get and thus different performance measures give us different economies. Arguably, a capitalist system that seeks to maximise return on productive capital will ultimately lose out to a capitalist system that seeks to maximise productive capital. It is the latter that will respond better to economic stimulus by expanding the productive economy and will persistently generate a trading surplus. The problem is compounded once speculative activity and capital is introduced. It is the economy which seeks abnormal returns which is likely to have the more sophisticated financial and capital markets and higher levels of speculative activity. According to international trade theory, nations with a comparative advantage in production will expand productive activity and capital whilst those with a comparative advantage in speculative activity will extend its speculative capital and activity. As seen by the 2008 financial crisis, this dichotomy into nations specialising in production and nations specialising in speculation may lead to the collapse of the nations specialising in speculation due to trading imbalances and unconstrained growth of the financial sector. Of course, the above analysis contains several assertions that require further investigation but the point is to try and represent economics in a way that explains observed phenomena and coordinates with accounting-based performance measures so that both economics and accounting are better understood. It is also possible that differences in the nature of performance measures helps to explain the relative growth of the public sector in the UK. For example, public sector performance measures such as the numbers going to university or hospital waiting lists can be improved by further investment; yet in the private sector, due to the law of diminishing returns (except where there is a knowledge breakthrough) additional investment can reduce returns and is consequently discouraged. Alternatively, in the private sector divestment can be used to boost returns. Barclays under Bob Diamond was an example of a company which made a promise of an exceptional (abnormal) rate of return to investors whilst seeking to divest those parts of the business which do not meet the target. In any event, the size of the private sector stalls whilst the public sector presses ahead.

Essentially, 4S is a performance measurement system that seeks to maximise absolute profit and capital whereas traditional measures focus on returns. Accordingly, 4S does not discourage additional investment provided the required rates of return on tangible and intangible assets are achieved. Moreover, 4S highlights the difference between production and speculation and restricts the incentive provided by speculative returns and speculative capital growth. It will be argued that these properties make 4S accounting more suitable for coordination with the needs of the economy. Relatively little attention has been paid to traditional performance measures as a source of our economic difficulties and global imbalances. Low interest rates have so far had little effect on rebalancing the economy. Instead, the low rates have been accepted as a source of returns in the productive sector without necessarily any new investment, whilst the speculative sector is sustained by artificially supported asset prices. The UK economy in particular has to date remained one dominated by trading imbalance, high rewards in parts of the financial industry and too much consumption relative to production. Economic stimulus alone may not solve this.

Conclusion

This chapter has introduced traditional accounting and traditional performance measures such as return on equity and return on capital employed which are based upon the traditional accounts. Traditionally, accounting recognises a single fund of equity although purchased intangibles and promises are separately identifiable. The chapter identifies difficulties in deciding how traditional returns should be calculated and interpreted in the context of intangibles and promises, both of which are key aspects of the new economy. The chapter goes on to question the relationship between traditional performance measures and the economy. The key issue is the differing behavioural incentives provided by absolute and relative returns.

Traditional but unsuitable performance measures still have a considerable influence on resource allocation. Only when these performance measures are abandoned can accounting start to come to terms with the needs of the company and the economy! The four slices approach abandons these traditional measures. It does not treat equity as a single fund but as four funds represented by traditional assets (fixed assets plus working capital less loans), intangibles, promises and prospects. The role and the calculation of these four slices of equity are discussed in Chapter 5. Chapter 12 shows how the 4S approach would be applied in the case of SMD to provide clarity as to the company's performance through a four fund business review. It is the treatment of intangibles and promises as distinct equity funds rather than their inclusion in a single fund which makes the four slices (four funds) approach more suited to the new economy. The current chapter has sought to demonstrate the inadequacy of traditional accounting when dealing with the intangibles and promises of the new economy. The next chapter further demonstrates this lack of suitability by reference to the well-known Enron case. The case serves to illustrate the feedback failures of traditional accounting.

3

Feedback Failures and the Need for a New Accounting

This chapter explores accounting's failure to articulate with, and feedback upon, the new economy business model. This exploration is done through the Enron case. The feedback failures are identified as being: (1) a lack of focus on the performance of intangibles; (2) no coupling of performance in the form of accounting profit with risk; (3) no separate reporting of the impact of legacy promises; and (4) no clear demarcation between current performance and future potential. These failings correspond to the features of the new economy business model reported in Chapter 1 as being a challenge for any new accounting.

Nearly every major challenge facing accounting today can be seen in the Enron saga. Enron and its management were widely lauded as having transformed an old economy utility company dominated by plant and equipment, into a market maker resembling a Wall Street bank; so much so that the demise of Enron could have signalled concerns for the future of Wall Street itself! Enron's innovation and expertise in making and managing markets in energy, water and communications, including its creation of an on-line market place, moved Enron firmly into the new economy. This was celebrated in the following terms by Enron (1999: 2):

> *We are participating in the new economy, and the rules have changed dramatically. What you own is not as important as what you know. Hard wired businesses such as energy and communications, have turned into knowledge based industries that place a premium on creativity. Enron has been and always will be the consummate innovator because of our extraordinary people. It is our intellectual capital – not only our physical assets – that makes us Enron. Move our assets to another company and the results would be markedly different.*

Enron (1999: contents page) viewed networks as crucial to its role as a new economy company:

> ENRON operates networks throughout the world to develop and enhance energy and broadband communication services. Networks, unlike vertically integrated business structures, facilitate the flow of information and expertise. We can spot market signals faster and respond more quickly. Networks empower individuals, freeing them to craft innovative and substantive solutions to customer problems. Networks are the foundation of our knowledge-based businesses and they provide exceptional returns and value for our shareholders.

Enron's Development Pathway

Enron's story of transformational change is set out in Table 3.1 which should be read from the bottom up. The left-hand column gives the key steps in Enron's development pathway whilst the right-hand column provides key features and consequences of each step.

Table 3.1   WLEC to WMM

Key steps	Key features and consequences
Trade/create market in broadband capacity	Needs knowledge of broadband, access to content
Purchase hard broadband assets	Assumes value increase will come from new market in broadband
Dispose utility assets	To become asset light, loss on disposal
Enron on-line	Loss making in early years, Enron is the counterparty, 18,800 products traded, needs capital to underwrite trades, originally opposed by Chief Executive
New markets in other utilities	Political influence avoids regulation
Create markets in natural gas	Wins business following deregulation by offering long-term fixed contracts, futures, options
Go international as utility producer/supplier	Political support of US government but did not do homework and overpaid for acquisitions
Expand to other utilities as producer/supplier	Asset heavy
Natural gas producer/supplier	Expands through acquisitions

Enron started as a natural gas producer and supplier which grew through acquisitions at first in the natural gas industry and then in other utilities. It was Enron's ambition to be the world's largest energy company (WLEC) and so its next stage of development was to expand internationally. Thus the early steps in its development pathway (bottom of Table 3.1) are utility acquisitions at first domestically and then later, internationally. The crucial step in its development was when, following deregulation in the US of the natural gas industry and the consequent volatility of gas prices, Enron started to operate as an 'investment bank' that made and managed markets in natural gas contracts. This heralded its change from old to new economy company. Table 3.1 is headed *WLEC to WMM*. This refers to the fact that as the company changed its strategic direction, Ken Lay, the company boss, changed his car number plates from WLEC 1 (World's Largest Energy Company 1) to WMM 1 (We Make Markets 1)!

Many of the natural gas producers from whom Enron purchased supplies were short of cash and so Enron lent them money secured upon long-term contracts for the supply of gas. These long-term contracts were used to enable Enron to offer its customers not only long-term supply contracts but also futures and options. The flexibility of options in a volatile deregulated market was attractive to Enron's customers. In effect, Enron repackaged its gas contracts in much the same way as Wall Street repackaged mortgages to create collateralised debt obligations (for a discussion see Fusaro and Miller 2002: 28–37) . Enron also offered swaps which allowed customers to swap a floating price for a fixed price and vice versa. Enron, like a bank, needed to manage its own exposure, and to hold precautionary cash to enable it to meet any unexpected shortage through a purchase in the spot market. The risks involved and the need to minimise capital tied up in precautionary assets meant it was critical for Enron to develop a risk management system similar to those of the Wall Street banks.

Table 3.1 shows that Enron went on to make and manage similar markets in other utilities. It also created Enron on-line which was a high-volume, low-margin business in which customers could write contracts with Enron on-line and thus Enron carried the counterparty risk. It was Enron on-line that generated much of the increase in turnover between 1999 and 2000 towards the end of the company's existence. Once it became a committed new economy company, Enron wanted to dispose of its legacy fixed assets. However, it had paid too much for many of these assets and could not dispose of them without a loss. To avoid disclosing the loss, Enron 'sold' at a 'profit' many of its fixed assets to a special purpose entity (SPE) which would inevitably incur losses. Enron's SPE's are discussed later but were designed by Enron so that any losses incurred by the SPE did not have to be included in Enron's accounts. Notwithstanding these sales, Enron still had significant fixed assets on its own books when it collapsed in 2001. The final step in Table 3.1 captures Enron's move into creating markets in broadband capacity. Enron's broadband business was seen by the stock market as having great potential and underpinned much of Enron's share price prior to its collapse. Table 3.1 is inevitably a very brief, roughly chronological summary and a fuller description can be found, for example, in *The Enron Collapse* by Hamilton and Francis (2003).

A Powerful Value Creation Story

Table 3.1 shows there are a number of key dimensions to Enron's *value creation story* which is a story of its transformation to new economy thinking. One is the external change provided by the deregulation of the gas market, and subsequently other utility markets. Of course, this is not entirely opportunistic with Ken Lay using his influential political connections to encourage such a change. Companies do try to influence their environment. Another dimension is the vision to see the market making opportunities that such an environmental change provided. This vision owed much to Jeff Skilling who joined the company from McKinsey and was a Harvard MBA. A third dimension is access to the necessary 'banking' and risk management expertise which Enron could obtain by recruiting from Wall Street. Ken Lay also used his political networking to ensure that the regulatory apparatus that applied to Wall Street banks did not extend to Enron's activities. The regulation of Wall Street banks, however, did not prevent much of Wall Street from its own demise some five or six years later. A further dimension is the leveraging of the ideas originally developed for natural gas into other utility markets, notably electricity and then broadband communications capacity. Of course, Enron needed to recruit expertise in these areas which were outside the company's original base in natural gas. As Enron moved its ideas into broadband communications it met competition from major communications companies who had already adopted Enron's ideas and had better access to broadband capacity (Enron developed its own capacity by putting optical fibre along its pipelines) and to potential broadband customers. Another dimension of the story is the development of contracts that could be entered into and traded on-line, taking advantage of the potential of the newly arrived internet. Finally Enron had a legacy issue. Like all transformational companies it had to manage its exit from its established business. This was not easy for Enron as it had in the past gone on an acquisition trail of utility companies worldwide and, like many acquirers, it had paid too much. It could not exit without showing a substantial loss.

In terms of the LEADERS business model, Enron's development is viewed as one of leverage, engagement, alignment and development. The gas bank leverages Enron's previous network of gas suppliers and customers and knowledge of the gas market into new derivative products. Its experience of the gas bank is subsequently leveraged into new utilities markets and into on-line contracting. It is the deregulation of gas and subsequently other utilities that makes Enron's propositions engaging for both suppliers and customers. The alignment of supplier and customer commitments was the responsibility of risk managers who were acquired as new stakeholders with new expertise. This pool of expertise existed already in Wall Street. Enron's development is based upon the adoption and adaptation of Wall Street ideas in response to new opportunities provided by a changing environment. Enron's value creation story is a powerful one of adapting ideas to a new situation, of accessing the necessary expertise and capacity to do this and leveraging the ideas into further new markets. However, every value creation story, no matter how convincing, needs to be evaluated in terms of its financial performance in order to assess and guide its progress and to inform the further reshaping of stakeholder propositions. The necessary evaluation was deficient not only in terms of the financial reporting by Enron but in terms of the financial analysis undertaken by stakeholders, including investors, and by those who influence stakeholders such as ratings agencies and business journalists. The next section focuses upon those deficiencies.

A Focus Upon Intangibles

An understanding of how the intangibles of this self-proclaimed new economy company were performing can be seen from the 1999 and 2000 reported financial numbers set out in Table 3.2. As is now known, these numbers were themselves, in a number of respects, a misreporting by Enron in order to flatter the company's performance. However, even the reported numbers give reasons to question Enron's performance as a new economy company. Residual income (profit) is the profit left after charging the accounting profit with a notional charge for the use of shareholders' funds (equity). If, for example, there is a notional 10 per cent charge for use of the shareholders' equity (equivalent to the recorded net assets) then Table 3.2 shows a residual profit that is negative in both years and getting worse. Having charged for the use of recorded net assets, the residual profit must logically be the return from the unrecorded assets, which are assumed to be the intangibles. If a more lenient rate of return required by shareholders of 5 per cent is assumed then it can be calculated that the residual profit, though now positive, still declines from $415 m to $405 m. Ideally, the analysis of residual profit should be based upon a more detailed scrutiny of the accounting numbers, similar to those conducted in later chapters. However, even the preliminary analysis conducted here shows that the self-proclaimed new economy company has failed to improve the contribution of its intangibles to its current profits, and the contribution may even be negative.

Table 3.2   The 2000/1999 numbers

	2000 $m	1999 $m
Revenues	100,789	40,112
Operating results (profits)	979	893
Total assets	65,503	33,381
Shareholder funds	11,470	9,570
10% notional interest	1,147	957
Residual income	(168)	(64)
Market capitalisation	62,416	
Market value added (MVA)	50,946	

Interpreting its results as an old economy company, a focus on the ROE reveals that Enron does not fare much better than it does as a new economy company. Revenues increase dramatically from 1999 to 2000 but margins (operating results/revenues) decline dramatically. This is partly as a result of the expansion of the high-volume, low-margin on-line business. This expansion has a dual impact upon the accounts since the result is a large number of derivative contracts for both the purchase and sale of the relevant commodities. Due to changes in the market price of the relevant commodities, many of these contracts have a positive value and are a substantial contributor to the near doubling of total recorded assets from $33,381 m to $65,503 m. However, the offsetting contracts with a negative value account for most of the increase in 'non-shareholder funds' which finance the expansion. The return on shareholders equity (ROE) declines from 9.3 per cent (893 / 9,570) in 1999 to 8.5 per cent (979 / 11,470) in 2000. It is likely, however, that shareholders would be looking for an increase, not a decrease, in their returns, so as to compensate for the increase in risk from 1999 to 2000. This increase in risk comes from the increased activity in 'on-line' derivative contracts to which Enron is the counterparty, and from the increasing dependence on the new broadband markets, in which Enron invested heavily but met stern competition from the telecoms majors.

The difference between the company's market capitalisation (share price times number of shares) and its book value is known as the market value added (MVA) and it represents the market's view of the value of unrecorded intangibles arising from both: (1) their current contribution to profit; and (2) their growth and development value in terms of increasing future profits. Enron's MVA is $50,946 m and this implies, at a required rate of return of 10 per cent, that residual income has the potential to increase to at least $5,094 m from its current negative $168 m. This is most difficult to justify for a company with a declining performance in terms of residual income. On this basis even a half competent analyst should have seen that Enron was overvalued but very few did say this publicly, at least not before it was too late. The investment community had bought big time into Enron's transformational story of opportunities to exercise its expertise in new arenas such as communications. What can be seen is that the power of the value creation story induced investors to disconnect the future performance of intangibles from the current performance revealed by the financial statements. Overwhelmingly, the market value of Enron was based on an unrealistic assessment of its future performance.

To avoid this, any assessment of Enron should have been grounded in the current contribution of the company's intangibles to accounting profit. Knowledge of the company's development path can then be employed to assess how this current contribution is realistically extended through the future development and exploitation of the intangibles. The value attributed to growth and development by the market capitalisation must be tied to this assessment. In the case of Enron we see that the development path based upon expansion of the on-line activities and the move into broadband could not realistically bridge the substantial gap between: (1) the current performance and performance trend of the intangibles; and (2) the growth and opportunity value attributed by the market capitalisation. Thus any fundamental analysis of Enron should have exposed a serious overvaluation of its MVA and the market price of its shares.

Fair Value Accounting

Since Enron was in effect operating as a financial institution, it followed Wall Street financial institutions when it came to accounting for its contracts. Wall Street employed fair value accounting which meant that contracts were valued at market value when they were traded in active markets (mark to market) and on the basis of a valuation model when active market prices were not available (mark to model). Basically, fair value accounting means that the financial institution's contracts are valued and shown in the opening and closing balance sheets with any increase (decrease) in value being recorded as profit (loss). Under fair value accounting, contracts do not have to be either fulfilled or sold in order to record a profit. However, the dangers of mark to market accounting for financial contracts have been exposed in the previous discussion of Enron's unrealistic share price, and were to be exposed again by the 2008 credit crisis in respect of collateralised debt obligations (CDOs). Markets are far from perfect and if mark to market is used for financial assets then users of accounts must recognise the speculative nature of the market price unless it is supported by fundamental analysis.

But the previous discussion of Enron's share price reveals another important issue. It is that most of the market value of Enron reflects the future performance of its intangibles rather than the present performance. Any accounting system needs to be clear as to when it is reporting current performance and when it is reporting anticipated future performance. In the case of equity investments, by basing profit on the change in market price, mark to market is, in effect, confounding present and future performance.

Many of Enron's contracts did not trade in active markets and were valued by models. This can be even more precarious than mark to market if the inputs which underpin the model can easily be manipulated. When Enron needed higher profits, managers were pressured to take a more optimistic view of the future (assume more optimistic model inputs) in order to identify a higher net present value. This was a process known within Enron as 'marking up the curve' (Hamilton and Francis 2003: 9):

Consider a contract that Enron has to supply gas to customers over several years. Traditional, conservative accounting in the old economy requires that there should be a sale and delivery before profit is recognised and recorded. In terms used previously in Chapter 1, this is phase one profit. Mark to market and mark to model accounting dispense with this conservatism and, by comparison with traditional methods, accelerate earnings. Under conservative financial accounting the profits are recognised over the life of the contract as the gas is delivered. Under mark to market or mark to model, in effect the present value of all the profits expected during the life of the contract is taken as profit upfront when the marking is done. This generates phase two profit. Future earnings are brought forward to the present period. When the value of the contract changes because of changing prices or a reassessment by the model, phase three profits are generated. Enron also generated phase four profits by charging fees for the creation of the contracts.

A Demarcation Between the Present and the Future

The previous discussion leads us to a further deficiency of existing accounting practice. There is not a clear demarcation between present performance and future potential. We need to distinguish those transactions which require current delivery from those transactions which are selling the future or making promises to be delivered in the future. A conservative accounting profit excludes the sale of future profits/cash flows as in a securitisation and the gains/losses that flow from changes in the value of promises such as derivatives. However, financial institutions do not follow such conservatism and moreover in many cases it is difficult to tell from the financial statements how much of the profit is phase one, how much is phase two and so on. This was most certainly difficult in the case of Enron. Such segmentation of the reported profit is important because it helps articulate the divide between the present and the future – between revenue and capital.

The need for conservatism is supported by authors such as LaFond and Watts (2008) who argue that Enron moved from traditional profit recognition (recognising profit upon delivery to the customer) to recognising profit when the idea was formed! This lack of discipline affects internal as well as external governance. Internally, employees rewarded or fired on the basis of profits booked had a huge incentive to go for long-term deals that could be optimistically priced to give high net present values and current profits. However, once the profits had been booked there was no incentive to ensure that the cash flows under the deals were achieved. Instead employees moved on to the next deal.

Fair values are not unimportant since management should be held to account not just in respect of current performance but also in terms of how they have positioned the company for the future. However, changes in the value of the company's future (speculative capital) should be clearly separated from changes in the value of its production capital invested in tangible and intangible assets.

Recognising Promises Embedded in Contracts

A key issue in Enron's demise concerns the role of the now infamous special purpose entities (SPEs). Enron created huge numbers of SPEs each designed to give effect to a particular transaction. For example, Enron was often short of cash and wanting to sell the future cash inflows that it expected to receive from a long-term contract for an upfront lump sum, a process known as securitisation. In fact, the right to receive the cash flows would be sold to an SPE set up and controlled by Enron. So that the SPE had the money to pay Enron, the SPE borrowed from a bank. To induce the bank to lend, Enron guaranteed the bank loan. Now, in principle, a sale to another entity (in this case the SPE) that is under your control is simply a sale to yourself and not one that should be recognised in the reporting of revenue, profit or cash flow. To deal with this, accounting theory says that Enron and the SPE should be 'consolidated' (that is, treated as one) for financial reporting purposes and any transactions within the consolidated entities ignored. In the United States at the time, however, the accounting rules that were supposed to put this theory into practice were not tightly drawn and Enron found a way round them. No consolidation took place. Enron included the profit on the sale of the future cash flows to its SPE in its (Enron's) current reported profit. Crucially, the existence and scale of Enron's guarantees of loans made by banks to the SPEs was *not* clearly articulated in the notes to Enron's accounts. The guarantees triggered if the expected cash flows under the contract did not materialise. They could bring down the company and they needed to be properly understood by investors.

It follows that there is a further deficiency in Enron's reporting and a further requirement for any new accounting for the new economy: it is that the value of promises embedded in (legacy) contracts must be recognised and their significance to the value creation story and the company's valuation explained. The failure to include the SPEs in Enron's consolidated financial accounts generates the need to subtract the value of the guarantees in the valuation of Enron. Each guarantee, if the details are disclosed, can be valued on the basis of: (1) the likelihood of the SPE defaulting; and (2) the expected loss to the bank in the event of default. The value of the portfolio of guarantees should take into consideration any correlation between the individual SPE default events. In the case of Enron, disclosure of the details of the guarantees was obscure and did not allow proper valuation or even recognition of the potential liability, by investors, especially since the financial condition of the SPEs was not disclosed. Moreover, it is important to understand the role of the guarantees in the development of Enron's business (the value creation story), for the reasons outlined in the next section.

Recognising the Relationship Between Risk and Value

The risks in Enron's business were increasing but did not appear to impact upon Enron's valuation. Enron was giving guarantees to banks in order to induce them to lend money to SPEs who were buying Enron's securitised cash flows, and hence providing capital to Enron. Enron's need for capital in the shape of cash or liquid assets was increasing, in particular due to the rapid expansion of the on-line business and its move into broadband. Enron was increasingly short of precautionary capital to underwrite its derivative contracts. This increased liquidity risk and should have provided downward pressure on Enron's value. As noted in Chapter 1, changes in value need to take into account changes in risk. Enron's business risk was also increasing because of its move from its traditional stakeholder base in utilities into broadband. Operational risks were increasing due to the internal incentive structures of Enron. The potential for these risks to impact profit was multiplied as a consequence of Enron's high financial gearing; a gearing that was obscured in part by the use of the SPEs to raise bank loans. However, this pattern of increasing risk did not appear to influence Enron's valuation by the market. This leads to a further requirement for a new accounting. It is that the new accounting must recognise the impact of increasing risk upon valuation.

Concluding Comments

In this chapter the well-known Enron case has been used to explore accounting's feedback failures and the shape of any new accounting for the new economy. Enron is a fascinating case. It contains a powerful value creation story that led to a disconnection between reported financial accounting numbers and valuation of the company. Traditional valuation disciplines had been abandoned by the investing community. Moreover, it is seen that Enron's accounting numbers were not so much a useful input to the valuation models of the investing community, but rather they were themselves the outputs from valuation models under the control of the company itself. Thus the reported numbers were unreliable. Finally, it has been seen that promises (in Enron's case the guarantees to the banks) can play an important role in understanding a business, the interests of stakeholders and the allocation of risk/reward between the company and its stakeholders.

The discussion of the Enron case has led to the following requirements that will influence the shape of any new accounting:

1.   The new accounting must provide a focus upon the current performance of intangibles.

2.   The new accounting must provide for a clear demarcation between current performance and future potential.

3.   In the new accounting the contingencies embedded in contracts in the form of promises must be separately recognised along with their relevance to the value creation story and the company's valuation.

4.   The new accounting must recognise the impact of increasing risk upon valuation.

It follows from the above four points that the new accounting will be more comprehensive than the current financial accounts. It is important that the new accounting allows the reader to connect market capitalisation with the current performance of intangibles, with the value creation story (in respect of growth and opportunity value), with contingencies (promises) and with the risks the company is facing. These are all key features of a new economy business model of which Enron is a classic example. Forthcoming chapters show how the Stakeholder Knowledge Network enables these connections.

4

The Stakeholder Knowledge Network

This chapter introduces the concept of the company as a (reshaping) Stakeholder Knowledge Network (SKN). The SKN is an example of what is called distributed cognition, whereby the understanding, interpretation and capability necessary for action resides in a network of human and non-human 'actors'. Following the LEADERS business model introduced in Chapter 1, the SKN is *reshaping* and this reshaping is designed to *leverage* the network, *engage* and *align* stakeholders in order to secure the network, and to *develop* the network with respect to its access to intangibles. These management actions are guided by both the strategic logic (Bingham and Eisenhardt 2008) that management is following and by the financial *evaluation* or feedback supplied by 4S accounting. This feedback is in terms of the impact of management actions upon company value. Thus the SKN provides a common framework for both the management and evaluation of the company. It sits at the heart of the analysis of the new economy.

The idea behind the SKN is that a company secures its knowledge base at a point in time through a set of relationships with knowledgeable stakeholders (The Stakeholder Knowledge Network: Figure 4.1). Some of this knowledge base is the property of the company itself and in this sense, as per Figure 4.1, the company is included as a stakeholder in its own network. For example, the company owns physical and intellectual property that constitutes knowledge in the sense of contributing to network capability. However, much of the network's knowledge base is not the property of the company and resides with stakeholders such as customers, suppliers, employees and management who have to some degree or another a measure of independence from the company. What matters is that the stakeholder propositions engage the stakeholders and thus secure access for the company to all stakeholder knowledge and capability required in the pursuit of enhancing company value, the pursuit of company sence being the proposition to the shareholders. Thus the knowledge must be embedded in a set of stakeholder propositions that both e stakeholders and align their contributions with the enhancement of company value. The matrix of stakeholder propositions illustrated schematically in Figure 4.1 is called a 'Stakeholder Knowledge Network'. It will be shown that the dimensions of the stakeholder propositions in Figure 4.1 (product, cost/price volume, knowledge, relationship, promises and prospects) must be aligned with each other and with the processes of company valuation and company development. Whilst from an old economy perspective financial performance is the company's success in building a stronger set of net assets recorded in the balance sheet, a new economy perspective sees performance as enhancing value through success in building (and leveraging) a stronger stakeholder knowledge network.

These dynamics of the LEADERS business model align with both the 'inside out' and 'outside in' views of strategy. Whilst leveraging and developing the knowledge network starts from the network the company has and is thus internally focused in the first instance (inside out), the engagement of stakeholders is focused on matching or exceeding the opportunities that stakeholders, especially customers, have in the external competitive market (outside in). Consideration must be given not only to what stakeholders do to satisfy the company's needs but also what the company does to satisfy the stakeholders' needs (Neely, Adams and Kennerley 2002). Satisfying stakeholder needs, especially those of customers, can only be achieved by understanding

1	2 Product performance	3 Price, cost, volume	4 knowledge	5 relationship	6 promises	7 prospects
customers						
employees						
suppliers						
company						
loan holders						
shareholders						
government						
management						

Figure 4.1   The Stakeholder Knowledge Network

the external environment that provides the context for the impact propositions have, both currently and prospectively, on the stakeholders.

In the SKN (Figure 4.1) product specifications in terms of performance form the first dimension. Product should be thought of in terms of the functionalities and experiences it delivers for customers, and one important form of innovation is rethinking how these functionalities or experiences can be delivered in other ways. All product designs must be aligned across stakeholders so that the inputs of non customer stakeholders are coordinated with the output for customers. The second dimension, being sales price in respect of customers (cost for other stakeholders) and volume, has to reflect market conditions if the propositions are to engage stakeholders. It is this dimension which leads to a focus upon traditional accounting that matches sales value and costs (Figure 4.2, column 3). Knowledge and relationships are the third and fourth dimensions. Knowledge is defined widely to include competence, ability and capability. Typically, in the literature on intangibles (for example, Viedma Marti 2007), intangible assets are categorised as human capital (assets of individual competence), structural capital (assets of internal structure) and relational capital (assets of external structure). In this schema the value of intangibles is attributed to the human competence, stakeholder relationships and organisational structures. Similarly, the network perspective of the SKN attributes competence to all stakeholders and the key is the ability to access this competence through appropriate relationships. These relationships are in turn a function of formal structures, processes, controls and incentives as well as company culture and informal practices. The ability to create appropriate relationships is taken to be a competence of management who are therefore a key stakeholder. Knowledge and relationships are the intangibles at the heart of the Stakeholder Knowledge Network and these two dimensions are discussed further in the next two sections of this chapter. Promises for the future form the fifth dimension and in accounting terms these take the form of contingencies or commitments. Promises reflect the 'business legacy'. They are covered in more detail in a subsequent chapter (Chapter 8), though Figure 4.2 (column 6) introduces some examples of typical 'promises'. Figure 4.2 shows that promises include the provision for asset replacement which is an implied promise if the business is to be sustainable under current market conditions. Prospects, being the sixth dimension, are also discussed in a later chapter (Chapter 9). Prospects reflect the aggregate future for the other five dimensions of the SKN.

If business is viewed as a constantly reshaping Stakeholder Knowledge Network then it follows that the network should be at the heart of corporate

1	2 *Product performance*	3 *Price, cost, volume*	4 *knowledge*	5 *relationship*	6 *promises*	7 *prospects*
customers		sales			warranties	
employees		wages			pension deficit	
suppliers		cost of materials			forward contracts	
company		depreciation			replacement	
loan holders		interest			forward contracts	
shareholders		dividends			share price	
government		tax			deferred tax	
management		salaries			share options	

Figure 4.2   The Stakeholder Knowledge Network with promises

development, an analysis of market capitalisation and accounting. This chapter demonstrates the centrality of the SKN and its crucial role as a control framework for the effective integration of these three elements.

Categories of Knowledge

Table 4.1 gives three forms that the product dimension of the stakeholder proposition can take – operational excellence, customer intimacy and product leadership. They were introduced by Treacy and Wiersema (1996) and align with three categories of knowledge (systematic, adaptive and innovative). Each category of knowledge in turn aligns with a different style of stakeholder relationship (formal, responsive and perceptive) consistent with an appropriate selection of structures, processes, controls, incentives, culture and so on.

Table 4.1   Three types of customer proposition, associated knowledge and relationship

Customer proposition	Operational excellence	Customer intimacy	Product leadership
Knowledge	systematic	adaptive	creative
Relationship	formal	responsive	perceptive

Each knowledge category is discussed briefly in turn. Systematic knowledge is knowledge that is detailed, well understood and most likely documented. A comparative advantage in systematic knowledge should lead to operational excellence and is leveraged to financial effect through high volumes and competitive prices. This reflects an emphasis on adding value by delivering the operational excellence to as many customers as possible.

Adaptive knowledge is the ability to apply a core of (systematic) knowledge to a variety of different customer needs or markets. A comparative advantage in adaptive knowledge both requires and leads to customer and/or market intimacy. Whilst adaptability leads to increasing volumes, it may also be leveraged financially through a price premium reflecting the emphasis on adding distinctive value to the customer. Thirdly, innovative 'knowledge' is the ability to create the substantially new. It should lead to a flow of leading-edge products leveraged in financial terms through premium prices associated with early mover advantage and subsequently, assuming the market is there, significant volume. Innovation can also come through the business model in the shape of innovative stakeholder propositions that enable new access to, leverage or development of intangibles. As previously stated, the different categories of knowledge are associated with different styles of stakeholder relationship and different modes of product specification. These issues are discussed shortly.

In Treacy and Wiersema the clarity of the product proposition serves as a key discipline (they call it a value discipline) throughout the company. Treacy and Wiersema argue that a successful organisation is a focused organisation and should therefore concentrate on only one value discipline for customers being operational excellence, customer intimacy or product leadership. However, each of the three different customer propositions are typically aligned with different categories of knowledge (systematic, adaptive, innovative) and a successful economy depends on the successful interaction of these different knowledge categories. For example, adaptive knowledge provides volume for a systematic knowledge base by applying the systematic knowledge to as wide a range of customers/markets as possible. Leading-edge products generated by innovative knowledge require to be brought to market through a systematic planning and monitoring process adapted to the particular circumstances of the new product and its market. In this regard, fast followers can outperform the original innovator in bringing new ideas to market. Systematic knowledge itself needs to be rethought periodically in anticipation of changing market requirements. This rethink comes through a mixture of innovation and experience gained by adapting the existing knowledge base to a wide range of circumstances. Many innovations take the form of being first to systematise previously unstructured knowledge. Over time as knowledge becomes better understood and more formally specified, it tends to migrate from being innovative to systematic.

To reconcile the need for focused organisational activity with the need for effective interaction between knowledge categories (value disciplines), companies develop a fourth form of knowledge, holistic knowledge, and a fourth value discipline, versatility. The 'fourth discipline' requires organisations to be able to respond to a holistic understanding of how different knowledge categories and the relationships that the different categories require, interact and fit together within the stakeholder network and between stakeholder networks. It is this holistic knowledge that forms the basis of the so-called organisational capital, an intangible which Lev, Radhakrishnan and Zhang (2009) find to be the most important contributor to corporate performance and growth. Organisational capital is the ability to put together different knowledge categories to form a successful Stakeholder Knowledge Network. It is the ability to align as well as to engage the stakeholders. Such holistic knowledge is tacit knowledge that is developed through the history of the organisation, is difficult for competitors to imitate and therefore forms a key source of strategic advantage for many companies (Kay 1993).

Thus as companies mature and grow it is common for their core competence to migrate to that of holistic understanding of how other competences fit together. A good example of this is given in Mouritsen, Hansen and Hansen (2001) who study a small Danish company in the business of property security systems. Over time the company is unable to maintain its detailed knowledge of each of the increasing number of rapidly advancing technologies that go into a security system. As a consequence it decides to concentrate on bringing the various technologies together into the overall system by setting the performance criteria for suppliers who specialise in the individual technologies. Of course, some knowledge of the individual technologies must be retained in order to be able to set appropriate performance specifications for the suppliers, but it is at a different level to the detailed knowledge of the suppliers themselves.

Relationships with Stakeholders

There are two views on the role of stakeholders such as customers, suppliers, employees and providers of capital. The first sees management's role in relation to stakeholders essentially as one of exploitation subject to the constraint of the need for continuing engagement. The highest prices are obtained from customers and the lowest prices from other stakeholders consistent with them continuing to buy and supply. In principle, shareholders as owners of the net assets are treated differently to other stakeholders since part of the proposition made to shareholders is that retained, recorded profits 'belong' to them. This is the traditional, old economy perspective on stakeholders and one that in terms of accounting ratios looks to leverage expenses by reducing each category of expenses, including per unit fixed asset expense, as a proportion of sales.

However, from a new economy perspective, stakeholders are seen as an important source of ideas, knowledge and capability, as well as buyers and suppliers (Doz and Hamel 1998). Witness the engagement (cooption) of customers by Dell in the online co-design of the customer's computer, an opportunity for engagement provided by the arrival of the Internet. From a new economy perspective, in order to secure access to stakeholder knowledge and capability, stakeholder engagement is deeper and the role closer to that of a network partner. Trust, fairness and understanding become key attributes and management of the stakeholder network moves centre stage in pursuit of a 'win win' wealth creation for all. Given the longer term, deeper nature of the relationships, management of the stakeholders and the stakeholder propositions from a new economy perspective, assumes a higher profile and importance.

Nevertheless, there is a spectrum of stakeholder relationships within the new economy. This spectrum may be illustrated by reference to Simons's four levers of control being diagnostics, interaction, beliefs and boundaries (Simons 1995). *Boundary* systems are formally stated rules and limits to define the authority of employees and other stakeholders. *Diagnostic control* systems are feedback systems that monitor a subordinate's (or other stakeholder's) performance against preset targets and measures. They are most useful for systematic activities which require tight activity processes. *Interactive control* systems require regular personal involvement of managers in the decision making of subordinates, for example in project management or other activities which are not systematic but require individual or unexpected circumstances to be taken into account. *Belief* systems represent a shared purpose or shared values which may be illustrated formally, for instance in mission statements, but perhaps are more effective when absorbed informally as part of the corporate culture. They are a form of social control. Belief systems may be important in shaping the direction of, and motivation for, new knowledge. In the context of innovation, mutual belief may be underpinned by an agreement between stakeholders to share in the risks and rewards associated with innovative activity. Hence, what is needed is not only the right combination of controls but the right combination of controls and incentives. Macintosh (1994: 144–7) provides a classic example of a control/incentive system for an advertising agency that is incompatible with innovative activity and therefore fails to deliver creative advertising. The advertising agency recruited its finance director from Ford who following his experience with Ford, promptly implemented a control/incentive environment appropriate to a systematic rather than a creative business. Thus whilst all four levers are likely to be of significance in all stakeholder relations, the emphasis will vary depending upon the nature of the knowledge which the stakeholder proposition is designed to access and foster.

A mix of beliefs, boundaries, interactions and diagnostics (Simons 1995, Widener 2007) has to be selected so as to generate a relationship that provides the degree of rigour/flexibility/creativity required by the nature of the product and its components. The stakeholder network covers not only intra-firm but also inter-firm relationships and controls (Caglio and Ditillo 2008, Mouritsen, Hansen and Hansen 2001). Constraints upon the content of stakeholder propositions and thus upon the degree of alignment achievable can come from cultural differences, from formal hierarchical structures, unequal power relations (Pfeffer and Salancik 1978), outside regulation and the state of contract law. Institutional structures and outside regulation should exist to facilitate and clarify propositions, not to inhibit their development except where they are manifestly unfair.

Each stakeholder proposition is now discussed in turn, starting with the customer proposition. Although other stakeholder categories can be included in the network (for example, regulators and alliance partners, trade bodies and even possibly competitors), the stakeholders illustrated in Figure 4.2 are customers, suppliers, employees, shareholders, other investors (taken to be loan-holders), government and management. In addition, the company itself is treated as a stakeholder in respect of its contribution to the network in the form of fixed assets, operational processes and intellectual property.

CUSTOMERS

Following Treacy and Wiersema, the product proposition will correspond to one of operational excellence, customer intimacy or product leadership each with different implications for product performance, price (cost)/volume, knowledge and relationships. If the product is one of operational excellence, then the relationship with the customer (column 5) is likely to be one of formal communication and there is likely to be high product specification (column 2). In this case, if the customer provides knowledge (column 4) to assist the product specification then it is within a formal context, for example through a generalised customer survey. Additionally, a level of knowledge or skill on the part of the customer may be necessary for the customer to operate the product, as would be the case for example with a motor car or indeed any complex piece of machinery. Branding can be an important element of formal relationships with customers (and with other stakeholders). 'Brands are like a contract with consumers to produce regular cash flows' (quotation reported in Holland 2006: 69). A brand gives a company access to customers, whilst through its reputation it gives customers knowledge of the product.

If the product is adaptive to customer needs then the knowledge of the individual customer in respect of product requirements is a key input to product design. This input takes place in a less formal interactive dialogue, for example through the medium of a customer service officer. For an innovative product the customer, or perhaps a focus group, may be part of the brainstorming process.

A customer warranty is given as an example of a promise (column 6) that forms part of the overall customer proposition, and may play an important role in supporting sales.

Prospects (column 7) are the future for each of the other dimensions of the customer proposition. Thus the prospects dimension captures the future development of the product, of knowledge and of the customer relationship and promises as well as the future of price and volume. Prospective product developments and price may be influential in determining whether customers are willing to buy now or prefer to delay. The prospect of a continuing and advancing relationship may encourage customer engagement. Clearly the prospects for product reliability affect the value of any warranty.

Customer power can force change in the propositions for other stakeholders. GAP, the US-based clothing company, provides a good example of the potential inter-dependence of stakeholder satisfaction. GAP suffered a sales collapse (customer disengagement) in the early 2000s and in part this was due to publicity given to the working conditions at its third world suppliers. GAP customers, spurred by media publicity, were not satisfied with the company's supplier propositions in terms of the prices paid and the consequent working conditions.

It is important to recognise the role of information technology advances in enabling new, innovative propositions. An example would be the advent of dynamic pricing by airlines, underpinned by computer pricing models. In traditional pricing arrangements a full fare ticket gives the customer the option (flexibility) to change the flights or to get a full refund for the ticket. Often airlines also offered standby tickets which gave themselves the option to take passengers at the last moment if the flight was not full. The value of the customer's option embedded in the full fare ticket is, following option pricing models, greater the longer there is to go before the flight. In dynamic pricing the ticket is inflexible once purchased and the price increases as the flight date approaches. This price increase reflects options pricing. For example, the passenger who opts for the inflexible deal is giving up the option embedded in the full price ticket and the value of this option declines as the flight date approaches. In this case the large discount given to a passenger who books an inflexible ticket well in advance reflects the value of the lost option.

EMPLOYEES AND SUPPLIERS

Employee and supplier propositions require from these stakeholders an input to production based on the requirements of the product design. The proposition made to the supplier by the company is equivalent to the proposition made to the company as customer by the supplier. The issues for the design of the supplier proposition are therefore equivalent to those influencing the design of the customer proposition. What is needed as input from the supplier may be operational excellence, adaptation to circumstances or, possibly, innovation. In each case the nature of the input has implications for the other dimensions of the supplier proposition, notably knowledge and relationships. In respect of promises it is quite possible to have a risk and reward sharing agreement with suppliers concerning the development of new parts. An example is provided by Rolls Royce whose suppliers can operate as risk and reward sharing partners (called RRSPs) in which case the supplier funds the development and design of parts for a new aero engine and in return shares in the profits from the engine's sales. Promises can also take the form of long-term contracts with suppliers at fixed prices (column 6). Such contracts have a current value contingent upon expected price changes and the remaining life of the contract.

Employees are suppliers to the company who as individuals enjoy certain statutory and contractual arrangements which frame their relationship with the company. In other respects the issues for the design of employee propositions are similar to those of suppliers. In particular, the relationship between employee and the company aligns with the nature of the input required. For example, the relationship of an employee who contributes to a routine production process will be more formal and specified than where the employee is expected to be adaptive to circumstances. Diagnostics play a large role in respect of the former and interactive controls with regard to the latter. With regard to promises, an example might be a defined benefit pension (column 6) which can be a considerable attraction for an employee (though also possibly a tie). Although many companies have discontinued new entry and in some cases further contributions, pensions are a long-term commitment and so the consequences of past promises will be significant for many years to come. The pension is a guaranteed promise by the company to the employee. In relation to employees, prospects are the prospects for the business and its potential for employment security and/or career development.

THE COMPANY

The company as a stakeholder provides fixed assets and other capabilities to the Stakeholder Knowledge Network. The fixed asset requirements can be proposed in terms of cost, volume and output characteristics. Knowledge is embedded in the machine design, the physical expression of which delivers the performance required. Moreover, sophisticated programmable machines allow for communication of the characteristics required and adapt accordingly. Thus they can exhibit flexibility that presents as adaptive behaviour. The replacement of fixed assets (column 6) can be treated as an implied promise if the company's current performance is to be sustainable. It will be shown in a later chapter (Chapter 8) that this can, in certain circumstances, result in the need to establish a (replacement) provision as part of NVP.

SHAREHOLDERS AND LOAN HOLDERS

Shareholders and loan-holders are suppliers of finance to the company, for which they are paid dividends or interest. A fixed interest loan is really a forward contract (column 6) in respect of the supply of finance. Like other forward contracts it assumes a value contingent upon the expected movement in price (interest rates). If there is an interest rates rise during the year, then, making the assumption that interest rates remain the same thereafter, the company will make a saving every year until the loan has to be repaid of the difference between the interest paid and the interest that would have been paid based upon the increased interest rate. This provides a basis upon which the forward contract can be valued.

It is important that the propositions meet shareholder/loan-holder needs as well as meeting company needs. Thus both shareholders and loan-holders should be treated as customers as well as suppliers. They are in effect customers for the company's financial products (issues of shares and debt), and each product has its own risk/return characteristics. The risk/return characteristics depend upon an assessment of all the propositions of the SKN and not just those made directly to the loan-holders and shareholders. They are crucially dependent upon the prospects for the business as a whole.

The relationship between the company and its shareholders is distinctive. In addition to the payment of dividends, shareholders receive a contingent benefit (loss) in the form of rising (falling) share prices. Company valuation is an attempt to value this promise made to the shareholder. In the UK the relationship with shareholders includes the right of shareholders to replace those at the top of management who are executive directors (non-executives can also be replaced but perform as supervisors/governors rather than executives). Shareholders, in principle at least, replace executive directors as part of their (shareholder) responsibility to exercise governance. Where the shareholder is working to systematic routines, for example with a tracker fund, then this governance relationship is distant and, quite probably, ineffective. At the other extreme, where the shareholder is operating a focus fund, for example, then dialogue is key, in order to realise the fund manager's knowledge/expectation as to how the company should be performing. If a company wishes to attract long-term as opposed to speculative shareholders then it needs to ensure that shareholders and hence the share price are fully informed.

GOVERNMENT

The government is a key stakeholder in any business with tax on current profits being charged (column 3) as an expense. Normally tax is regarded as an expense though it might also be considered as a distribution of profit to the government since the size of the tax is a function of profit. In return for the taxation, government provides the social and economic infrastructure that business needs. If part of the tax charge on current profits can be deferred (column 6) then the deferral represents a 'promise' to pay the tax in the future. This deferred tax, on which no interest is payable, may not itself be payable until an uncertain time in the future. For example, if the deferral is allowed because the company has currently made capital investment entitling it to capital allowances in excess of its depreciation, then payment of the deferred tax will in effect be contingent on the pattern and extent of future capital expenditure.

Government may consider themselves to have an interest, on behalf of stakeholders, in any of the SKN's propositions. For example, they may place restrictions on the employee propositions in terms of conditions, hours or pay rates. Such regulatory interference may be appropriate where there are unequal power relations between the two parties (Pfeffer and Salancik 1978), but care must be taken by government not to stand in the way of innovation in proposition development that might be beneficial to both parties. It must be recognised that stakeholders are defined by the propositions they enjoy rather than the other way around. Innovative propositions may imply new categories of stakeholder for which existing legislation may be inappropriate.

MANAGEMENT

Senior managers, and in particular executive directors, play a key role in formulating, in the context of market conditions, the proposition for each stakeholder group. Part of the management proposition is that management collectively possess and maintain sufficient knowledge of stakeholders and stakeholder markets to do this. In crafting these stakeholder propositions on behalf of the company, management may require some stakeholders to work systematically, and others to work adaptively or creatively, in order to generate the necessary stakeholder coalition. Management use their holistic organisational knowledge (capital) to combine all the stakeholders and stakeholder propositions into an effective stakeholder coalition. The contribution of this holistic knowledge is crucial to the management proposition. Such holistic knowledge itself might be routine, adaptive or perhaps innovative by putting different stakeholders and knowledge categories together in new ways. The nature of management's holistic knowledge should fit management's relationship with shareholders and vice versa. For example, it may be difficult to manage an innovative company unless there is dialogue with shareholders. In terms of this book the key to the management proposition is that management possess the abilities required of them by the LEADERS business model.

It is essential that shareholders possess and seek the knowledge that enables them to exercise governance over the management proposition, since this proposition like the others is initially crafted by management. In particular, governance is needed when there are incentive schemes for managers. In these cases, both promises and prospects (columns 6 and 7) can become a crucial element of the management proposition. Inappropriate incentives for banking executives and senior employees have been blamed, at least in part, for the 2008 credit crisis.

Prospects (column 7) are themselves influenced by the overall shape of the company, and hence form a recursive element within any evaluation. In other words, improvement in prospects improves engagement that improves the shape of the company and hence returns a further improvement of prospects. Prospects are not only determined by the shape of the company but by technology development, macroeconomic variables and competitor activity that may be significantly outside the control of management.

Summary

This chapter has introduced the Stakeholder Knowledge Network as a representation of business which is seen as a reshaping set of stakeholder propositions. The reshaping is designed to engage and align stakeholders with the development and leverage of the intangibles within the stakeholder network. These intangibles are stakeholder relationships and knowledge. Management's ability to make innovative propositions is itself an important intangible asset. It is the set of stakeholder propositions that secure access to stakeholder knowledge and the chapter has discussed the key issues for each stakeholder proposition. The next chapter introduces the process of understanding the SKN as a conceptual framework for accounting. The reshaping of the SKN is to enhance shareholder value and the next chapter starts with the relationship between the SKN and the market capitalisation of the company.

5

Accounting for Distributed Knowledge

The previous chapter introduced the idea of knowledge being distributed around a network of stakeholders with business seen as a reshaping stakeholder network. It was seen that the SKN serves as a framework to capture a stakeholder network's product, sales and expenses, intangibles (knowledge through relationships), promises and prospects. This chapter shows how the equity stake – the market capitalisation – of a company is linked to this framework. The market capitalisation is taken to be the sum of values attributed to: (1) traditional assets; (2) intangibles; (3) promises; and (4) prospects. In this chapter these four slices of equity will be referred to respectively as: (1) ESTA; (2) CUVI; (3) NVP; and (4) GOV. ESTA is the equity stake in traditional assets, CUVI is the current use value of intangibles, NVP is the net value of promises and GOV is prospects taken as growth and opportunity value. The chapter sets out how these four funds (four slices) are valued. The 'four slice' analysis of market capitalisation has been coordinated with the dimensions of the SKN. Intangibles, promises and prospects are key components of both. The price/cost/volume dimension of the SKN derives the accounting profit which links to ESTA and traditional accounting.

The Valuation Analysis

The starting point for a discussion of the process of analysing market capitalisation is a widely used valuation model, the residual earnings model (see for example, Ohlson 1995). This model relates the firm's equity value to: (1) assets in place financed by equity (fixed assets and working capital less loans); plus (2) the growth potential. If the equity value is taken to be MC (market capitalisation), fixed assets plus working capital less loans is ESTA (equity stake in traditional assets) and the growth potential is GOV (growth and opportunity value), then:

$$MC = ESTA + GOV \qquad \qquad \text{equation (1)}$$

In the residual earnings model, the growth potential (GOV) is taken to be the present value of all expected *future* residual earnings. Residual earnings are the profits left after charging for an appropriate return on ESTA, the equity invested in traditional assets, and are attributed to the intangibles of the business (Lev 2001). 4S accounting, however, adapts equation (1) to respond to key feedback failures of accounting for the new economy business model identified in Chapter 3. These include the impact of intangibles, of risk and reward sharing, and the separate identification of productive and speculative capital.

Firstly, given the key role of intangibles, assets in place are not just the traditional accounting net assets but also the intangible assets. The value of the intangibles is taken to be the capitalised value of the *current* residual earnings based upon the current reported profit. The current residual earnings are valued as a perpetuity assuming current business conditions persist. They are based upon sustainable accounting profit. 'One off' profits or losses that will not recur even if current business conditions persist are excluded. The value of intangibles derived on this basis is called CUVI (the current use value of intangibles) and values them on the basis of their current performance (current use) rather than their future potential. The revised equation is:

$$MC = ESTA + CUVI + GOV \qquad \qquad \text{equation (2)}$$

In this equation GOV no longer includes all expected future residual earnings but rather it values future increases (or decreases) in the current level of residual earnings. The reason for splitting future residual earnings into: (1) those which are a continuation of current earnings (CUVI); and (2) changes to current earnings (GOV) is to distinguish intangibles that form productive capital based upon the profitability of current production from speculative capital based upon future changes in the profitability of intangibles. The Enron case demonstrates the importance of this distinction. ESTA, CUVI and GOV are discussed in more detail in the following paragraphs.

CALCULATING ESTA AND CUVI

ESTA is the first slice of equity and is equivalent to fixed assets and working capital taken at their book value, less loans. Shareholders are assumed to require a return on their stake in the traditional assets appropriate for the risk inherent in this investment. The return required depends upon the business uncertainties that existed during the year. As previously discussed, the current (sustainable) profit which is in excess of the amount required to give the return on ESTA is known as the residual profit or residual income and is assumed to flow from the equity stake in intangible assets. This residual profit can be capitalised as a perpetuity using an appropriate rate of return and this gives CUVI (the current use value of intangibles). It is assumed that the rate of return required for the equity stake in intangible assets is higher than that required for fixed assets/working capital since the intangibles are in general more susceptible to business risks. ESTA and CUVI together form the equity stake in 'assets in place'. Together they are the capitalised value of current profits in perpetuity. In other words, they are the current value of an income stream that maintains the company's present 'standard of living'. GOV represents the value today of any future increase or decrease in that standard of living.

THE NATURE OF GOV

Capitalising current profit in perpetuity assumes that the pattern of business conditions and uncertainties experienced during the current year will continue forever. Of course, the current year's business conditions will not continue, or at least not for long, and the value of the current profits in perpetuity merely serves as a platform or benchmark from which the company will either grow or decline. GOV is the current expected value of this future growth, or decline. The importance of such a benchmark based upon current actual achievement, and assuming current business conditions persist, is in particular brought out in the Enron case.

One plausible interpretation of continuing business conditions is that current growth rates are assumed to continue in perpetuity. However, 4S accounting adopts a less demanding interpretation of continuing business conditions. Maintaining the current level of activity under management is less demanding than maintaining a constant growth in activity. Consequently, the interpretation of continuing business conditions that is used implies not a constant growth in activity but the maintenance of current activity levels. This is the more conservative approach and consistent with the requirement for conservatism identified in Chapter 3.

CALCULATING GOV

The difference between the value of the company (MC) and the capital value of the current profits in perpetuity (ESTA + CUVI) is the company's growth and opportunity value (GOV). It is known that in most circumstances when there is no takeover in prospect, market share price and hence market capitalisation tends to understate the value of the company as a takeover target. Nevertheless, as a working assumption, company value is taken as being its market capitalisation. GOV is positive when the prospects are good and negative when they are unfavourable. Growth and opportunity value adjusts the capital value of current profit for the expected future changes in the company's SKN in response to changing business conditions and opportunities.

CALCULATING THE THREE SLICES OF EQUITY: AN EXAMPLE

Returning to equation (1), Table 5.1 provides an illustration based upon J D Wetherspoon's 2006 accounts, which show book equity invested in fixed assets and working capital of £202 m and a profit after tax (assumed to be sustainable) of £39.9 m. The amount required to provide shareholders with a return on ESTA is £16.2 m, being an assumed required rate of 8 per cent applied to the equity invested in fixed assets and working capital (ESTA). This leaves shareholders with a further residual profit of £23.7 m. Assuming a required rate of return by investors on intangibles of 10 per cent, residual profit is capitalised to give CUVI at £237 m. Growth and opportunity value (GOV £246 m) is the difference between the sum of ESTA and CUVI, and the market capitalisation at the year end (share price times number of shares).

Table 5.1   J D Wetherspoon: three slices of equity

	2005 £m	2006 £m	Required rate of return	Profit (2006) attributed
Equity in FA + WC	247	202	8%	16.2
CUVI	116	237	10%	23.7
GOV	114	246		
Market cap*	477	685		
Profit after tax	31.4	39.9		39.9

* using 153.776m (2005 172.877m) shares at 445.5 p (2005 276 p)

Introducing Promises

The assessment of future annual sustainable profit, assuming existing business conditions continue, is based upon the most recently reported accounting profit. This accounting profit should be net of a charge for the value of promises made to stakeholders during the year in order to help secure their engagement. Thus sustainable profit in future years is also net of a charge that allows (retains funds) for the value of promises made in each future year. However, charges to sustainable profits in perpetuity going forwards do not allow (provide funds) for the obligations at the latest balance sheet date in respect of outstanding promises made in past years. Insofar as assets have not been set aside to meet these outstanding promises, then the (net) value of these promises must be subtracted from the company's valuation. In effect, if shareholders want to receive the current profits in perpetuity then they must pay in as capital an amount sufficient, together with any assets set aside, to meet past years' outstanding promises as they fall due.

By way of illustration consider the case of defined benefit pensions. Each year the cost of an additional year of pensionable service by employees is charged to current accounting profit which is therefore sustainable given constant business conditions. Thus sustainable profit achievable in future years is net of the cost of each future year's pensionable service, and the capital value of sustainable profit takes into account the pension obligation in respect of future years of service (on the assumption that present business conditions continue). However, future sustainable profits do not provide funds for obligations at the balance sheet date in respect of past pensionable service. This outstanding pension obligation in respect of past years of service has to be met from assets already set aside for that purpose. Insofar as there is a pension fund deficit, then there is a deficiency of funds set aside and the value of the deficit should be a reduction in the company's valuation. Of course, pension promises are a special case in the sense that assets are specifically set aside in a protected fund for the purpose of meeting the obligation. However, in principle, obligations in respect of all past promises are the same though in practice many do not have (non-operating) assets specifically set aside.

It follows that the excess value of outstanding promises made, over and above the precautionary non-operating assets available to meet such promises (the net value of promises), is a reduction from company value. Thus, assuming the net value of promises (NVP) is negative:

$$\text{COMPANY VALUE} = \text{ESTA} + \text{CUVI} - \text{NVP} + \text{GOV} \qquad \text{equation (3)}$$

There are now four slices of equity which are known by the acronyms ESTA, CUVI, NVP and GOV. If market capitalisation (MC) is taken to be the value of the company then the GOV implied by the market is:

$$\text{GOV} = \text{MC} + \text{NVP} - \text{ESTA} - \text{CUVI}$$

It should be noted that when promises such as pension deficits and deferred taxation are introduced into the reported accounts then fixed assets plus working capital less loans no longer equals recorded book equity (share capital plus retained profit) but equals recorded book equity plus promises. Promises can become a source of funding for traditional assets. However, ESTA continues to be calculated as fixed assets plus working capital less loans. ESTA represents the shareholder stake in the fixed assets and working capital either through past capital paid in, through retained profits, or through funds in effect borrowed from promises and to be repaid from equity in future.

EQUITY SLICES: TWO BY TWO ANALYSIS

Table 5.2 illustrates equation (3) and its presentation as a two by two analysis. Market capitalisation is the sum of ESTA, CUVI, NVP and GOV. Under present accounting, as shown in Chapter 2, traditional assets (ESTA) plus (most) promises (NVP) are combined together as a single slice of equity in the reported balance sheet. CUVI and GOV are excluded from the currently reported balance sheet and hence together form the market value added – being the difference between the balance sheet (book) equity and market capitalisation. ESTA and CUVI derive their value from the profitability of current production and are therefore productive capital. NVP and GOV are both valued on the basis of expectations and are speculative capital.

Table 5.2   Combinations of the slices of equity

ESTA	NVP	Approximates to the current balance sheet
CUVI	GOV	Market value Added
Productive capital	Speculative capital	Market Capitalisation

ILLUSTRATING THE FOUR SLICES OF EQUITY

Table 5.3 provides an illustration of the four slices of equity based upon Halma plc's 2007 accounts, which show fixed assets/working capital of £94 m and a profit after tax (assumed to be sustainable) of £44 m. Halma had no loans at the time. Halma provides shareholders with a return on ESTA of £6.6 m based upon an assumed required rate of return of 7 per cent on the fixed assets/working capital of £94 m. It also provides a further (residual) profit of £37.4 m for the equity holders. Assuming that the required rate of return on Halma's intangibles is 9 per cent then this is capitalised at a CUVI of £416 m. Halma has promises, primarily its pension deficit, with a net value of £ 32.3 m. GOV (£344.1 m) is calculated as the market capitalisation (£821.8 m) plus the NVP (£32.3 m) less the ESTA (£94 m) and less the CUVI (£416 m). It should be noted that Halma is considered less risky than J D Wetherspoon and hence lower required rates of return have been used.

Table 5.3   Halma plc: four slices of equity

	2006 £m	2007 £m	Required rate of return	Profit (2007) attributed
ESTA	94.5	94.0	7%	6.6
CUVI	367.0	416.0	9%	37.4
GOV	272.4	344.1		
NVP	(40.5)	(32.3)		
MC*	693.4	821.8		
PROFIT	39.6	44.0		44.0

*approx 373.2 million (2006 369.3m) shares at 220 p (2006 188 p)

ADJUSTMENTS TO CALCULATE SUSTAINABLE PROFIT

The calculation of residual income and hence CUVI should be made on the basis of sustainable accounting profit. To calculate sustainable profit might require a number of adjustments to the reported accounting profit. These potential adjustments are only required where they are material and are discussed in the following paragraphs.

For the column of the Stakeholder Knowledge Network (Figure 4.2, column 3), headed 'price/cost, volume' to yield a sustainable accounting profit the expenses shown in column 3 need to be increased by the value of any promises for the future made during the year in order to secure stakeholder engagement in current business activity. Such promises are not 'one off' and will need to be repeated in order to secure continuing engagement. This will be looked at more carefully in a later chapter (Chapter 8) on accounting for promises. Charges in respect of such promises are often already made in reported profit and, if so, no adjustment to reported profit is required. For example, reported profit will already have been charged with the value of any defined benefit pension promises accrued through employee service during the year.

It should be noted, however, that where the reported profit includes an amount for the gain or loss during the year in the value of legacy promises (as can happen, for example with the movement in value of certain types of derivative contract) then that movement should be excluded from sustainable profit.

Furthermore, to give 'sustainable' profit it is necessary to adjust current profit in respect of 'one off' events that have impacted upon profit during the year but will not recur every year even if current business conditions persist. This avoids capitalising a profit or loss that it is known will not recur. Suppose for example that a company's business consists of a single long-term contract and through securitisation the company takes all the profit to be earned on the contract up front. This will result in accelerated profit in the year the contract is signed. This (speculative) profit is not sustainable and reported profit must be adjusted accordingly. In practice, the company is likely to have a mix of contracts in different stages of completion and the size of the adjustment will be determined by the age profile of the contracts. In the extreme, given a perfectly balanced age profile then the adjustment will be zero. For example, there could be ten, ten-year contracts and one retires (and is renewed or replaced) each year.

The illustration (SMD), first introduced in Chapter 2 in terms of traditional accounts and completed in Chapter 12 in terms of 4S accounts, gives two common examples of 'one off' events: profit on disposal of assets and an impairment charge. These are items which should be excluded from sustainable profit.

Coordinating Business Value with the SKN

Figure 5.1 summarises the relationship between the SKN and the value of the business. Items in the column headed 'cost/price volume', less the charge for promises given during the year, give the accounting profit on the basis of which sustainable profit is assessed. The capital value of this sustainable profit is the starting point for the analysis of market capitalisation. As discussed, this capital value is split into the equity stake in fixed assets and working capital (ESTA) on the one hand and CUVI on the other. ESTA is directly impacted (increased) by the accounting profits and in Figure 5.1 sits under the column headed 'price/cost volume'. CUVI is the current use value of intangibles and in Figure 5.1 is identified with the two 'intangible' columns of knowledge and relationship. ESTA and CUVI together derive their value from (sustainable) profits which in turn rest upon the value of outputs (sales) less matching inputs (expenses). The column headed 'promises' has two accounting impacts as shown in Figure 5.1. Firstly, it generates the charge for the value of promises given during the year to help secure stakeholder engagement. Secondly, the value of outstanding past promises less precautionary assets (the net value of promises or NVP) is a reduction in the valuation of the company. The column headed 'prospects' in Figure 5.1 is identified with GOV, since it is these prospects that drive the growth and opportunity value. Thus the columns of the SKN and the elements included in the analysis of business value have been co-developed so that the one is a reflection of the other.

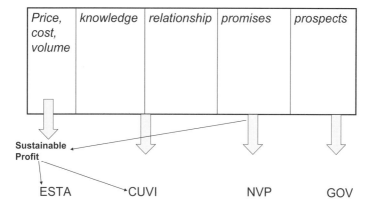

Figure 5.1   **The SKN and valuation analysis**

The Fair Value Debate

There are two accounting models in current usage (Penman 2007a). The first computes accounting profit as the difference between the value of outputs and the value of inputs necessary to create the products sold. The second takes the fair value of assets (less liabilities) at the beginning of the period away from the fair value at the end of the period and the difference is accounting profit. The two accounting models are used to value different elements of the equation: MC = ESTA + CUVI − NVP + GOV.

4S accounting uses the first accounting model (matching) in respect of the flow of product to arrive at sustainable 'profit'. This in turn is used to value ESTA plus CUVI. Together ESTA and CUVI are called the productive capital since their value is a consequence of current product flow. 4S uses the second accounting model (fair value) in relation to the 'overhang' of past promises. The value of this overhang is the result of: (a) changes in the value of the promises in the time since they were incurred and charged against profit; (b) the spending of the assets retained in the business as a consequence of these charges, on items other than the discharge of the obligations incurred by the promises; and (c) movements in the value of the assets retained in order to meet the promises made. Often the value of the overhang is negative but it can of course be positive if the value of the promises falls and/or the value of the retained assets increases more than was anticipated. Thus it is possible, for example, to have defined benefit pension surpluses as well as deficits. The second accounting model (fair value) is also used to value market capitalisation (MC) which is based upon the market value of shares. Since GOV is valued as a residual after taking the other three slices of equity away from MC, it follows that GOV is a hybrid of the two accounting models.

Thus 4S views each of the two accounting models (fair value and matching) as having their place. They are complementary rather than competing. A contribution of the mapping of accounting onto the SKN is that it gives a clear understanding of the roles of traditional matching (transactions) based accounting and (fair) value accounting.

Working, Precautionary and Opportunity Cash

The foot of Figure 5.2 highlights the four demands for cash (and other liquid assets). First, underneath the column headed 'profits, costs, volume' is the working cash that in particular supports the propositions to employees, customers and suppliers in respect of cash payments and stock deliveries. Second, there is the need to *maintain* the intangibles of relationships and knowledge at their current level. Third, as has already been recognised, a company should carry cash or other suitable assets set aside (precautionary capital) to allow it to meet the promises it has made (contingencies and commitments) as they fall due, without disrupting the flow of operations. These assets form a reserve similar to that carried by insurance companies to meet its insurance claims. If suitable assets are not available or cannot be liquidated as required, then the company carries a liquidity risk. In Figure 5.2 precautionary assets are shown under the promises column. Fourth, underneath the prospects column is the 'opportunity' cash (and other non-operating assets) required to take early advantage of knowledge breakthroughs without having to negotiate outside finance. Opportunity cash is also held to enable the company to respond to acquisition opportunities. In many of the forthcoming analyses of companies it is difficult, due to lack of information, to identify separately the size of the four different demands for cash, and assumptions must be made. In particular it is assumed that cash needed to maintain *relationships* is part of working capital and cash required to maintain *knowledge* is part of the opportunity capital needed to deliver prospects. 4S accounting therefore works with three rather than four demands.

The management of working cash is well documented in accounting texts. In addition, precautionary/opportunity cash needs to be carefully managed to reduce disruption to the current operations and future prospects of the company. The assessment of required precautionary/opportunity cash is a

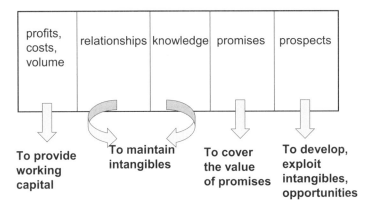

Figure 5.2   The SKN and the demands for cash

difficult judgment. Where a company has low financial gearing it may be able to borrow in order to meet any precautionary/opportunity needs and hence its need to hold precautionary/opportunity cash is lower. Even well-established intangibles-based companies, such as those in the pharmaceuticals industry, can exhibit low gearing, to allow them to borrow if they need to support a new development quickly. It is impossible to predict the success of a research project and the pharmaceuticals firm wants to avoid having to postpone the next stage of a drug's development due to financing constraints at just the time when the value of continuing the project is at its highest. However, access to borrowings is not as secure as actually having the surplus liquid assets in hand, and the liquidity risk is consequently somewhat greater where there is reliance upon a low gearing than where the company already has liquid assets.

Cash balances at the year end can be allocated first to meet working cash requirements and then the need for precautionary cash, with the balance being available to promote opportunities as they arise. In 4S it is the precautionary cash balance which is subtracted from the outstanding promises to give NVP, whilst working cash is part of ESTA and opportunity cash is part of GOV. In circumstances where there is a clear deficiency of the working cash necessary to sustain profit, or of precautionary cash to underwrite the outstanding promises or of opportunity cash to support growth and opportunity value then it is necessary to consider the increase in risk (liquidity risk), a topic addressed in the next chapter.

Returning to the formula MC = ESTA + CUVI – NVP + GOV, it should be noticed that ESTA is invested in fixed assets plus working capital to support operations and excludes other (non-operating) assets held for precautionary or opportunistic purposes. Consequently, income from cash or other assets held for precautionary or opportunistic reasons should be excluded from sustainable profit and the additional cash generated by such income added to the fund of precautionary or opportunity cash.

Conclusion

Chapters 2 and 3 introduced four business issues which have led to accounting's feedback failures. They are: (1) the coupling of risk and reward; (2) the importance of intangibles; (3) recognising the role of promises; and (4) accountability as both current performance and positioning for the future. The valuation analysis provided by 4S accounting addresses these issues. The coupling of risk and return comes from the calculation of CUVI as the risk adjusted value of residual income in perpetuity. Risk is of course also part of the assessment of GOV. The importance of intangibles is recognised by the inclusion of intangibles as assets in place. The role of promises is separately recognised and understood in terms of both its impact on current accounting profit and the generation of future exposure. Current performance is identified with the value of assets in place (ESTA plus CUVI) whilst positioning for the future identifies with the net value of promises and the growth and opportunity value (NVP plus GOV). Thus both the present and future dimensions of accountability are covered. Assets in place (ESTA plus CUVI) represent the value of future profits at a level which maintains the company's 'living standards'. GOV less NVP indicates whether current living standards are expected to increase, and gives the expected value of that increase. The assets in place (ESTA plus CUVI) are the company's productive assets/capital measured in terms of current profit from product flow. NVP plus GOV constitutes the company's speculative assets/capital being based upon future expectations of change. This chapter has introduced the value profile (ESTA/CUVI/NVP/GOV) which forms the basis of the financial analysis used in future chapters.

6

Distributed Risk

The previous chapter has shown the linkage between the Stakeholder Knowledge Network and an analysis of market capitalisation into four slices (4S) of equity (ESTA, CUVI, NVP and GOV). The analysis integrates accounting returns and risk and thus requires consideration of risk as an input. For instance, the current use value of intangibles (CUVI) is dependent upon both the required rate of return on the equity stake in fixed assets/working capital (ESTA) and the required return on intangibles. The risk associated with these two slices of equity (ESTA and CUVI) has to be evaluated as a basis for judging the required returns. The value of NVP is influenced by the risks that impact upon the respective promises contained therein and in turn influence the need for assets held as precautionary capital. The assets held as precautionary capital should be very low risk but no assets are entirely risk free. The value of GOV depends upon the risks that impact on the future of the company. The chapter proceeds through a brief overview of the overall average required rates of return on equity based upon past experience of returns. These returns need to be modified according to the (business) risks faced in the specific business under evaluation. The remainder of the chapter provides a framework for the assessment of business risk. This framework translates the framework for understanding the business (coordinating strategy, stakeholder knowledge network, four slices of equity) into an equivalent framework for the understanding of business risk.

Returns Required for ESTA and CUVI

In the calculation of CUVI there are two required rate of return judgments, one for the rate of return on equity invested in tangible assets/working capital, the other for intangibles. The former is anchored on the long-term rate of return for equity invested in companies dominated by fixed assets (for example utilities) and the latter is anchored on the long-term equity return in companies dominated by intangibles (for example software, biotech). For the illustrations in this book, 8 per cent has generally been used for the former and 10 per cent for the latter, on the assumption that these approximate to the long-term equity returns in each case. Stewart (2001) estimates that the average expected return premium of high knowledge intensive industries is 6 per cent above 'risk free' which, assuming a typical risk free rate of say 4 per cent, gives a required return of 10 per cent on intangibles. However, these anchor rates of 10 per cent for intangibles and 8 per cent for fixed assets and working capital may be a little low. Penman (2004: 646) reports that the historical average return to investing in all US equities has been about 13 per cent per annum. However, this long-term average has by 2007 (Penman, 2007b: 686) fallen to 12.5 per cent. Thus the long-term rate at least up until the financial crisis had been falling.

It is assumed that a higher return is required for intangibles rather than tangibles on the assumption that intangibles generally carry a higher risk. A risk premium for the intangibles of 2 per cent (10 per cent less 8 per cent) has been assumed. Lev (2007) reports that impairment (write offs) is higher for goodwill than for physical assets over a wide range of industries. At the knowledge frontiers it is notoriously difficult to predict the outcome of research projects. All of this suggests that intangibles are riskier. However, in relation to tangibles, specialised assets that can only be used to apply a single idea are as vulnerable and risky as the idea itself. Much depends upon the flexibility of the assets concerned. Risk reduces with flexibility. Property can probably be used for a wide variety of purposes and some ideas may have a wide range of applications in different products. It is therefore necessary in practice to consider the nature of the tangible and intangible assets concerned. However, for illustrative purposes the general assumption that intangibles are riskier than tangibles, has been followed.

ADJUSTING FOR THE FUNDAMENTALS

The required returns for ESTA and CUVI are anchored upon the historical long-term returns on equity. They are the average of periods of differing economic uncertainty. Thus these average long-term returns may not reflect the risks inherent in current business conditions. If current uncertainty is historically high then the required return for the current year should be higher than the long run average. In particular, if the risks inherent in a company's current year business conditions have changed from those facing the company last year then the required returns need to be adjusted from those used last year. If the specific risks faced by a company increase then, all else being equal, so should the required rates. This adjustment has been made for example, in a later chapter, for Croda International following its debt financed acquisition of Uniqema. Following the acquisition in 2006 the rates for Croda are moved up from 8 per cent to 9 per cent to reflect increasing risk from the substantially increased financial gearing of the company.

Insofar as current uncertainties differ between companies then the anchor rates of 8 per cent and 10 per cent should be adjusted to reflect the specific risks faced by the company under examination. In Chapter 5 this adjustment was made in the case of Halma considered to be a relatively low-risk company. For Halma the rates were reduced to 7 per cent and 9 per cent.

An additional benchmark for the assessment of the required returns on a company's ESTA and CUVI is the company's weighted average cost of capital (WACC). An indication of WACC is disclosed in the note included in most companies' financial statements on the impairment testing of goodwill. For this impairment testing a discount rate based upon WACC is generally used to calculate the value in use of a cash generating unit by discounting the unit's forecast cash flows. For example in the case of Rolls Royce the discount rate based upon WACC is disclosed as 12.75 per cent in both 2007 and 2008. Halma used a discount rate based upon WACC of 8.4 per cent in 2008 up from 8 per cent in 2007. These discount rates are pre-tax (that is, applied to pre-tax cash flows) and need to be significantly reduced to give the company's actual (post-tax) WACC. WACC is based upon the weighted average of the cost of debt and the cost of equity and therefore does not reveal directly the cost of equity. The cost of equity will be somewhat higher than (post-tax) WACC whereas the cost of debt will be lower than WACC. Thus the pre-tax discount rate used for impairment of goodwill requires at least two judgmental adjustments to give the cost of equity. Firstly, it needs to be adjusted to give the equivalent post-tax rate and, secondly, it needs to be adjusted to allow for the fact that WACC is an average of return on equity and return on debt. Finally, the cost of equity arrived at by these adjustments needs to be split into the required return on ESTA and on intangibles.

These adjustments are not easy to make from outside the company. It would therefore be helpful if directors were to consider their firm's cost of equity and disclose and explain it (Armitage and Marston 2008: 322–6), preferably distinguishing between the returns on ESTA and on CUVI, and explaining year on year movements. Movements in WACC do not necessarily correspond to movements in the cost of equity. For example, the WACC for Croda

International decreases following the debt financed acquisition of Uniqema since debt is cheaper than equity. However, the risks facing the company might increase as a result of the higher gearing and if so these increased risks increase the required return on equity.

Risk determines the required rate of return on equity and the remainder of this chapter puts forward a framework for thinking about risk based upon distributed risk and cognition. Just as an understanding of business comes through the coordination of three representations of business – business as strategy, business as a Stakeholder Knowledge Network and business as value – so the understanding of business risk comes from the coordination of the three equivalent representations of business risk. These are shown in Figure 6.1 as strategic risk, stakeholder network risk and value risk. Each of these is discussed in turn starting with the stakeholder network risk. The next five sections discuss the six risks corresponding to the six dimensions (columns 2 to 7, Figure 4.2) of the SKN (relationships and knowledge are discussed in the same section). The chapter then proceeds to consider the risks to value associated with ESTA, CUVI, NVP and GOV, and the risks associated with strategic choice (strategic risks). Understanding risk comes from the coordination of the three representations of business risk. Thus our understanding of risk does not flow solely from an analysis of risk into the three categories but also from the connections and correlations between the risks that are identified. The impact of relationships between the three representations of risk is introduced as they become relevant. Similarly, the stakeholder network provides a risk matrix and the connections and correlation between the different cells of the matrix are discussed.

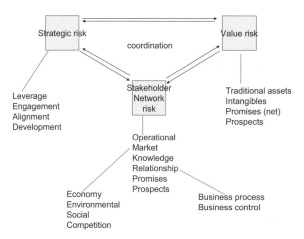

Figure 6.1   Business risk

Stakeholder Network Risks

For each of the six dimensions the discussion considers: (1) the chance of *underlying events* occurring which have the capability of impacting value; and (2) the *potential impact* on value of those underlying events should they occur. A high chance of an underlying event with a small impact might be a low risk overall, whereas a low risk of a catastrophic event that cannot be insured might be considered a high risk. The discussion also considers where relevant: (3) the likely effect of *contracts already in place* (pre-event) to accentuate or mitigate the impact; and (4) the likely effect of *post event responses* that can be taken to accentuate or mitigate the impact. Any uncertainty of an event, the impact of an event or uncertainty of response to an event increases the risk. Contracts already in place include loan contracts (leading to financial leverage), long-term contracts for sale or purchase, risk sharing propositions agreed with stakeholders and (other) derivatives. Post-event responses are particularly relevant to a consideration of the risks inherent in GOV since such responses are often relevant in respect of future events if they should take place. The available responses are the 'real options' to transfer knowledge and/or tangible assets to additional or alternative product markets and/or to renegotiate stakeholder propositions thus reshaping the stakeholder network.

PRODUCT (OPERATIONAL RISK)

Operational risk can come from internal problems or as a result of operational problems at a supplier or other outside stakeholder. In this section the discussion is in terms of internal problems. Operational risk impacts upon value through its effect on the uncertainty of profits.

Underlying events and uncertainty of impact

In respect of the product column of the SKN, operational risks can result in product specifications not being met in the way that was proposed by the company to its customers and other stakeholders. Risk is concerned with uncertainty of outcome before the event. For example, J. Sainsbury is a company that in the early 2000s notoriously suffered from supply chain difficulties that sometimes resulted in empty supermarket shelves, and a poor customer experience. Its information technology (IT) systems were implicated in this failure. Thus in the early 2000s these operational risks were creating uncertainty as to Sainsbury's financial performance. This higher risk would have driven a higher required return for both ESTA and the calculation of

CUVI. Higher required returns, other things being equal, result in lower values for CUVI. Operational uncertainty depends on one or both of two factors being present. The first is uncertainty as to the performance of the IT systems and the second is uncertainty as to the impact any performance failure of the systems will have upon profit.

A further example of operational difficulty and accompanying uncertainty is given by the difficulties experienced at City Link, the parcels business of Rentokil. This example combined two risk 'events' that are common in operational failure; problems in integrating an acquired company (in this case Target Express) and failure in the (new) IT systems.

PRICE/VOLUME (MARKET) RISK

Underlying environmental events and uncertainty of impact

Market risk is concerned with the potential for changes in market size due to environmental factors and the potential for change in market share due to competitive factors. The discussion in this section is limited to price/volume (market) risks associated with changes in the environment, though competitive risks can be equally important. Market risks have their origins in potential change regarding the social, political or economic environment and need to be considered in two parts being: (1) the risk of the change; and (2) uncertainty regarding the impact of the change upon volumes and/or prices. For example, what is the chance of gross domestic product (GDP) changing and what impact would such change have upon volumes and prices? As with knowledge breakthroughs, some political, social and economic changes are not incremental. These rare and dramatic events are difficult to predict in both timing and effect (Taleb 2008). The recent credit crunch is a classic example. Although the chance of such a happening might be low, its impact can be dramatic.

An example of risk coming from social change is as follows. In the mid-2000s pub chain J D Wetherspoon (JDW), in common with other pub chains, was facing the prospect of the introduction of a ban on smoking in pubs. This event was known to be coming and was the continuation of a trend that started with clean air in offices, but there was attendant uncertainty as to its effect on sales volumes. This would give a high-volume risk for future periods. However, in 2005 the ban had yet to be introduced and hence it was not a risk factor for the 2005 profits, but became a risk factor for 2006 when the ban was introduced with the impact of the ban being uncertain. It should be noted that it is the current risk conditions that influence the required returns for ESTA and CUVI, whilst future risk conditions influence the assessment of GOV. J D Wetherspoon's volumes are also at risk from other social factors such as increasing concern over the adverse behaviour and health effects of alcohol consumption, and from the increasing competition from supermarkets/home drinking. The (potential) action(s) of competitors is another key factor influencing market risk.

Mitigation through correlation

It is important to judge price/volume risks in the round across all stakeholders by considering the relationships between the cells within the price/volume column of the SKN. For example, if price rises from suppliers can generally be passed on to customers without impacting upon volumes, then the impact upon sustainable profit of any supplier price rise (and consequently the price/volume risk) is low. Mitigation of market risk can also be organised through derivative contracts.

Mitigation through derivatives and forward contracts

Price risk for example is mitigated by the use of options or propositions with option-like qualities. Forward contracts normally protect against the risk of prices moving in one direction. If prices move in the opposite direction, however, then the use of the forward contract causes a loss in comparison to buying on the spot market. Thus when using such contracts the nature of the exposure is changed but risk remains. It should be noted that risk reduction through the use of derivatives only lasts for the period of the contract. The effect is to mitigate the impact of the underlying risk in the price/volume column of the SKN but consequently the underlying risk has an impact on risk attaching to the column on promises.

Uncertainty as to response

Finally, it is important to consider the adequacy of working and opportunity capital. A shortage might inhibit the company's ability to respond to changing market conditions.

RELATIONSHIP/KNOWLEDGE (INTANGIBLES) RISKS

Risk events and mitigation

The next two columns of the SKN relate to stakeholder relationships and knowledge. Stakeholder risk events include a breakdown in the stakeholder relationship, perhaps due to a takeover, a dispute or the stakeholder getting into financial difficulties. These stakeholder (counterparty) risk events can be a particular concern in the case of derivative contracts. In the case of lending activities by a company, the credit risk associated with the borrower getting into financial difficulties can be mitigated by taking a charge over the borrower's assets. In respect of borrowing activities by a company, a particular source of concern during the credit crunch has been the refinancing of loans. The risk is one of disengagement by a key stakeholder (the loan-holder) who might not be willing to reissue loans when they become due. Relationship risks are in general mitigated by staying close to the key stakeholders so that there is trust and no surprises.

There might also be the risk of insufficient attention given by or to a major stakeholder due to unequal power relations. In the case of Rexam, one of the world's largest canning companies, there is a risk due to the importance of Coca Cola as a customer. To mitigate that risk, Rexam must ensure that its proposition to Coca Cola adapts to changing circumstances such as a steep rise in aluminium prices and that it is able to service Coca Cola's strategic initiatives by servicing any new markets that Coca Cola develop. Rexam stays close to its major customer. Losing touch is a relationship/knowledge risk.

Inherent risk that is difficult to mitigate

Knowledge risk is not only a question of access to, and understanding of, stakeholders. Human knowledge and understanding of the world is bounded and although those boundaries extend over time, significant shifts in the form of knowledge breakthroughs are difficult to predict. For example, businesses such as pharmaceuticals which, as patents expire depend on new blockbuster drugs, are inherently risky. Indeed, Jack (2008) writing in the *Financial Times* reports that shares in established drug makers are (in 2008) trading on profit multiples that largely discount any value in their portfolio of future medicines. The greater the gap between a company's present knowledge and the knowledge it needs to implement its business objectives, the greater the risk. Externally, it is also necessary to look at the competition. Are they better placed to make the knowledge breakthrough? A knowledge breakthrough at a rival company or a new entrant can have a dramatic impact. Knowledge breakthroughs and their impact are difficult to predict and hence generate uncertainty and risk in the new economy. One way to mitigate knowledge risk is by having a portfolio of products and projects underpinned by different branches of knowledge.

PROMISES AND PRECAUTIONARY CAPITAL

Promises play an important role in reshaping the risk and reward profile of the stakeholder network by mitigating (or accentuating) the impact of underlying risk events. For example, a fixed price long-term purchase contract reduces the negative impact of rising purchase prices but removes the positive impact of falling prices. The risk of being hit by rising prices is mitigated but a risk of missing out on falling prices is introduced. Much depends upon the likelihood of the underlying event (rising or falling prices). Similarly, looking at relationship risk, the long-term contract mitigates the risk of losing access to the supplier whilst at the same time removing the option of moving to another supplier if it were favourable to do so.

Risks associated with promises need to be considered in respect of each stakeholder category. This is also a consideration for other risks but is particularly important for promises since there are substantial differences in the nature of the risks associated with promises depending upon the stakeholder category. For example, the risks associated with the defined benefit pension fund (the behaviour of equity prices, interest rates, longevity and so on) are the result of macro events whereas the warranty risk is micro and dependent on the behaviour of the company's own products. There may be very little correlation between these two risks.

Defined benefit plans are highly leveraged, accentuating risk

The pension promise is a major risk category for many UK businesses. For instance, a small percentage drop in the value of equities can have a disproportionate impact on the pension surplus or deficit. In effect, the pension fund deficit/surplus is high in financial leverage and a major source of risk for the company. By providing a defined benefit pension, the company has written a valuable option for its employees. Such options have a high leverage effect accentuating risk.

The greater the size and volatility of the net value of promises, then assuming NVP is negative, the greater the precautionary capital required. If the assets held to provide this precautionary capital are also volatile then once again this requires precautionary capital to be increased. Any deficiency of precautionary capital reduces the value of the company. The impact of volatility can be considered in respect of the pensions promise. Volatile equity markets and interest rates lead to volatility in the size of the pension deficit/surplus and in theory this volatility might require precautionary assets over and above the assets set aside within the fund itself. In effect, volatility increases the value of the option that has been written by the company in favour of its employees, but the value of this option is not generally recognised in the calculation of the deficit/surplus. In principle, precautionary assets should be held to cover the value of this option.

Correlation between rows

It is important to examine whether there is correlation between the various promises (the cells in the promises column) since this too will impact on the precautionary funds that are necessary to underwrite the promises portfolio as a whole. For example, interest rate changes will impact on the pensions promise, on the savings from fixed interest loans and the value of interest rate swaps. If deferred tax were valued on a discounted basis, interest rates would also have a significant impact on that item. If precautionary assets are inadequate in the light of the overall value and volatility of promises then there is the risk (liquidity risk) of the business getting into difficulties due to a shortage of funds.

The impact of financial leverage (gearing)

Loan contracts are promises that create or accentuate risk due to financial leverage (gearing). Like many other promises it is not so much a risk in its own right but rather it operates to accentuate the impact of underlying risk events. It is well known that the impact of changing volumes and prices upon sustainable profit is accentuated when a company has high levels of loans relative to book equity (financial gearing). Thus gearing accentuates pre-existing price/volume risks. In a similar manner, any other fixed contractual commitments, including leases, that inhibit a company from responding flexibly to new volumes or prices, can also accentuate market risk. Operational gearing occurs when a company cannot respond flexibly due to its purchase of fixed assets. The impact of traditional financial gearing upon risk arises most clearly when the interest charge on loans is at a fixed rate and thus, unlike dividends, cannot be varied in response to financial performance. It is a payment that has to be met before dividends can be paid. Thus the risk attaching to profits after interest (net profit) is accentuated by high gearing. If profit before interest (PBI) dips then net profit will dip by a greater percentage depending upon the extent of the gearing. However, if the underlying event (a dip in profit before interest) is unlikely since the profitability is not volatile then the high gearing can be undertaken with little risk. Thus gearing does not of itself create risk but accentuates a pre-existing risk.

As regards loan-holders, the risk for them attaching to their interest payment depends upon the volatility of profit before interest (PBI) and the size of the 'cushion' provided by the number of times PBI exceeds interest. This cushion is known as the interest cover. If PBI is volatile and the cover is thin then the interest payment is at risk and loan-holders are likely to seek higher rates. Interest cover is closely related to the size of interest bearing loans relative to shareholder book equity as shown in the traditional accounts (old economy gearing).

PROSPECTS AND GOV

The risk attaching to the prospects for the future of the business is a function of the risks affecting future operations, future markets, the future for the intangibles and future promises. It is necessary to consider how today's risks are going to change in the future. Whereas it is today's risk conditions that provide the context for the valuation of sustainable profit (a valuation which assumes that current conditions continue), it is the future risk conditions that impact upon prospects.

In assessing GOV it is necessary to consider the risk that prospects do not materialise. The evaluation of risk for GOV is not concerned directly with the current risk environment but takes into account future threats (and opportunities) associated with anticipated future business conditions and the possible management responses. For GOV, risk is concerned with the diversity of possible futures. If we are expecting to move into a riskier, more uncertain business environment (with less certainty as to what future SKNs will look like), then, all else being equal, the value of GOV should be adjusted downwards.

Mitigation through real options

GOV should also reflect the flexibility of expected future investments in fixed assets and intangibles in terms of alternative uses. Other things being equal, the greater the real options for these assets then the lower the risks associated with the future.

Response difficulties

Assessment of GOV should also take into account liquidity risk, being the risk that a shortage of opportunity assets impedes the future progress and development of the company. In general, the need for opportunity capital is lower when there is lower financial gearing.

    The remaining sections of the chapter (re)present risk in terms of value relations (ESTA, CUVI, NVP and GOV) and strategic choice (leverage, engage, align, develop).

Value Risks

In essence, the risks for ESTA flow through from the product and market risks of the stakeholder network, risks to CUVI flow from the risks to ESTA plus those associated with knowledge and relationships and risks for NVP and GOV flow from the promises and prospects columns respectively of the SKN as a risk matrix. In addition, it is necessary to consider the value relations between the four slices of equity, notably between ESTA and CUVI, and CUVI and GOV.

THE RELATIONSHIP BETWEEN ESTA AND CUVI (NEW ECONOMY GEARING)

The return to ESTA as a charge on sustainable profit prior to reaching residual profit has a very similar effect on risk to the effect of interest as a charge in reaching sustainable profit. Like the interest charge which leaves (net) profit as a residual, the charge on ESTA is met ahead of the return on intangibles. Whether the return on ESTA is at risk depends upon the volatility of the sustainable profit and the size of the 'cushion' or cover provided by the number of times sustainable profit exceeds the ESTA return. If the sustainable profit is volatile and the cushion is small then there is a high risk that sustainable profit will dip below the required return so that the ESTA return cannot be met. The cover for the ESTA return is closely related to the size of ESTA relative to the size of CUVI (a relation that can be called 'new economy gearing').

As regards CUVI, the risk attaching to residual profit is accentuated by high 'new economy gearing'. If the new economy gearing is high then ESTA is high relative to CUVI and thus the ESTA return is high relative to residual income. Thus, other things being equal, a high new economy gearing is associated with low cover for the ESTA return. If sustainable profit dips then residual profit will dip by a greater percentage depending upon the extent of the new economy gearing. New economy gearing can be thought of as the extent to which the company has had to invest equity in traditional fixed assets so as to exploit ideas and other intangibles. High gearing serves to accentuate other (pre-existing) risks, but if those pre-existing risks are low then high gearing is less of an issue.

For example, a high ESTA relative to CUVI suggests high (new economy) gearing but it also suggests an old economy company and such companies often have far less volatility in their earnings than companies dependent upon intangibles. If there is low earnings volatility then the company can take a higher gearing.

RELATIONS BETWEEN CUVI AND GOV (FUTURE ECONOMY GEARING)

The life cycle of a strategic choice impacts upon risk. During the start-up phase of a strategic choice we expect a relatively low CUVI and a relatively high GOV. This is risky since it puts pressure on achieving future prospects and much can happen to interfere. It is important that the value of GOV, though relatively high, takes into account this risk. Towards the end of the life of a strategic choice we expect a relatively high CUVI and low GOV. This is risky since the company needs a new strategic direction and it might be hard to find. This time it is important that the low value of GOV takes the uncertain future into account. Companies in the start or finish stages are, other things being equal, riskier relative to a company where CUVI and GOV are well balanced. The relative rates of change of CUVI and GOV are also a consideration. Other things being equal, when GOV is rising faster than CUVI, there is a prima facie risk that the share price is overvalued, whereas when CUVI is rising faster than GOV the share price might be undervalued.

CORRELATION AND GOV

There were two previous examples of correlation between the *rows* (stakeholders) of the SKN. The first example for price risk was where price rises from suppliers could be passed on to customers. The second example for the risk associated with promises was when interest rates impact upon the pension deficit (employees), the value of interest rate swaps (suppliers) and possibly deferred taxation (government). In relation to GOV it is important to consider the correlation between the *columns* (leading to four slices of equity) of the SKN. In the valuation analysis the four slices of equity are the equity invested in fixed assets and working capital (ESTA), the current use value of intangibles (CUVI), the net value of promises (NVP) and growth and opportunity value (GOV). Thus the overall valuation might be thought of as a portfolio of these four slices (a fund of four funds). Like any portfolio, the portfolio risk is lower when the risks associated with each slice are negatively correlated and greater when the risks are positively correlated. Given the same expected returns, it follows that a portfolio with negative correlation offers the same reward for lower risk and hence has a higher value. If we regard GOV as the residual value that makes up total value, then GOV should be adjusted upwards when there is negative correlation between the four slices of equity and downwards when there is positive correlation. To find out about correlation between the slices of equity it is necessary to look at correlation between the columns. For example, interest rate changes impact pensions but they also impact upon the business itself, notably on sales volumes and costs. A rise in GDP can increase volumes for the company and increase the pension fund surplus due to a rise in equity prices generally.

Strategic Risks

The nature of the strategic choice also impacts upon the relevance of the risks (corresponding to the six dimensions of the SKN). For example, if the strategy depends upon engagement, it is particularly important that the relevant relationship and the effectiveness of the knowledge that the relationship gives access to hold up since these are the strengths to be leveraged. The potential impact of relationship and knowledge risks is accentuated through leverage. We shall see that most strategic choice involves leverage in the shape of higher volumes and/or margins and such leverage accentuates pre-existing risks. Leverage in the sense of higher volumes and/or margins can put stress on relationships and expose any weaknesses.

Conclusion

Chapters 1 and 2 introduced four business issues. They were: (1) the coupling of risk and reward; (2) the importance of intangibles; (3) recognising the role of promises; and (4) accountability as both current performance and positioning for the future. The 4S (four slices) valuation analysis addresses these issues. The coupling of risk and return is facilitated by the use of the same representational frameworks for both the understanding of business and the understanding of business risk. In particular, the Stakeholder Knowledge Network serves as: (1) the risk matrix for the assessment and understanding of stakeholder risk; and (2) the medium for coordination of stakeholder risk with value risk and risks consequent to strategic choice.

The chapter started with a discussion of the required rates of return on: (1) equity invested in tangible (traditional) assets; and (2) equity invested in intangible assets. There is a substantial literature on required rates of return but little confidence that the appropriate rates are known accurately and so more work could usefully be done in this area (See Penman 2004: 644–71). The rates are anchored in the long-term experience of equity returns, but where there is reason to, the long-term rates are adjusted for the fundamentals of each company. The size of this adjustment is largely a matter of judgment based upon an analysis of the company's risk profile. This chapter has discussed the use of the SKN as a risk matrix to profile the risks associated with the stakeholder propositions including correlations and response uncertainties. The risks associated with each of the columns of the SKN as a risk matrix flow through to form the risks associated with each of the four slices of equity. It is also necessary to consider how the business risk associated with each of the four slices is impacted by value relations (between ESTA and CUVI, CUVI and GOV) and, directly or indirectly, by strategic choice.

The assessment of risks associated with the six dimensions of the SKN is in four parts. First, there is the uncertainty as to the underlying event with the capacity to change value. Second, there is the impact any change will have on the company's valuation. Third, there is the effect of contracts in place that accentuate or mitigate the impact. Fourth, there is the impact of post-event responses designed to accentuate or mitigate the impact. It is important to consider the SKN as a whole. For example, in the event of a rise in interest rates or GDP then many of the cells in the SKN are impacted, creating correlation. It is therefore necessary to allow for correlation when considering the exposure to interest rates, inflation or GDP. These are not easy judgments to make, but the chapter has sought to set out a framework within which the judgments can be made.

7

Accounting for Intangibles

This chapter briefly considers the nature of intangibles. It then, again briefly, reviews the rather inconclusive debate on accounting for intangibles in the academic literature. Next, an overview is given of how intangibles are treated under current accounting standards. This leads to consideration of impairment and the impact of impairment on sustainable profit as used in 4S accounting. The remainder of the chapter then considers two case studies – DMGT and Halma – to demonstrate the accounting for intangibles, and the interpretation of the performance of intangibles, in accordance with 4S principles.

The Nature of Intangibles

We will regard intangibles as existing essentially in the two SKN dimensions of: (1) knowledge; and (2) stakeholder relationship. Knowledge leads to capability whilst the stakeholder relationship leads to access. The existence of intangibles can be given formal expression or it can be informal. Knowledge includes formal knowledge that can be written down in an explanation, manual of procedures or formula and the informal tacit knowledge of competencies, capabilities and skills. Access can also be formal or informal. Formal expression can be in the form of licences, brands or patents. A licence gives access to knowledge and/ or to stakeholders. A brand gives access to customers and it gives customers 'knowledge' of the product. A patent gives improved access to knowledge (and to customers for that knowledge) in the sense of shielding that knowledge from competitors. Access to stakeholders and their knowledge can also come informally through relationships that build over time through the enactment of transactions. That there is a wide range of intangible assets is made clear in the following quote by a media company executive. The quotation is taken from Holland (2006: 121):

> *Our tangibles are bricks and mortar. The near-tangibles are things like the TV licences which, if they were to shoot up from £5 million to £10 million for the cost of renewal, then this would affect our share price. The next category we can move on to are the valuable intangibles such as top management qualities, track record, brands and relationships with other TV firms and advertisers with our viewers and our readers. These particular categories are amongst our important intangibles; they directly affect value. The top management part of these involves our ability to facilitate deals and acquire new businesses. This increases our revenue and cash flow. It will increase the EBITDA before exceptional items and, of course, this will help us improve our share price. So the valuable intangibles are pretty important. The final group, the intangible intangibles such as celebrity talent, are less valuable here.*

There is therefore a spectrum of assets with first tangible assets and then categories of intangible asset all of which have different risk characteristics in terms of their potential impact upon profit and ultimately the value of the company. Intangibles range from those such as licences with characteristics not dissimilar to fixed assets through to 'intangible' intangibles such as 'celebrity' talent.

The Debate on Intangibles

In the new economy intangibles have been recognised as a crucial factor in business success and a key part of the value creation story that management communicates to the analysts and investing community (Holland 2004, 2006). The importance of intangibles in the evaluation of a company has led to accounting for intangibles becoming a major and sensitive issue for standard setters (Alfredson 2001). In essence, the issues are those that typically face standard setters, being which (intangible) assets to include in the balance sheet, whether they are included at cost or value and what disclosures to require outside of the balance sheet in the notes to the accounts or in other reports. In respect of disclosures much of the early work on intangibles measurement may be relevant. Such early work comes from intellectual capital theory (Viedma Marti 2007) and includes the 'Skandia Navigator' (Edvinsson and Malone 1997), the 'Intangible Assets Monitor' (Sveiby 1997) and the 'Balanced Scorecard (BSC)' (Kaplan and Norton 1992). Scorecards such as the BSC have the potential to feed disclosures but they do not directly seek to value intangibles or put them on the balance sheet; rather they serve to help managers develop the link between measurable characteristics of intangibles and subsequent financial success. Score-carding also facilitates benchmarking (Viedma Marti 2001) in which companies can benchmark their intellectual capital against their 'world class' competitors. Many of a company's intellectual resources are not captured within mandatory financial accounting metrics and are reported therefore on a voluntary basis (Stiukova, Unerman and Guthrie 2008). Stiukova, Unerman and Guthrie provide an empirical examination of intellectual capital disclosure practices by UK companies.

There is a continuing debate as to whether the inclusion of intangibles on balance sheets is feasible and Kaplan and Norton (2004: 52) describe the valuation of intangibles as the 'holy grail of accounting'. Value relevance is part of the debate and Dahmash, Durand and Watson (2009) examine value relevance during the period 1994 to 2003 in Australia when it was possible to report internally generated goodwill and identifiable intangible assets, including R and D, on the balance sheet. In accord with prior studies they found that the balance sheet disclosures were value relevant though, due to accounting arbitrage between goodwill and identifiable intangibles, they may not have been reliable. The finding of value relevance is consistent with Lev, Nissim and Thomas (2007) who claim that expenditures on intangibles such as R and D should be capitalised and amortised. However, Dahmash, Durand and Watson (2009: 132) also report that for high-performing companies with sustainable abnormal operating earnings (AOE, being similar to residual income), the reporting of goodwill and identifiable intangibles is no longer viewed as market relevant whilst the AOE variable becomes highly significant as a basis for valuing intangibles. This is consistent with Lev (2001) who has suggested a means of valuing intangibles by capitalising residual income. Skinner (2008) provides a summary of the debate and takes issue with those who argue for the reform of accounting for intangibles, claiming there is little evidence that the current reporting arrangements have adverse effects on capital markets. A critical view of the literature on intangibles is given by Zeghal and Maaloul (2011).

Current Accounting: Purchased Intangibles Through Takeover

A common way of accessing intangibles is through the acquisition of another company (a takeover). Upon a takeover the difference between the fair value of all *identifiable* assets of the business acquired (both tangible and intangible) and the cost of the acquisition is called goodwill, and is described as such in the consolidated balance sheet. Goodwill therefore represents the non-identifiable intangible assets of the acquired company. The relevant accounting policy of Halma plc, for example, explains goodwill as follows (Halma 2007: 42):

> *Goodwill in respect of acquisitions after 4 April 2004 represents the difference between the cost of an acquisition and the fair value of the net identifiable assets of the business acquired, and is recognised as an intangible asset in the Consolidated balance sheet. Goodwill therefore includes non-identified intangible assets including business processes, know-how and workforce-related industry-specific knowledge and technical skills.*

Goodwill is subject every year to an impairment test to establish whether the net present value of the future cash flows it is expected to generate is lower than the recorded amount for goodwill in the balance sheet. If it is found to be lower then the goodwill is 'impaired' and is reduced in the balance sheet to the net present value of expected future cash flows.

Upon a takeover, all of the intangibles in the acquired company that can be separately identified are included in the consolidated balance sheet as other intangible assets (that is, other than goodwill) and shown at fair value. Those 'other intangibles' in the balance sheet that are expected to have an indefinite life are subjected to an impairment test. Other intangible assets with a finite life are first amortised over the expected useful life and then the net book value (un-amortised cost) is subjected to an impairment test.

Intangibles Not Acquired Through Takeover

In addition to their purchase through takeover, intangibles can be purchased directly or they can be internally generated. The practice is for some of these intangibles not acquired through takeover to be capitalised and some to be expensed. There are commentators and academics (such as Lev, Nissim and Thomas 2007) who advocate the capitalisation and amortisation of all intangibles expenditure but this chapter shall discuss and work with the current practice whereby the accounting treatment depends on the nature of the intangible. The distinction in current practice between what is capitalised and what is expensed is somewhat arbitrary. Table 7.1 shows how different intangibles are normally treated. Those which are capitalised are subjected to impairment testing.

Table 7.1   How intangibles are treated

Expensed	Capitalised
Research and some development	Development, in-house research acquired through acquisition
Customer acquisition/retention	Licences
Advertising and marketing	Patents
Training	Trademarks
Relocation	Software developed for internal use

EXAMPLE OF IMPAIRMENT TESTING

For example, a licence with five years to run is acquired for £5 m. It does not matter whether the licence is bought directly or acquired upon a takeover. On a straight line basis the licence will be capitalised and amortised to £4 m after one year in operation. If the net present value of future cash flows from the licence is judged at the end of year one to be only £3.8 m then the licence is reduced in the balance sheet to £3.8 m and the charge against profit for year one is increased by £0.2 m to £1.2 m. It should be noted that if the net present value of the licence were judged at the end of year two to be £3.1 m, the year two balance sheet would show the licence at the un-amortised cost of £3 m and the charge to profit would be only £0.8 m. In essence, this accounting treatment of purchased intangibles is the same as the accounting treatment of purchased tangible assets for which the net book value is also subject to an impairment test. In terms of sustainable profit, however, the charge to profit should be £1 m each year. In year one, for example, an assessment of sustainable profit requires that the charge is reduced from £1.2 m to £1 m through an 'add back' to reported profit of £0.2 m. In essence, the process of impairment accelerates future anticipated losses to the current year. The 4S argument is that such an anticipated decline in future profits corresponds to an anticipated decline in future business conditions and in the four equity slices is recognised though a fall in the GOV and not by reducing current (sustainable) profits and hence CUVI. Sustainable profit and CUVI are predicated upon existing business conditions continuing.

The amortisation of the licence of £1 m per year remains as a charge in the assessment of sustainable profit since this is necessary to be able to renew the licence, assuming licence costs do not escalate. The basic rules for the calculation of sustainable profit as used in 4S accounting, therefore, are:

a)   impairments are 'one offs' and therefore adjusted in the assessment of sustainable profit; and

b)   amortisation charges are not 'one offs' and therefore there is no adjustment.

However, an adjustment in respect of amortisation will be necessary if there has been double charging. There is double charging if an acquired intangible through acquisition of a subsidiary (for example customer acquisition costs) is identified, capitalised and amortised, but subsequent expenditure on the maintenance of that intangible (the cost of replacing customers lost through churn) is also expensed.

In relation to impairments being 'one offs', the adjustment is to remove asymmetrical conservatism. Asymmetrical conservatism occurs when expected future losses on a line of business are accelerated so as to (decrease) current profits, as is the case with impairment, but expected future profits are not accelerated so as to be included in current profits. The asymmetry relates to the different treatments of favourable and unfavourable expectations. 4S accounting wants to retain the conservatism of not accelerating profits in calculating sustainable profit but does not want the asymmetrical conservatism of accelerating future losses. This is because 4S requires a clear distinction between current and future performance. Future performance is captured by GOV, and it is of course possible if desired to carve out for separate disclosure that part of GOV that constitutes the impairment.

Two cases involving intangibles are now investigated. The first case (DMGT) has intangibles typical of the media industry and uses a significant amount of loans to finance its intangibles. The second case (Halma) has intangibles typical of an innovative engineering company and at the time of consideration it has no long-term loans. It is unusual for a company of its size in being a portfolio of 80 or so subsidiaries and therefore effective governance/parenting skills is an important intangible.

The Case of DMGT 2006/2007

In the 2006 annual report of DMGT (DMGT 2006: 11-12) its strategy is described by the Chief Executive in the following terms:

The Group's objective is to be the owner of high quality sustainable media properties, reflected in premium commercial positions, thereby generating a premium return for shareholders. Over the past decade the strategy has been to extend the Group's media activities so as to reduce its dependence on UK newspapers, which are heavily dependent upon advertising, and, due to their strong market position, much regulated.

The Group's newspapers remain highly profitable and we are continuing to invest in them in order to maintain their market-leading positions. The stability of these businesses has underpinned the manner in which we have built a re-balanced group: by deployment of capital most successfully in DMG Information, recently in Euromoney through its acquisition of Metal Bulletin and in DMG World Media and DMG Radio.

DMGT was incorporated in 1922 but has origins dating back to the launch of the *Daily Mail* in 1896. It is one of the longest-established media companies in the UK and now sees itself as a successful information provider. DMGT has substantial intangible assets in licences for radio, mastheads and of course editorial quality. The company is investing in new media properties, and hence there are substantial intangibles on the balance sheet as a result of acquisition. Its strategy is to acquire new media intangibles, whose financing is 'underpinned' by the stability of its newspapers business. The following paragraphs look more closely at how the acquired intangibles are funded.

In Table 7.2 sustainable profit is assessed based upon the reported profit from continuing businesses before tax and after interest. Sustainable profit is the profit that can be maintained assuming the pattern of business conditions experienced in the current year were to be maintained in perpetuity. Impairment charges being a 'one off' are adjusted, as are 'one off' exceptional costs. Non-operating gains shown in the company's income statement are also treated as 'one off' income. Often such income relates to profit on disposals of assets. In practice, the circumstances giving rise to other income should be investigated to assess whether or not it should be included in sustainable profit. Table 7.2 shows tax charged on the calculated sustainable profit at 30 per cent though in practice the company's effective tax rate might be used.

Table 7.2   DMGT sustainable profit

	2006 £m	2007 £m
Profit from continuing operations before tax	311.5	142.1
Impairment	59.2	52.7
Exceptional costs	41.1	28.1
Non-operating gains	(188.6)	(35.7)
Sustainable profit before tax	223.2	187.2
Tax (30%)	(67.0)	(56.2)
Sustainable profit	156.2	131.0

THE NEW ECONOMY BALANCE SHEET

DMGT's balance sheet can be reconfigured to clarify the financing of intangibles. The reconfigured balance sheet is shown as Figure 7.1. In Figure 7.1, fixed assets and working capital have been taken to include the amounts shown in DMGT's balance sheet in respect of:

> *fixed assets, joint ventures, associates, inventory, trade receivables, cash, trade payables and current tax payable. Loans are the other financial liabilities. Recorded intangibles are Goodwill and other intangibles. Promises in the shape of contingencies and commitments are taken to be net of precautionary assets and to include available for sale assets, deferred tax assets and liabilities, retirement benefit assets and obligations, derivatives, put options and provisions.*

Figure 7.1 assumes that financial management from a new economy perspective would apply loans first to the financing of fixed assets and working capital, whilst equity (along with NVP) is applied first to the funding of intangibles. This is because from the new economy perspective it is the investment in intangibles that is key to the business and the investment in fixed assets is made in order to leverage those intangibles. Following this assumption, Figure 7.1 demonstrates that in 2007 fixed assets/working capital is, for DMGT, wholly funded by loans (ESTA is zero), whilst the recorded intangibles are funded 45.2 per cent by loans, 48.7 per cent by equity and 6.1 per cent by promises (NVP). The equivalent percentages for 2006 are 40.2 per cent for loans, 42.25 per cent for equity and 17.55 per cent for promises. Thus loans are a significant part of the funding of intangibles. The equity percentage is on an upward trend, showing that retained profits are playing at least some part in the company's expansion into new intangibles.

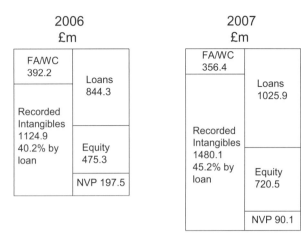

Figure 7.1   DMGT's reconfigured balance sheets

Since the equity stake in the traditional assets of fixed assets/working capital is nil, there is no required return to shareholders in this regard and sustainable profit, which is net of interest, becomes the residual income. At a required return on intangibles of 10 per cent, CUVI based on sustainable profit (Table 7.2) is £1,310 m at the end of 2007 and £1,562 m for 2006. This, along with the continuing impairment charges, suggests a company in modest decline. This is especially so when one recognises that the 2007 CUVI has the benefit of CUVI in the subsidiaries acquired during 2007. The share price for DMGT's 375.4 m non-voting shares was 631.5 p at the 2007 year end. There were also 19.9 m voting shares which retained control with the founding family and carried at that time an approximate premium of 50 per cent. These numbers give DMGT a 2007 year end market capitalisation of £2,559 m. The market capitalisation at the 2006 year end is £2,460 m based upon a share price of 607 p. These market caps in turn give a 2007 GOV of £1,339.1 m and a 2006 GOV of £1,095.5 m. The calculation is as follows:

GOV = Market Cap + NVP – CUVI – ESTA.

2007 GOV = 2,559 + 90.1 – 1,310 – NIL = 1,339.1

2006 GOV = 2,460 + 197.5 – 1,562 – NIL = 1,095.5

These balance sheet date GOVs are, of course, before the market has had an opportunity to assess the relevant financial figures. The share price by April

2008 had dropped to around 420 p. If the fall had been in line with the media sector then the DMGT price would only have dropped to 500 p. This suggests that the market was not impressed with the 2007 performance and prospects based upon its 2007 financial results.

Table 7.3   DMGT 4S balance sheets

	2006 £m	2007 £m		2006 £m	2007 £m
FA/WC	392.2	356.4	loans	844.3	1,025.9
CUVI funded by loans	452.1	669.5	NVP	197.5	90.1
CUVI funded by equity	1562.0	1,310.0	Equity (market cap)	2,460.0	2,559.0
CUVI	2,014.1	1,979.5			
GOV	1,095.5	1,339.1			
	3,501.8	3,675.0		3,501.8	3,675.0

Table 7.3 gives the 4S 'comprehensive' balance sheet for DMGT; comprehensive in the sense that it deals with the full year end value of equity as indicated by the market capitalisation. Loans have been included as a separate item in view of their importance in financing intangibles. Consequently, the 'assets' side of the balance sheet includes FA/WC and CUVI plus the cash flows associated with the growth potential (GOV). On the right-hand side of the balance sheet are the claims on those assets in respect of loans, promises (NVP) and the claims of shareholders (equity at market cap). In the discussion of the funding structure, loans are taken to have funded firstly the fixed assets and working capital, and then CUVI. CUVI is split between that which is funded by loans and that 'funded' by equity. NVP is taken to have funded GOV, or to put it the other way around, the future cash flows of GOV are assumed to be applied firstly to the payment of promises and then to support the value of equity. Following this structure, GOV supports £1,249 m of the value of equity whilst CUVI supports the other £1,310 m of equity (£1,249 m + £1,310 m = £2,559 m).

The 4S balance sheet shows the proportion of intangibles measured as CUVI to be funded by loans in 2007 as 669.5/1979.5 = 33.8 per cent, up from 22.4 per cent in the previous year. The conventional balance sheet of Figure 7.1 only shows those intangibles that are capitalised and it shows them at purchase cost less amortisation and impairment. The 4S balance sheet shows all intangibles, whether or not they are capitalised in the conventional balance sheet, and it shows them at current value in terms of profits. It is interesting to compare the intangibles in the two balance sheets. In 2006 the ratio of intangibles at value to acquired intangibles at cost (less impairment and amortisation) is 1.8, being 2014/1124. In 2007 this ratio drops to 1.34 (1979/1480) due to a drop in the performance of intangibles and an increase in acquired intangibles through acquisition. DMGT has more intangibles and they are performing less well. Table 7.3 shows that GOV has increased whereas CUVI, in spite of CUVI bought through acquisition, has fallen. These are likely pre-conditions for a fall in the share price to adjust GOV downwards. In 2007 the ratio of GOV to CUVI (funded by equity) is 1.02 up from 0.7 in 2006. It has been noted that from the year end in October 2007 to April 2008, the share price fell from 631.5 p to 420 p. By the time the 2011 results came out the share price had fallen to 400 p and the premium on the controlling shares was down to 12 per cent. Market capitalisation stood at £1,580 m and the 4S analysis is shown as Table 7.4.

Table 7.4   DMGT 2011

	2011 £m		2011 £m
FA/WC	251.6	Loans	861.3
CUVI funded by loan	609.7	NVP	301.0
CUVI funded by equity	686.3	Equity (MC)	1,580.1
CUVI	1,296.0		
GOV	1,194.8		
	2,742.4		2,742.4

Compared to 2007, CUVI has dropped by 34.5 per cent from £1,979 m to £1,296 m, whist GOV has dropped by only 10.7 per cent from £1,339 m to £1,195 m. The story has moved on from 2007 since the old media properties are no longer providing the cash flow to fund the investment in new media. Indeed DMGT have been trying to sell the regional newspapers without success. It looks as though DMGT has held on too long to the old media and the transformation from an old economy to a new economy company has consequently stalled. For the investor it is hard to justify the GOV of £1,194.9 m shown by the 2011 4S accounts. The 2007 and 2007 4S accounts suggested that DMGT was not a good buy in 2007 and the 2011 accounts would appear to confirm that verdict.

Halma: 2005 to 2009

Halma's value creation story is one of exercising high-quality parenting skills (for a discussion of such skills see Goold, Campbell and Alexander 1994) as 100 per cent owner of 80 or so subsidiaries worldwide, all operating in the growth sector of health and safety products. It is this parenting capability together with the management of risk and reward for the portfolio as a whole which is the key intangible asset of Halma. Indeed, Halma may be thought of as an activist long-term investor in a specialist sector. The 2007 Annual Report explains how Halma operates in the following terms (Halma 2007: 21):

> We cultivate a highly decentralised operating culture which encourages our businesses to focus on establishing market leadership in their selected niche within a global market. Each subsidiary is led by a management team who enjoy genuine autonomy and the freedom to grow in an entrepreneurial environment.

Important contributions of Head Office are to encourage collaboration between subsidiaries so as to develop new products, and to provide management development across the Group subsidiaries.

At the level of the individual subsidiary, innovation is critical. In its 2007 annual report (Halma 2007: 33) it states:

> Innovation is a critical ingredient for Halma's growth. Continually refreshing our intellectual property leads to new products and processes and helps us maintain the strong market positions held by many of our companies. Innovation is not just the responsibility of the R and D department but is integral to all commercial activities within the business. Innovative ideas can range from a novel way to enter a new or remote market to administration process improvements speeding the delivery of products to customers. All employees within the Group have the opportunity to deliver innovative ideas to help their company and the Group achieve the growth objectives.

Thus Halma's intangibles include research and development, its innovative employees and parenting skills in respect of its subsidiaries together with the management of the portfolio. Parenting is exercised through a set of relationships with subsidiaries that enables the innovation of its employees and the productivity of research and development. It is this productivity that is now investigated. Table 7.5 shows the output from Halma's intangibles in the form of residual income and CUVI for the five years up to and including 2009. It also shows the administrative and R and D expenditure each year during that period. Residual income has been calculated using a 7 per cent required return on the fixed assets and working capital, being set 2 per cent lower than the 9 per cent return for Halma's intangibles. The rate of 9 per cent is based upon the discount rate Halma used during the relevant period to calculate the net present value of recorded intangibles for impairment testing. Since in the years up to 2007 Halma does not have any long-term loans then all of its fixed assets/working capital during that period is taken to be funded by equity and the 7 per cent is applied to the whole of the fixed assets/working capital.

Table 7.5   Halma's intangibles record

	2005 £m	2006 £m	2007 £m	2008 £m	2009 £m
FA/WC	105.8	94.5	94.0	79.4*	111.3†
Profit post tax	33.5	39.6	44.0	48.3	52.6
Return (7%)	7.4	6.6	6.6	5.6	7.8
Residual income	26.1	33.0	37.4	42.7	44.8
CUVI (9%)	290.0	367.0	416.0	474.0	498.0
CUVI increase		26.5%	13.4%	13.9%	5.1%
Recorded intangibles	94.8	134.2	144.9	194.5	239.0

*£79.4 m is FA/WC of £144.8 m less loans of £65.4 m
†£111.3 m is FA/WC of £190.9 m less loans of £79.6 m

THE PRODUCTIVITY OF INTANGIBLES

The movement in CUVI provides an overview of the performance of the intangibles during the year. Table 7.5 shows that the best year was 2006 with a 26.5 per cent increase, and 2009 the worst with a 5.1 per cent increase. The movement in CUVI can be explained by the movement in residual income together with any change in the required rate of return for intangibles. In the Halma case a constant 9 per cent required return has been assumed throughout the period and thus the percentage change in CUVI from year to year equals the change in residual income.

Residual income equals the intangibles spend times the productivity of the intangibles, where productivity is residual income divided by intangibles, as follows:

Residual income = intangibles spend * residual income/intangibles spend,

and residual income/intangibles spend = productivity.

It follows that change in residual income can be examined by looking at changes in the intangibles spend and changes in the productivity of the intangibles. Intangibles spend for Halma (Table 7.6) is either taken as R and D or as R and D plus administration costs. Administration costs is a proxy for the costs of management and its inclusion provides a measure of intangibles spend similar to that reported in Hope and Hope (1997: 179–80) and used by Paul Strassman, the former Chief Information Officer at Xerox. He regarded management costs, taken to be SGA (selling, general and administrative), in the new economy company as being primarily the cost of managing intangibles and he added this cost to R and D expenditure to provide the denominator for his productivity measure. More recently Lev, Radhakrishnan and Zhang (2009) have also used SGA as a proxy for spend on intangibles in the form of 'organisational capital'. It is not clear how good a proxy this is for the costs of maintaining organisational capital.

Table 7.6   Halma's R and D record

	2005 £m	2006 £m	2007 £m	2008 £m	2009 £m
Residual income (RI)	26.1	33.0	37.4	42.7	44.8
Development capitalised	1.1	2.5	3.9	3.8	3.8
R and D	10.6	11.7	11.4	14.8	19.1
Total R and D	11.7	14.2	15.3	18.6	22.9
Admin	33.3	38.1	43.2	50.1	55.7
R and D plus admin	45.0	52.3	58.5	68.7	78.6
RI/ (R and D plus admin)	58%	63.1%	63.9%	62.1%	57%
RI/ R and D	2.23x	2.32x	2.44x	2.3x	1.96x

Table 7.6 indicates that the expenditure on administration plus R and D increased steadily over the period under review. However, the productivity of

these intangibles hit its lowest point in 2009 with a productivity of 57 per cent. The productivity of R and D alone is investigated in Table 7.6 by a ratio using just R and D costs as the denominator, whilst retaining residual income as the numerator. Residual income is as follows:

Residual income = R and D * Residual income / R and D,

where the term residual income / R and D is R and D productivity.

Thus any change in residual income can also be examined by looking at changes in the R and D spend and in its productivity. Productivity is at its lowest in 2009 with a productivity of 1.96. It should be noted that R and D productivity can be broken down further into the multiple of two terms being: (1) Sales / Rand D; and (2) Residual Income / Sales. The first term is the reciprocal of Rand D / Sales (the percentage of sales spent upon R and D is commonly used as a signal of commitment to R and D) and the second is the margin on sales (in terms of residual income). This breakdown is the new economy equivalent of the well-known Dupont formula. As discussed in Chapter 2, Dupont breaks down the productivity of assets into the multiple of asset turnover and margins.

What is good to see over time in a well-managed, innovation-dependent company is a steadily increasing R and D expenditure, but with the productivity of R and D at least being maintained, and preferably increased. Halma does have increasing R and D expenditure, though the productivity of R and D falls in 2009 to 1.96. This is because the increase in residual income in 2009 has not kept pace with the increase in R and D. The drop in productivity is not altogether bad news if the increase in R and D expenditure is expected to be successful in due course. If so this should reflect in an increase in GOV (rather than CUVI).

If residual income is identified with the exploitation of intangibles, and R and D with the exploration of new knowledge, then the R and D productivity ratio can be taken as the exploitation/exploration ratio. There is a significant literature on the need for firms to leverage/exploit existing knowledge whilst at the same time building/exploring new knowledge. This has been referred to as the need for organisations to be ambidextrous (Tushman and O'Reilly 2002). Moreover, Levinthal and March (1993), and Volberda and Baden-Fuller (2003), for example, stress the need for organisations to actively manage the balance between exploration and exploitation. This can be done in a multi-unit firm like Halma by buying and selling subsidiaries with different exploitation/

exploration ratios. In Halma, the investment in R and D remains high relative to many of its peers, in part because of an overall uplift in the technology level of Group companies due to merger and acquisition (M & A) actions which dispose of lower/older technology companies in favour of higher/recent technology companies. However, such M & A activity can depress reported R and D productivity since the high-technology acquired companies tend to have a relatively lower R and D productivity ratio than Halma's existing portfolio due to relatively high recent R and D expenditure. The issue might also be examined by looking at the ratio of CUVI to recorded intangibles. From Table 7.5 it can be seen that this ratio has fallen from 3.1 (290 / 94.8) in 2005 to 2.1 (498 / 239) in 2009 showing that the performance (exploitation) of intangibles has not been rising as fast as the purchase of intangibles largely through acquisition.

OPPORTUNITY FUND

It is in the nature of research that breakthroughs happen unpredictably and therefore opportunities to take forward new developments are also unpredictable. A research-dependent company should retain opportunity cash/capital to ensure that it is able to move quickly on any good development opportunities thrown up by its research. In terms of long-term loans, Halma has low gearing allowing it to raise loans quickly for any opportunities that arise. Indeed up to and including 2007 Halma had no long-term loans at all. Low gearing reduces the need of a company to keep liquid assets as opportunity capital. However, low gearing is not the same as actually having the cash available especially during a credit crunch. It is interesting to note that Halma have since 2008 taken on long-term loans to provide a fund enabling it to move quickly, not so much on opportunity thrown up by its R and D, but on opportunities to acquire suitable subsidiaries. Increasing the number of subsidiaries is important leverage of Halma's parenting capability. In the 2006 financial year Halma purchased three subsidiaries for which they paid £30.4 m in cash plus some deferred compensation, and in 2007 they purchased five companies for £21.4 m again with a small amount of deferred compensation. Clearly, a significant part of the cash balance held by Halma over time has been in the nature of an opportunities fund.

IS HALMA A GOOD BUY?

Table 7.7 gives Halma's 4S comprehensive balance sheets for the five years to 2009.

Table 7.7   Halma's 4S comprehensive balance sheets

	2005 £m	2006 £m	2007 £m	2008 £m	2009 £m
FA/WC	105.8	94.5	94.0	79.4*	111.3†
CUVI	290.0	367.0	416.0	474.0	498.0
GOV	234.6	272.4	344.1	200.4	27.0
NVP	(36.6)	(40.5)	(32.3)	(34.8)	(50.7)
MC	593.8	693.4	821.8	719.0	585.6

* £79.4 m is ESTA being FA/WC of £144.8 m less loans £65.4 m

† £111.3 m is ESTA being FA/WC of £190.9 m less loans £79.6 m

There is a strong argument that Halma is significantly undervalued at end of March 2009 (GOV = £27 m). Halma is a holding company for 80 or so wholly owned subsidiaries around the world, producing a wide range of health and safety products, many of which are prominent in their own niche markets. Some of these products are for the construction industry and therefore were at substantial risk from the recession. However, with so many subsidiaries and products Halma remains reasonably well diversified across industries, and health and safety continues to have the 'winds of regulation' behind it. Halma's CUVI trend, although slowing down in 2009, continues to be positive showing the successful leverage of intangibles. Moreover, CUVI is substantially in excess of GOV over all five years. Halma's Board and central management team exercise governance through which each subsidiary is encouraged to leverage and develop its intangibles effectively. In Halma, leverage takes place at two levels. First, there is the leverage of the intangibles held by each subsidiary. Second, there is the leverage of Halma's governance skills through the acquisition of new subsidiaries.

Until 2007 Halma had no long-term borrowings yet managed to reduce its equity investment in fixed assets/working capital whilst increasing CUVI. During this period it was a highly effective 'conceptual' company, being a company that can expand without needing new investment in traditional assets. The company then decided to take on borrowings to provide opportunity cash for acquisitions, since acquisitions allow the Board to leverage its governance expertise. In 2008 these borrowings served to reduce the equity stake in fixed assets/working capital whilst CUVI continued to increase, giving Halma the status of a 'quasi-conceptual' company. A quasi-conceptual company is one that can expand through increases in loan capital and does not need new equity. However, in 2009 the equity stake in fixed assets/working capital rose faster than the rise in CUVI and therefore Halma was potentially losing its status as a conceptual or quasi-conceptual company. As a consequence there might at first sight be a concern as to the future status of the company, but further examination of the statutory accounts does not give too much cause for alarm. Firstly, the increase in fixed assets, over half of which is due to exchange adjustments, is matched by the increase in borrowings. The increase in FA/WC can therefore be attributed to an increase in working capital. However, the increase in inventories and trade receivables is in line with the increase in sales, whilst the increase in cash (mostly opportunity cash) is largely due to exchange adjustments. The only out-of-line item is the decrease in trade payables, suggesting that there may have been a change in the supplier propositions. Alternatively, it may be a temporary phenomenon. Because the accounts do not contain any assessment of the need for working capital it is difficult to know.

SO WHAT HAPPENED IN 2010?

In 2010 CUVI increased substantially from £498 m to £557 m whilst fixed assets and working capital both declined slightly. This looks like a story of successful (volume) leverage but in fact revenue was flat and the improved profits which drive the CUVI increase were attributable to cost reduction (including headcount reduction) and consequently improved margins. There was only one small acquisition during 2010. Cash generation was excellent and used not for acquisitions but to pay down debt. Consequently, the equity stake in fixed assets and working capital increased significantly from £111.3 m to £147.2 m. So in brief, 2010 was not a year of leverage through volume but one of caution in a difficult business environment. In September 2010, five months after Halma's year end, based upon a share price of 278 p Halma was sporting a market capitalisation of £1,040 m, giving a GOV of approximately £385 m. Given that further cost reductions may be difficult then this looked like an optimistic GOV/share price and dependent upon a return to leverage. However, such optimism was well founded since in 2011 leverage was back on track with 2011 sales revenue increasing by 12.9 per cent from 2010 and profit by 19.9 per cent. The share price has improved substantially since March 2009 reflecting: (1) an improved stock market; (2) Halma's diversified overseas earnings which have been a protection from problems in the UK economy; and (3) its involvement in growing Asian markets, notably China.

Conclusion

This chapter has reviewed current practice in accounting for intangibles. It has subsequently looked at how the accounting might be improved to give greater insight into firstly the financing of intangibles and secondly the performance of intangibles. A study of DMGT has been used to focus on the former and a study of Halma focuses on the latter. The two companies are in different sectors, both with important but quite different intangibles. The DMGT case shows how a 'new economy' perspective that concentrates on the financing of intangibles can lead to a 'comprehensive' balance sheet that explains the financing of fixed assets plus working capital, CUVI and GOV, through loans, promises and equity measured at its market capitalisation. It is seen that DMGT uses loans to pay for a significant part of its intangibles. Halma, however, makes little use of loans and largely uses internally generated cash to fund acquired and internally developed R and D. The Halma case shows how to account for the performance of intangibles through the rise of CUVI; a rise explained in terms of intangibles spend and intangibles productivity.

Promises

8

In general the new economy is higher risk and higher reward than the old economy. There are a number of factors pushing us to transform further into a higher risk, higher reward new economy. In particular, in the face of old economy activities moving to the lowest cost producers internationally, it has been necessary for activities based in developed countries to move to higher risk activities to maintain living standards. Again, because of the rising cost of commodities there has been a push to discover new technologies that use commodities in more efficient ways. Given the move towards the new economy, it is logical for shareholders to share the higher risks and higher rewards with other stakeholders. Stakeholder propositions that include promises serve to spread the risks and rewards of new economy activity and bind the Stakeholder Knowledge Network. This chapter looks at current accounting practice in respect of various promises that form part of stakeholder propositions. By way of illustration the chapter looks at customer warranties, the defined benefit pension fund (employees), forward contracts (suppliers or customers), the need to replace fixed assets, fixed interest loans, deferred tax (government) and share options granted to management (Figure 4.2). It is found that the accounting disclosures and the accounting treatment of these promises (contingencies and commitments) is less than ideal in some cases. This chapter is not concerned with short-term promises in connection with trading transactions (debtors and creditors) that form part of working capital. It is concerned with promises to purchase or sell in the future (for example, orders, long-term and forward contracts) insofar as they create current value due to expected changes from the contract price.

Accounting practice for different promises does vary. However, in principle the accounting is the same for all promises. The value of the promise at the time it is made to secure stakeholder engagement in current business activity is a charge against current profits. In principle, this charge sets aside assets (creates a fund) available to meet the obligation at the time it falls due. The charge to current profit is the estimated size of the obligation upon discharge, discounted at the rate of return expected on the assets set aside. At the time of making the promise there is no net liability since the funds set aside (plus returns) are expected to match the obligation when it falls due. However, over time a net liability (NVP) can arise due to: (1) the estimated size of the obligation upon discharge is revised; (2) the actual or expected returns on the assets change; or (3) ring-fenced assets are not set aside (no fund is established) and so such assets are diverted to another purpose. In practice, outside of pensions, funds are rarely set aside for specific promises but a pot of precautionary cash, or other liquid assets, might be held as cover for the portfolio of promises as a whole.

Customer Warranties

Table 8.1 is indicative of the accounting treatment for warranties. The value of the opening provision is the best estimate at that time of the cost of outstanding obligations under warranties issued. During the year, the cost of fixing products under warranty is charged to the opening provision. At the end of the year the balance on the provision is adjusted in line with a new assessment of the overall outstanding warranty obligation. This adjustment is in two parts. Firstly, there are the warranties issued during the year on the current year's sales. Secondly, there are the unexpired warranties from previous periods. Both of these are assessed (reassessed) on the basis of up-to-date experience of the product's performance. Both parts of the adjustment are charged to accounting profit as warranty expenses. Is this the appropriate charge to profit for purposes of assessing sustainable profit? Strictly it is only the estimated cost of the warranties issued on sales during the year that should be a charge to profit for it to be sustainable. The adjustment to the provision for unexpired warranties is a prior year adjustment. However, in most cases the breakdown into the two parts of the adjustment is not available in the published accounts and/or the prior year adjustment is not material and so the reported accounting profit is taken to be sustainable (in respect of warranties). The closing balance, representing the value of outstanding warranty obligations, is included in the valuation of net promises at the year end. Unless the warranties run for a long period, it is not normal practice to discount the estimate of the cost of obligations under outstanding warranty claims. Hence the closing balance is not a discounted number. Furthermore, companies do not normally hold dedicated funds specifically to meet warranty costs.

There are ways other than warranties through which the risks and rewards of product success or failure can be shared between seller and purchaser. For instance, an advertising agency's contract with its client might include the sharing of profits from extra sales resulting from an advertising campaign devised by the agency.

Table 8.1   Warranties

	Balance £m	Charge to profit £m
Opening balance	100	
Cost of fixing products during year	(20)	
Reassessment of warranties from previous years	25	25
Estimated cost of warranties issued during year	<u>30</u>	<u>30</u>
Closing balance	135	<u>55</u>
Charge to sustainable profit		30

Defined Benefit Pensions

These are a major item for many UK companies, even when they have been closed to new members. Pension obligations *are* discounted and dedicated funds (assets) *are* held with a view to discharging these obligations. A surplus/deficit on a pension fund is made up of scheme assets less (discounted) obligations to scheme members. A surplus cannot be applied to any other contingency or commitment. Where a company operates more than one scheme, a surplus on one scheme cannot be applied to a deficit on another.

BT is an example of a privatised company which has a substantial pension fund deficit, a potential problem which may not have been fully taken into account at the time of privatisation. BT has been making substantial 'deficiency contributions' to tackle the deficit and its attempts to recover some of these costs through charging other telecoms companies for the use of BT networks has been resisted by the regulator. Its 2010 deficit was £5,671 m, being liabilities of £43,293 m less assets of £35,429 m less deferred tax of £2,193 m: deferred tax arises because if the company were to pay into the fund to eliminate the deficit then the expenditure would be allowable for corporation tax purposes.

The movements on pension fund liabilities is illustrated in Table 8.2 which reproduces the relevant part of the pensions note (note 29 retirement benefit plans) for BT Group plc's 2010 accounts. In basic terms, the value of the outstanding obligation at the beginning of the year (the scheme liability of £33,326 m) is increased by the current service cost (£206 m) necessary to engage employees during the year. Since pension obligations are discounted, it is also increased by the unwinding of the interest (£2,211 m). To explain this item it is necessary to appreciate the unwinding of interest takes place for any future liability that has been discounted to present value. When a year passes, the liability is one year nearer and increases in present value terms simply through the passage of time. A further change in the pension obligations (and assets) takes place because the actuarial assumptions upon which the fund valuation is based are reassessed at the end of the year in respect of matters such as the discount rate, inflation, longevity and salary growth. This gives rise to actuarial gains and losses. For BT there is an actuarial loss of £9,481 m which increases the obligation. There is also an actuarial gain which increases the assets by £5,157 m (see Table 8.3).

Table 8.2   BT defined benefit pension obligation

	2010 £m
Opening defined benefit obligation	(33,326)
Current service cost	(206)
Interest expense	(2,211)
Contributions by employees	(15)
Actuarial loss	(9,481)
Benefits paid	1,948
Exchange differences	(2)
Closing balance	(43,293)

On the assets side (Table 8.3), the opening fair value of the assets of £29,353 m is increased by £1,932 m being the return, both capital and income, expected to be earned during the year (this accounting treatment is set to change from 2013 onwards). Both assets and obligations are reduced by the amount of £1,948 m paid out to pensioners during the year. Both assets and obligations are increased by contributions of £15 m from the employees. Scheme assets are increased by contributions of £916 m from the employer, of which £525 m is paid in to help meet the pension fund deficiency.

Table 8.3   BT pension scheme assets

	2010 £m
Opening fair value of scheme assets	29,353
Expected return	1,932
Actuarial gain	5,157
Regular contributions by employer	391
Deficiency contributions by employer	525
Contributions by employees	15
Benefits paid	(1,948)
Exchange differences	4
	35,429

In the published accounts actuarial gains and losses are taken to other comprehensive income (OCI) in the statement of comprehensive income (this is not comprehensive income as used in 4S accounting) and not to the profit statement. However, the current service cost (£206 m, table 8.2) is charged to accounting profit, being the current value of the pension promises made during the year to help secure the engagement of the employees. This charge is necessary if profit is to be sustainable. In the published accounts the interest cost on scheme liabilities (£2,211 m) less the expected return on scheme assets (£1,932 m) is also charged to accounting profit as part of the financing cost. This charge reflects movements on outstanding assets and liabilities in respect of pension promises made and provided for in previous years. It is a legacy item and is part of the movement in NVP. Reported profit should, therefore, be adjusted accordingly in arriving at sustainable profit for 4S accounting. Under the present accounting standard it is the *expected* returns on scheme assets (less interest) that are credited to profit, whilst any shortfall when the actual returns are considered is taken to OCI in the Statement of Comprehensive Income in the published accounts. As previously stated, actuarial gains and losses are also taken to this statement. Thus higher reported profits can be achieved through higher expectations and arguably this lacks rigour (again this will change from 2013 onwards due to a new standard on pensions).

The amount in 4S accounting for the net promises in respect of pensions is the fund surplus or deficit and all movements relating to pensions are taken to the pensions section of the NVP fund. In view of the fact that surpluses cannot be applied to other contingencies there is an argument that a fund with a surplus should be counted at zero. In today's pensions environment it is unlikely that firms will ever again feel able to declare pensions holidays in order to access surpluses. However, the existence of a substantial surplus reduces the risk of future deficits, and is in effect a precautionary asset in this regard. Funds with surpluses are therefore normally shown as assets whilst funds in deficit are shown as a liability using the deficit value. Whilst taking the declared pension deficit as the appropriate valuation is the practical step, it should be noted that many commentators have questioned the use of a discount rate in pension fund calculations based upon investment grade bonds, rather than a risk free rate. The choice of discount rate makes a substantial difference. A further point is that the declared pension fund surplus or deficit does not allow for the option value of the pension. Even when a fund is in balance (zero deficit or surplus), the pension arrangements have positive options value for the employees and negative options value for the employer since it may well go into deficit in the future. If it does, the employees have the right to call upon the company to make up the deficit. This option value *is* taken into account by any insurance company that might be willing, at a price, to take over the pensions liability from the company.

Forward Contracts

In Figure 4.2, which sets out the SKN, the proposition to suppliers is a forward contract. Let us assume that it is in fact a fixed price contract for long-term purchases over several years. If the current (spot) price moves ahead of the fixed price in the contract and is expected to stay ahead, then the contract becomes valuable. If, however, the current price falls then the contract is a burden and has a negative value. You would have to pay another company to take it over. Thus the present value of such a forward contract that has a number of years to run is contingent upon expected price movements. Such contracts may be made in respect of purchases or sales and the accounting issues are the mirror image in each case. The following example, taken from UBS (2007: 37–8) can be used to illustrate different ways of accounting for a long-term contract.

The example is as follows. At the end of the accounting year a company has four years left on a five-year contract to supply a commodity of 100 units each year at a price of £10. The spot price of the commodity at the start and finish of the accounting year was £8 and £8.5, respectively. The cost of producing the commodity is £3 per unit. The value of the contract at the beginning of the year is £200 (the 'excess' profits) for five years @ say a 5 per cent discount rate, giving £865.9. At the end of the year the value of the contract based upon the higher spot price is £150 for four years @ 5 per cent discount rate giving £531.9. The contract loses £334 of value during the year moving from £865.9 to £531.9.

In practice, accounting for such sale (or purchase) contracts does not recognise any value of the contract and reported profit follows the first column of Table 8.4 (profit £700). This simply takes sales at the contract price less the cost of sales. As UBS (2007: 38) explain:

> ... *the problem with this is that it gives a misleadingly flattering measure of performance, given that when the current advantageously priced contract comes to an end and production must be sold at the spot price, revenues and profits will inevitably decline.*

In other words, the operating result of £700 is not sustainable and 'cannot be used successfully to value this business without having additional information about the contract' (UBS 2007: 38).

Table 8.4   Accounting for the contract: reporting alternatives

(1) Historical cost		(2) Fair value		(3) Sustainable profit	
	£		£		£
Revenue	1,000	Revenue	1,000	Revenue	850
Cost	300	Cost	(300)	Cost	300
Profit	700	Value loss	(334)	Sustainable Profit	550
		Profit	366		
				CUVI 550 pa @ 5%	11,000
				Closing contract value	532
				Company value	11,532

An alternative presentation would be to recognise the contract at fair value (the second column of Table 8.4). This is not how it is currently treated under accounting standards unless the contract contains a degree of optionality that makes it a derivative. Fair value accounting would, as per the second column of Table 8.4, generate a profit of £366. This adjusts the £700 profit for the loss in value of the contract. Again this would not be sustainable since the fair value charge of £334 is unlikely to recur at the same amount and will not recur at all outside the period of the contract. As UBS (2007: 38) state *'it is impossible to derive the value of the business directly from this measure'*. This measure of £366 combines the transactions profit of £700 and the contract loss in value of £334. Thus it combines traditional and fair value accounting.

The value of the business is derived in Table 8.4, column 3. This shows that the value of the business is the capitalised value of sustainable profit based upon the closing spot price, plus the closing contract value. The sustainable profit is £550 (8.5 − 3 = 5.5 * 100 = 550) giving a capital value, at a 5 per cent required return, of £11,000. Adding this to the closing contract value of £532 gives a closing company value of £11,532. By the same method, based upon a capitalised sustainable profit of £10,000 derived from the opening spot price and an opening contract value of £866, the opening value of the company is £10,000 + 866 = £10,866. Unfortunately, current accounting does not easily allow these calculations since sufficient information on long-term contracts and spot prices is not generally disclosed. 4S accounting, however, would give the value of the business analysed into the value of the sustainable profit (equivalent to CUVI if there is no fixed assets/working capital) and the value of the contractual promise. 4S comprehensive income (Table 8.5) shows the change in the value of the sustainable profit (change in CUVI) and the change in the contract value (change in NVP). Chapter 10 provides a much fuller exposition of the 4S comprehensive income for this example developed so as to deal with the introduction of both ESTA and GOV.

Table 8.5   Contract 4S comprehensive accounting

	Opening £	Closing £	Difference £
ESTA	Nil	Nil	Nil
CUVI	10,000	11,000	1,000
NVP	866	532	(334)
		Comprehensive income	666
		Dividend	700
		Total shareholder return	1,366

Fixed Asset Replacement

The replacement of fixed assets may not be an obvious candidate for the net promises section of the company's analysis of value. However, maintaining the production capability of the company is an implied commitment of the assessment of sustainable profit (and its capital equivalent) based upon the assumption of current business conditions continuing in perpetuity. The value of this implied promise depends upon the capital expenditure (capex) profile of the company. It is necessary to consider the two extremes of a spectrum. On the one hand, Table 8.6 features a 'smooth' profile where the company's assets last for five years and one fifth of its fixed asset stock is replaced each year. In this case, each year the 'free' cash flow from depreciation equals the capital expenditure on replacement plant. The net book value (NVB) of the fixed assets is constant at £125 (cost £250 less cumulative depreciation £125). The constant NBV gives not just sustainable profits but sustainable residual income and CUVI.

Table 8.6   Smooth capex profile

	Year 1 £	Year 2 £	Year 3 £	Year4 £	Year 5 £
Cost £5@50	250	250	250	250	250
Cumulative depreciation	125	125	125	125	125
NBV	125	125	125	125	125
Depreciation charge	50	50	50	50	50
Free cash	50	50	50	50	50
Fixed asset additions (capex)	50	50	50	50	50

Table 8.7   Lumpy capex profile

	Year 1 £	Year 2 £	Year 3 £	Year 4 £	Year 5 £
Cost 1@250	250	250	250	250	250
Cumulative depreciation	50	100	150	200	250
NBV	200	150	100	50	Nil
Depreciation charge	50	50	50	50	50
Free cash	50	100	150	200	250
Fixed assets additions	250	Nil	Nil	Nil	Nil*

* £250 additions at beginning of year 6

On the other hand, Table 8.7 features a 'lumpy' profile where the company has one major asset (original cost £250) which is replaced every five years. The net book value of the fixed assets declines from £250 to nil over the five years, causing sustainable profit to yield an increasing residual income and increasing CUVI over this period for no other reason than the ageing of the asset. The intangibles appear to perform better (a higher CUVI) because they use older fixed assets, with a lower book value, to generate the same profit. This increase is not sustainable beyond the life of the fixed assets. During the five years the free cash from depreciation each year exceeds capital expenditure by £50. Eventually, if the free cash is retained as liquid assets within the business, this provides for the asset's replacement. At the end of say year 3, the NBV of the asset is £100 and the accumulated free cash should be £150 (equal to the accumulated depreciation provision) if the asset replacement is to be achieved from free cash. This ignores possible returns from investing the cash. Unlike pensions there is no requirement for a company to keep funds in order to provide for the replacement of lumpy assets and the free cash generated in the first three years is likely to have been spent on other things such as expanding the business. This financial flexibility is important but the company's financial managers and its investors must keep in mind the need to finance up and coming commitments, including fixed asset purchases.

In practice, a major company will have some activities that are associated with a smooth fixed asset profile and some which are associated with a lumpy profile. The total fixed asset schedule produced as a note in the accounts does not segment the fixed assets on this basis. Hence there is a shortage of information from which the 'lumpiness' of the company's fixed asset profile can be deduced. However, an assessment of lumpiness is important for two reasons, being: (a) to understand how much of the change in CUVI is a function of fixed asset ageing; and (b) to assess the need for a replacement promise to be included in NVP. As a lumpy fixed asset is depreciated there is, under 4S accounting, an equivalent increase in the value of the replacement promise which is reduced by the (free) cash set aside for replacement. The replacement promise represents the shortfall of free cash flow that 'should' have been saved if lumpy fixed assets are to be replaced without the need for additional capital. It serves to reduce the valuation of the company. No one, for instance, wants to buy a company and then be faced with a further large investment to replace its fixed assets, just as no one wants to buy a company and be faced with the need for an injection into the pension fund; unless of course it is allowed for in the purchase price.

There are two other points to consider in relation to fixed assets. Firstly, if the replacement cost of lumpy fixed assets has risen since purchase, then the value of the 'replacement' promise has also risen and should be based upon current replacement prices (that is, it should include what students of replacement cost accounting will recognise as 'backlog depreciation'). This is equivalent to the obligations of a defined benefit pension fund increasing due to salary levels increasing (most schemes base the pension upon final salary). In principle, whether the assets are lumpy or smooth, the annual depreciation charge in the calculation of sustainable profit for 4S accounting should, if material, be increased to current cost levels as it would be under replacement cost accounting.

The second point relates to finance leases. When access to fixed assets comes through a finance lease, accounting standards require that the asset is brought on to the balance sheet and depreciated as though it had been purchased. Much of the rationale for this is that a company leasing its assets can then be directly compared with a company that owns its assets, through performance measures such as return on assets employed. Such performance measures, however, are rooted in old economy thinking. From a new economy perspective the rental under the lease is sufficient to give the required rate of return on the deal for the finance company which has made the investment in the fixed asset, and the rental charge is thus the right charge for calculating the lessee's residual income. The rental should be charged, like any other supply contract, against the profits of the lessee as being the cost of the use of the fixed asset. The finance lease should be treated as a forward contract to capture the element of commitment and in contradiction to present practice for finance leases, the fixed asset should not be brought on to the balance sheet. The argument is that leases are a different (stakeholder) proposition to ownership and therefore there should be no problem with their accounting treatments being different.

From the point of view of the discussion on lumpy versus smooth, an activity that leases its assets is equivalent to a smooth profile. There is no need to save for the replacement of leases. However, like any other long-term supply contract, the rental charge should be based upon the charge in new (replacement) leases and the value of the savings expected under the existing lease treated as additional value in the net promises column.

A final point for noting is that if the sale of capital goods was given an accounting treatment that was symmetrical to the purchase of capital goods (that is the sale was taken to the seller's revenue and profit over the effective life of the asset) as suggested by the author in the preface, then similar 'lumpy versus smooth' issues would apply, this time in relation to the pattern of sales.

Fixed Interest Term Loans

Fixed interest loans are forward contracts. Like forward contracts for sales and supplies they offer protection against price (interest rate) increases. They change in value as interest rates rise or fall. As with forward contracts for purchases or sales, this value change is not generally captured by current accounting practice. Current practice is to report loans on an historical cost basis without recognising the impact of interest rate changes.

For a variable interest loan, changes in interest rates do not affect the value of the loan. However, a variable interest loan can be turned into the equivalent of a fixed interest loan through an interest rate swap. An interest rate swap potentially generates future savings when interest rates rise and additional future interest expense when interest rates fall. The value of these savings/expenses changes the value of the swap. The swap is treated as a derivative under current accounting standards and thus its fair value change may be recognised in the accounts. It follows that a company with a fixed rate loan may be treated differently to a company that achieves the same through the use of a swap. This highlights the difficulty in traditional 'one fund' accounting of recognising some fair value changes (for derivatives) but not others (for fixed rate loans).

The difficulties faced by one fund accounting are highlighted in the particular circumstance of the company paying higher interest rates on current loans due to a drop in its credit rating. This would cause the market value of its established fixed rate loans to decrease, and it is not felt appropriate by many that a company should be able to report a decrease in its liabilities (in the shape of the savings generated by its fixed rate loans) as accounting profit when the driver is bad news. But this bad news can be more appropriately reported with 4S. It does not impact all slices of the reporting framework in the same way. In terms of the 4 slices, promises (NVP) will reflect the value of the prospective interest rate savings through having fixed rate loans. However, the reduction in the credit rating is likely to reflect an already weakening sustainable profit (CUVI) and GOV, to be accentuated by the consequent increase in interest cost (on current and future borrowings). Thus although the bad news might impact favourably on the value of promises, it impacts unfavourably on the other dimensions of the 4S valuation analysis. The accounting for the bad news has to be seen comprehensively. The fact is that when rates rise, those with fixed rate loans make a saving for the remaining period of the loan and these savings have a discounted value. In 4S accounting the value of these savings is captured in NVP, whilst the weakening of the business reflected in the credit rating change impacts CUVI and GOV. The original value of the loan is subtracted from the fixed assets/working capital in the calculation of ESTA. It is assumed that the loan will be rolled over when its term expires. There is a risk (a rollover risk) that this will not be achievable and this risk is particularly concerning during a credit crunch. The assessment of sustainable profit should recognise the current interest rate and not the fixed interest rate associated with the term loan. In many cases, however, this adjustment may be difficult to quantify due to a shortage of information regarding the company's current interest rates, or it may not be material to sustainable profit. If necessary an estimate can be made.

Deferred Taxation

Deferred tax can arise for a number of reasons including: (1) the revaluation of an asset in which case tax on any gain is deferred because it need not be paid until the asset is sold; and (2) the deferral of tax on accounting profits due to 'accelerated capital allowances'. The discussion focuses on the latter. The idea of accelerated capital allowances is to encourage companies to invest in fixed assets by allowing them to write off early much of the investment against profits for tax purposes. When capital allowances exceed depreciation, taxable profit is less than accounting profit and vice versa when depreciation exceeds capital allowances. The effect of accelerated capital allowances is to allow payment of some of the tax payable as a result of current accounting profits, to be deferred into the future. Thus tax ultimately payable as a result of current accounting profits consists of: (1) current tax payable within 12 months and shown as a current liability in the balance sheet; and (2) deferred tax shown as a non-current liability. The timing of the obligation to pay deferred tax is contingent upon what the business does in the future, particularly in respect of future capital expenditure (investment in fixed assets). Future tax payments might continue to be deferred if capital expenditure, and hence capital allowances, continue to increase. The deferred tax opening balance for the year represents tax as a result of previous years' profits, not yet required to be paid. The balance is increased by any deferral of the tax payable as a result of the current year's accounting profit. It is reduced by any transfers to current tax in respect of past deferrals that have become due for payment within 12 months. The closing balance on deferred tax can be taken as the value of the commitment in the SKN's promises column, although under international accounting standards it is not discounted and is to that extent overstated.

One difficulty for discounting is the uncertain timing of the future crystallisation of deferred tax. However, if the company were able to pay someone else to take over its deferred tax liability then the discount would be brought into the price. It is likely the price would also depend upon some stochastic modelling of capital expenditures.

The tax charge against profits reported in the company's profit statement represents the tax payable (whether current or to be deferred) as a result of those profits. In the UK, for listed companies, this tax charge for 2011 works out at around 26 per cent of the year's accounting profits, 26 per cent being the main corporation tax rate for 2011. The main corporation tax rate was 28 per cent in 2010 and reduces to 24 per cent in 2012 and 23 per cent in 2013. The actual rates charged (the effective tax rate) can be a little lower (or possibly higher) than the main corporation tax rate if the company does a significant amount of its business through overseas subsidiaries subject to non-UK tax regimes. As far as the analyst is concerned, accounting profits before tax are adjusted to give sustainable profit (before tax) and once this has been assessed, it can be subjected to the company's effective tax rate.

Share Options

Share options and share-based payments have become an important element in the proposition made to senior executives and especially directors. The discussion looks at share options by way of illustration. Under accounting standards, the value of the options at the grant date is amortised (charged against profit) over the period from the grant date to the vesting date, being the date after which the options can be exercised. This is typically a period of a few years. It is an appropriate annual charge in the sense that the option serves to engage management for this period and therefore the cost of the option is part of the cost of engagement. It arguably also serves to align the interests of management and shareholders, insofar as the value of the option increases as the share price increases. Options can be valued using well established mathematical techniques in which the value depends not only upon the difference between share price and exercise price (this difference is the intrinsic value) but upon the volatility of the share price and the time left before exercise is possible. When the exercise date is reached, the option value approximates to intrinsic value (the share price at the exercise date less exercise price).

The annual charge is based on the cost/value of the option at the grant date. The double entry to the charge is usually a 'share payments accrual' within equity which is transferred to retained earnings when the option is exercised. As time passes, the value of an outstanding option changes until at the exercise date its value approximates to intrinsic value. In practice, the share payments accrual is not adjusted in respect of the changing value of the option. Thus the share payments accrual will often fall short of making up the difference between the exercise price and market price of the share at the exercise date. This shortfall is the legacy loss experienced by the existing shareholders through the use of options. However, it may be offset by increases in the share price over the vesting period.

4S accounting would show the current value of outstanding options within NVP, until they are exercised. Each year the charge to profit in respect of options is based upon the current value of the options. The options section of NVP is increased (decreased) by amounts necessary to bring the options section of NVP to the current value of the options. No cash needs to be set aside to pay for share options since when the options are exercised and the promise is fulfilled, the company finally pays for the work in respect of which the options were granted by taking lower share proceeds.

Case Studies

The chapter now looks at two case studies based upon reported accounts. The first, FKI, concerns the implied promise to sustain production capability. The second, Rolls Royce, focuses upon the 'promise' of derivatives.

FKI: HIGHLIGHTING THE FIXED ASSETS ISSUE

FKI plc was a UK-based diversified engineering group taken over by Melrose plc on 1st July 2008, an acquisition which increased the size of Melrose's non-current assets by approximately six times. According to FKI's annual report (FKI 2007: 1):

> *FKI plc is a major international diversified engineering group. The Group is driven by value metrics, principally return on invested capital, and actively manages the strategy and performance of its businesses. The Group's objective is to maximise the value of the portfolio as a whole and to deliver growth in shareholder value through increased focus on businesses that have superior and sustainable market positions in sizeable, attractive markets, leading brands and world class technology.*

According to its 2009 Annual Report (Melrose 2010: 7) the strategy of Melrose is to:

> *Look for businesses where our combination of increased management focus and strong but selective investment is likely to produce above average returns for investors. This strategy will include the sale of these businesses at the appropriate time, normally in a three to five year period, with proceeds being returned to shareholders in the most efficient way possible.*

No mention here of world class technology or leading brands! It is interesting to note the performance measures embedded in the two statements of strategy. FKI is concerned with 'return on invested capital' and 'maximising the value of the portfolio' and Melrose with 'above average returns to investors'. However, the routes to these returns are different with Melrose seeking to achieve the return through an exit sale. In this sense Melrose' return is absolute rather than relative.

The balance sheet is summarised in Table 8.8 split between, in the first column, goodwill/intangibles (£376.7 m) and the equity stake in fixed assets plus working capital (minus £2 m), and in the second column those net promises that are shown in the financial statements (£94.8 m). Any (negative) value overhang in respect of lumpy fixed assets (represented by the question mark in Table 8.8) is not shown.

Table 8.8   Summarising FKI's 2007 balance sheet

	£m	£m
Property, plant, equipment	226.1	?
Goodwill/Intangibles	376.7	
Associates and other	5.7	
Deferred tax assets (net)		11.5
Pension deficit (net)		(108.8)
Loans	(491.6)	
Derivatives (net)		30.5
Provisions		(28.0)
Working capital	257.8	
NVP		(94.8)
Goodwill/intangibles	376.7	
ESTA	(2.0)	

Lumpy fixed assets could be an issue for FKI since included within property, plant and equipment (Table 8.8, £226.1 m), is plant, equipment and vehicles having a net book value (NBV) of £102.4 m. This is the cost of £451.4 m less cumulative depreciation of £349 m. Cumulative depreciation is 77.3 per cent of cost, indicating ageing assets and a lumpy profile. At one extreme it is possible that all the assets are lumpy. In this case, assuming there is no surplus cash set aside for asset replacement, £349 m should be provided in NVP for replacement of the lumpy assets and this amount would have a substantial impact on company valuation. At the other extreme, we can assume that as many as possible of the assets are on a smooth profile. The assumption is that all of the net book value of £102.4 m relates to a smooth profile being cost of £204.8 m and accumulated depreciation of £102.4 m. It is then also assumed that the remaining assets, cost £246.6 m and cumulative depreciation £246.6 m, are about to need replacement. On this basis the value overhang is £246.6 m or possibly more if replacement costs have risen. Again this is a material sum.

The question arises, are there any precautionary assets available to meet such a value overhang and contribute to the replacement of fixed assets? FKI was a highly geared company with loans of £491.6 m and equity of £279.9 m at the end of the year. The equity number can be arrived at from Table 8.8 by subtracting the NVP (£94.8 m) from the sum of goodwill (£376.7 m) and ESTA (minus £2 m). The published consolidated cash flow statement shows that loan repayments during the year were £43.2 m with new loans of only £16.9 m. In 2006 the figures were repayments of £61 m and no new loans. FKI had been reducing its debt but debt remained at very high levels and it should not be assumed that there was any appreciable precautionary capital for fixed asset investment. It is most likely that the remaining cash and short-term deposits shown in the accounts (£125.5 m) were already committed to working capital and further debt repayments.

Table 8.9 assesses FKI's sustainable profit. Two adjustments have been made to the reported profit. The published profit statement includes net finance costs of £3.6 m on pension schemes. This is the interest cost on pension scheme obligations less the expected return on scheme assets and is excluded from finance costs in Table 8.9. Secondly, finance income excludes the fair value gains (£6 m) on financial instruments included in the published profit statement.

Table 8.9   FKI 2007 sustainable profit

	£m
Operating profit before the following:	100.6
Minority interest	(0.2)
Finance costs	(36.8)
Finance income	10.8
Sustainable profit before tax	74.4
Tax (30%)	22.3
Sustainable profit after tax	52.1
8% (say) return on ESTA	Nil
Residual income	52.1
CUVI (10%) return	521
bid (500) = ESTA (nil) + CUVI (521) – NVP (94.8) + GOV	

The potential materiality of the fixed asset replacement is highlighted at the bottom of Table 8.9, where there is a calculation of the GOV implied by the takeover price (£500 m) offered by Melrose on the assumption that the fixed asset replacement is not allowed for. The bid values GOV at £500 m less £521 m plus £94.8 m equals £73.8 m. This does not seem like a generous price for FKI's GOV. However, if a commitment to replace ageing fixed assets is included as part of the NVP, then the GOV implied by the takeover price is far more generous. Indeed, if the value overhang in respect of ageing fixed assets is £246.6 m (the most favourable profile for Melrose) then the bid effectively values GOV £246.6 m higher at £320.4 m, implying a future increase in sustainable profits of say £32 m. Subsequently, Melrose has shown itself well capable of achieving that.

The property, plant and equipment note of Melrose (note 13 in the 2008 accounts) shows the fair value of the plant and equipment acquired from FKI (£107.1 m) as the acquisition cost. This is in line with accounting standards but there is no split between cost acquired and depreciation acquired and thus the age of Melrose's equipment is not disclosed. Indeed, Melrose shows its plant and equipment at 31st December 2008 as £234 m and accumulated depreciation of £56.6 m being a mere 24.2 per cent of cost, a ratio generally associated with a much younger asset age profile. It needs to be remembered in any 4S assessment of Melrose, that there is a material off balance sheet implied commitment in respect of renewing the fixed assets.

The 2009 annual accounts of Melrose provide an update on the fixed assets situation. There has been excellent cash generation but a slowdown in capital investment which in 2009 was at 0.7 times depreciation. There had been no attempt yet to provide the necessary improvement in the fixed assets profile implied by the bid price. The finance director of Melrose reports (Melrose 2010: 22) that:

> Inevitably during 2009 capital expenditure opportunities were reduced due to the economic environment ... The net capital spend to depreciation ratio is expected to increase in 2010. The five year Melrose average annual net capital spend is comfortably in excess of depreciation at 1.3 times.

This at least indicates that Melrose is concerned with the state of the fixed assets profile.

ROLLS ROYCE: HIGHLIGHTING DERIVATIVES

Rolls Royce reported an accounting profit of £733 m in 2007 turning to a loss of £1,892 m in 2008. These reported profit/loss numbers are after net financing which, as well as interest receivable and payable, includes movements in the value of promises, such as derivatives and pensions. For Rolls the main movement in the value of promises is the hedging of sterling through the purchase of future foreign exchange contracts. At the time Rolls held future contracts to cover around 2.5 years of dollar denominated sales. The movement in the value of these contracts during 2008, in accordance with accounting standards, is taken to the reported profit in Rolls Royce's statutory accounts through the item 'net financing'. During 2008 Rolls suffered huge unrealised losses on these contracts due to the unexpected strengthening during the 2008 credit crisis of the dollar against sterling. It is these losses which turned Rolls' reported 2007 profit into a reported loss in 2008.

These losses are the result of movements which 4S accounting does not deal with through (sustainable) profits and the CUVI fund but through the NVP fund. For 4S, these movements are excluded from (residual) income and hence CUVI. Table 8.10 gives the calculation of sustainable profit, residual income and CUVI based upon Rolls Royce's 2007 and 2008 results. Although this will be discussed later, for the moment the movements in contracts undertaken as hedges (hedging instruments) are along with movements in other derivatives and pensions, taken to the NVP fund.

Table 8.10   Rolls Royce sustainable profit, residual income and CUVI

	2007 £m	2008 £m
Profit before financing and taxation	512.0	852.0
Transfer from hedging reserve	(149.0)	(80.0)
Interest receivable on working cash	22.0	15.0
Interest payable	(89.0)	(69.0)
Other adjustments	22.9	(174.5)
Sustainable profits before tax	318.9	543.5
Tax (28%)	89.3	152.2
Sustainable profits after tax	229.6	391.3
Return on ESTA 10% on 956 (2007 9% on 946)	85.1	95.6
Residual income	144.5	295.7
CUVI: required return 12% (2007 11%)	1,314.0	2,464.0

In calculating sustainable profit as the basis for CUVI, Table 8.10 starts with the profit (£852 m) reported in Rolls' income statement *before* the item in the published income statement described as net financing. An analysis of net financing is given as a note in Rolls' financial statements. The relevant interest received, being interest on working cash, and the interest payable are taken from net financing into the calculation of sustainable profit. Most other items in net financing are legacy items associated with derivatives or with pensions and do not belong in CUVI which is based upon sustainable profit from production activity. Some items in net financing are, however, included in the 'other adjustments' in Table 8.10. Table 8.11 shows the overall movement in NVP between 2007 and 2008 as (£2,017 m), and most of this relates to the fall in value of foreign exchange contracts. Of course, exchange rates are not expected to remain constant and expected future changes in the value of the contracts can be separately identified in GOV. In this way management can show their belief that the mark down in the NVP fund is temporary.

The item in Table 8.10 'transfer from hedging reserve' is an adjustment to reduce reported profit necessary because Rolls had a legacy hedging reserve when it abandoned hedge accounting some years earlier. Hedge accounting allows the movement in contracts designated as 'hedges' to be taken to a reserve which is then released to profit when the hedge unwinds. In 2008 an amount of £80 m was transferred from this reserve into profit, but again this item relates to (past) movement in the value of derivatives which under 4S are not included in sustainable profit. By 2009 this transitional hedge reserve had been extinguished.

Table 8.11   Rolls Royce changes in the four slices of equity

	2007/2008 £m
Increase in ESTA	10
Increase in CUVI	1,150
Change in NVP	(2,017)
Decrease in GOV	(3,357)
Increase in precautionary/opportunity cash	464
Decrease in MC	(3,750)

In Table 8.10, sustainable profits for 2008 after tax of £391.3 m are reduced by a 'normal' return on book equity of 10 per cent to yield residual income of £295.7 m. This is then capitalised as a perpetuity using a required return on intangible assets of 12 per cent to give a CUVI of £2,464 m, compared to a 2007

CUVI of £1,314 m. The current use value of intangibles (CUVI) is the capitalised value of residual income based upon a required rate of return that responds to risk. Thus CUVI couples risk and reward. The required returns for both equity invested in tangibles and equity invested in intangibles have been increased by 1 per cent from 2007 to 2008. This is because the risks facing Rolls Royce have increased during 2008 due to various uncertainties, notably the impact of both the credit crunch and oil prices upon airlines. If no adjustment was made to the required rates of return, CUVI would have increased to £2,688 m in 2008. Given the importance of interest rates to capital values this interest rate effect needs to be clearly reported in the business review.

ACCOUNTING FOR HEDGES UNDER 4S

In the above 4S analysis the contracts used as hedges, being promises, are dealt with in the NVP fund. A preferred alternative approach might be to allocate the hedging contracts to the funds which contain the items to be hedged. At first sight this might appear to require a contract designed to hedge productive assets and liabilities designated in another currency (a net investment hedge) to be allocated to ESTA. However, if changes in the value of the net investment are treated as a backlog deficit or surplus and therefore taken to NVP, then the hedging contract should also be part of NVP. Similarly, contracts designed to hedge other promises designated in another currency would be dealt with within NVP. Contracts, like many of those entered into by Rolls, designed as a hedge against expected future business designated in another currency (such as a 'cash flow' hedge) would be allocated to GOV. When the cash flow hedge is unwound and the gain or loss on the hedging contract realised, any gain would sit in the GOV fund as an increase or reduction in opportunity cash. If opportunity cash was surplus to requirements then it might be used to support a 'one off' distribution.

However, realised gains and losses are not part of sustainable profit since even if current business conditions including exchange rates continue, those gains or losses do not continue. They should not therefore be capitalised as part of CUVI. Indeed it is argued in Chapter 10 that gains or losses on fixed price future contracts are a wealth transfer rather than a part of production.

In the case of Rolls as a manufacturer of capital goods there is a further twist. The sale of say $2,000 of aero engine that lasts for 20 years is really the annual sale of the service the engine gives each year for 20 years but with all the payment up front. Whereas current accounting treatment recognises the entire sale and attendant profit on day one, it might be more properly regarded as a case of deferred revenue. Spreading the sale over the economic service period matches the expense of the engine by the airline and balances the production of the service by the aero engine with consumption. If, when received, the $2,000 is converted into say £3,000 then the annual sale for the next 20 years is effectively locked in at the price and exchange rate ruling when the up front payment is received. The terms of the sale contract where the price is fixed and cash is received up front serve to hedge both price and exchange rate risk.

THE VALUE OF PROMISES AND PRECAUTIONARY CASH

Table 8.12   Rolls Royce NVP before precautionary cash

	Dec 2007 £m	Dec 2008 £m	2007/2008 difference £m
Deferred tax (net)	(264)	378	642
Pension deficit (net)	(123)	(142)	(19)
Other financial assets (net)	126	(2,451)	(2,577)
Assets for sale	7	12	5
Provisions	(301)	(369)	(68)
NVP	(555)	(2,572)	(2,017)

Table 8.12 shows the value of promises with the pension deficits being shown on a net basis. Table 8.12 is based upon balance sheet values and, because of the difficulty in valuation, excludes off balance sheet contingencies related to the financing of sales. However, ideally this promise, though off balance sheet, would also be included.

It is unclear from a company's annual report how much cash (or surplus realisable assets) is available to meet the value of outstanding promises (assumed to be negative for purposes of this discussion). The company needs cash for working capital, for precautionary capital in respect of promises and for opportunity capital to underwrite prospects. The annual report does not contain detailed analysis in respect of any of these cash needs and if it did then that would be a notable step forward. In Table 8.13 an arbitrary amount equivalent to one month's cost of sales has been taken as the need for working cash. In practice, working cash would also be needed to cover prospective 'lumpy' interest, dividend and tax payments but this has not been taken into consideration in Table 8.13. In the 2007 strategic review accompanying the 2007 preliminary results (Rolls Royce 2008: 4) the directors highlighted the need for opportunity cash as follows:

> We continue to believe that a strong balance sheet will remain essential for a long term business such as ours. The Group has to compete against large competitors on programmes where returns are measured over decades and where the Group's competitive advantage depends upon its ability to make substantial investments and long term commitments to customers, not always at a time of our choosing. Financial flexibility in periods of uncertainty is desirable especially as there may be opportunities to develop the business further.

Table 8.13   Rolls Royce demand for cash

	2007 cash £m	2007 interest £m	2008 cash £m	2008 interest £m
Total	1,897.0	83.0	2,471.0	59.1
Working capital	500.0	21.9	610.0	14.6
Precautionary	139.0	6.1	643.0	15.4
Opportunity	1,258.0	55.0	1,218.0	29.1

In Table 8.13 the need for precautionary cash has been arbitrarily set at 25 per cent of NVP. This leaves opportunity cash of £1,218 m and since no contrary information is given in the annual report, this is assumed to be adequate. Precautionary cash of £643 m might look slender against a liability of £2,572 m but most of this liability relates to foreign exchange futures, and in Rolls' case can be met from higher future sterling cash flows that would result if the change in the expected exchange rate that causes the negative value of the futures is realised.

Conclusion

This chapter has examined the role of promises (contingencies and commitments) in shaping the Stakeholder Knowledge Network, and the impact of various promises upon both sustainable profit and the net value of promises as used in the 4S valuation analysis. Promises can be either made or received and therefore have either a positive or negative effect on both sustainable profit and the net value of promises. For convenience this section discusses the issues by reference to promises that have a negative effect.

The value of the promise at the time it is made to secure stakeholder engagement is a charge against (sustainable) profit since further equivalent promises will have to be made in future years if current profits are to be sustained. Liquid assets equivalent to this charge could be set aside to settle the promise when it becomes due. If so, the charge and hence the sum set aside is that which, together with expected returns, allows the promise to be settled in full on the due date. However, if the assets are used for another purpose, or they lose their value or expected returns are not realised, then the outstanding promise generates a liability at the balance sheet date – a liability (NVP) that reduces the company's (market) valuation. A liability also exists if the value of an outstanding promise has increased from the amount originally charged, due to a change in the environment. In this case, even if the assets set aside are kept for the purpose of discharging the promise and they keep their value and realise the expected returns, they will still fall short of what is necessary to discharge the promise at the settlement date. These issues are most clearly seen in relation to defined benefit pensions, which, in spite of some outstanding issues such as the appropriate discount rate, might be regarded as the 'Rolls Royce' of commitment accounting. However, the issues that apply to defined benefit pension funds apply in principle to all promises.

Promises such as fixed price contracts and derivatives have very little value at the time the promise is made (that is, nothing need be charged or set aside at the time of the promise) and the impact of such promises comes primarily from subsequent changes in their value due to changes in market conditions. Overall, the value of outstanding promises net of precautionary cash needs to be recognised as a separate slice of equity and movements in their value excluded from sustainable profit.

Whilst the above paragraphs set out the ideal position, current accounting practice for dealing with promises is variable and in many cases less than ideal. With the advent of fair value accounting the value of many outstanding contractual promises (for example pensions, derivatives) is recognised in the 'one fund' balance sheet and for some (for example most derivatives) the movement in fair value is included as reported profit. There are separate rules for derivatives that qualify as hedges but ultimately gains on hedging contracts also end up in profit. Stock options are charged to profit and credited to a share payments accrual within equity based upon their value at the date of issue (grant date) but subsequent changes in value are not recognised. Deferred tax and other provisions are charged at the time they are incurred, based upon estimates, and subsequent changes in the estimates are recognised in both the balance sheet and reported profit. The estimates do not allow for discounting. Pensions are the one promise where it is compulsory to set aside funds and discounting is taken into account. A charge is made to profit in respect of current service and changes in the pension fund surplus/deficit are recognised in the balance sheet. However, apart from current service and finance costs (expected returns less interest), changes in the surplus/deficit do not impact upon reported profit but are taken directly to equity or to other comprehensive income (OCI). Pension fund surplus/deficit is based upon discounting and is highly sensitive to the discount rate used. The value of expected savings (losses) from long-term fixed rate loans and other forward contracts are not shown in the balance sheet. The annual savings (losses) impact upon reported profit which is therefore not sustainable beyond the period of the contract. Finally, it should be noted that any implied commitment in respect of fixed asset replacement is not considered at all by current accounting practice.

This diversity of treatments for different promises reinforces the need for each promise to be evaluated in its own terms for purposes of analysing company valuation. The net value of promises with positive and negative values, less any precautionary assets held to meet such promises, must be included in the valuation analysis. It represents the expected future impact of commitments and contingencies already established as a consequence of past business activity. The growth and opportunity value of future business activity is considered separately in the next chapter.

9

Strategic Connectivity

Chapter 4 introduced the concept of business as a constantly reshaping Stakeholder Knowledge Network (SKN) with the network at the heart of corporate development (strategy), value analysis and accounting. The SKN plays a crucial role as a control framework for the effective integration of these three elements. In Chapter 5 the role of the SKN was explored in relation to the valuation of the company by the market (market capitalisation). The outcome was an analysis of market capitalisation through 4S accounting where the four slices of equity were identified with the dimensions of the SKN. In this chapter the focus is upon the relations between the SKN and corporate development and its relationship in turn to both strategy and market conditions. The chapter starts with an exploration of the relations between strategic choice and the LEADERS business model which was introduced in Chapters 1 and 4 as a mnemonic for the strategic management of the stakeholder network. Strategy directs management action and LEADERS requires that a company excels in one or more, of leverage, engagement, alignment and development and/or the company excels in combining these. The aim is to create a strategic blend of leverage, engagement, alignment and development that is distinctive, superior, difficult to imitate and that works from a financial perspective. The chapter starts by looking at LEADERS as a strategic framework, in the context of Bingham and Eisenhardt's (2008) strategic logics.

Bingham and Eisenhardt give corporate examples to support their analysis. The chapter goes on to give further examples that illustrate strategic blending in response to various market challenges and opportunities. Examples are taken from Halma, J D Wetherspoon, GSK (Glaxo Smith Klein) and Rexam. The chapter then considers how the execution of strategic choice generates further knowledge development within the network and as a consequence new strategic choices emerge for the company. Formula plc is a pedagogic case illustrating a company as knowledge development through a succession of emerging strategic choices. For Formula the strategic choices made are represented as a 'development pathway', the construction of which is then further illustrated by the development of J Sainsbury plc up to 2003. J Sainsbury is employed to illustrate a 'financial pathway' developed in tandem with the 'development pathway' and demonstrating the relationship between strategic choice and financial performance. J Sainsbury is chosen because unlike most other business reports the 2003 business review provides much of the information necessary for the required analysis.

The development and leverage of the stakeholder network is a case of inside-out strategy. Stakeholder propositions respond to the opportunities that the existing knowledge base brings. It is equally important to consider outside-in strategic responses. These occur when the existing stakeholder propositions are unsuited to new market conditions as is the case with the examples of GSK and Rexam. In these cases, new stakeholder propositions are developed in response to outside circumstances. The Formula and Sainsbury examples also illustrate the importance of market conditions since it is how the company is placed with respect to each emerging market opportunity that dictates whether the opportunity is taken up.

4S accounting requires an assessment of growth and opportunity value (the fourth slice of equity) and this in turn requires a projection into the future of the current combination of market conditions, strategic choice and financial performance. The Stakeholder Knowledge Network is the intermediary vehicle bringing these elements together. In principle, the historical development pathway in terms of strategic choice and market conditions, together with the historical financial pathway expressed as 4S accounts, provide a platform for this projection of the future financial pathway. In practice, current business reviews do not generally give a clear understanding of the pathways. The best that can be hoped for is some indication of the directors' view of the future. This can be used as the basis for an assessment of growth and opportunity value and the chapter illustrates this with an estimate of Rolls Royce's 2008 GOV based upon information given in the 2008 annual report and accounts. Hindsight gives an idea of the difficulties inherent in this estimate.

The final opportunity in Formula's development is an acquisition to take the retail concept overseas. Acquisition is a popular strategic move for the development of a company and the chapter uses Croda's 2006 acquisition of Uniqema to indicate how 4S accounting can help the evaluation of a strategic acquisition. Hindsight gives us an opportunity to reflect on this acquisition.

Leaders as a Strategic Framework

In order to coordinate the stakeholder network with strategy it is necessary to describe strategic choices, highlighted by the strategy literature, in terms of the leverage, engagement, alignment, development and reshaping of the stakeholder network. Bingham and Eisenhardt (2008) provide a suitable synopsis of strategic choices. They categorise strategic choice in terms of leverage logic, position logic and opportunity logic. Consequently, each of these strategic choices is discussed in terms of LEADERS to illustrate a blending of leverage, engagement, alignment and development that results in success given particular market conditions.

LEVERAGE LOGIC

Leverage logic is based upon the ideas of Prahalad and Hamel (1990) and Collis and Montgomery (1995). These suggest that competitive advantage comes from specific core resources which are rare, valuable, non-substitutable and difficult to imitate.

Leverage occurs when such specific core resources are combined with complementary resources to give superior and inimitable performance in new product markets. The example often given is of Honda leveraging its specific core engine technology into the automobile, motorcycle, lawnmower and motorboat markets. Such leverage logic achieves higher volumes by deploying existing resources into new markets and/or products. Insofar as this requires existing resources to work with new complementary resources, then such leverage logic can be regarded as requiring development of the stakeholder network as well as pure leverage in the form of higher volumes. In terms of the stakeholder network, it is inimitable access to scarce or valuable resources, rather than ownership per se, which is key to competitive advantage. Leverage logic therefore requires that the terms of engagement for stakeholders with rare and valuable knowledge are difficult for competitors to replicate so as to give a continuing advantage. Bingham and Eisenhardt (2008: 245) argue that leverage logic applies to moderately dynamic markets and that the duration of competitive advantage is likely to be medium term. Under leverage logic the emphasis is upon *engagement* to give access to scarce knowledge, and *leverage* of that knowledge.

POSITION LOGIC

Position logic is based upon the idea of Porter (1996) that comparative advantage comes from executing different activities to the competition or executing the same activities in a different way. This strategic logic requires that resources are tightly linked together in mutually reinforcing systems known as activity systems (Porter, 1996; Rivkin, 2000; Siggelkow, 2002) in order to achieve an inimitable position in the market. In a case such as Southwest Airlines it is the low cost, no frills customer proposition that provided a differentiated product in the market place, and the idea is implemented through the strict alignment of other stakeholder propositions with the customer proposition. All stakeholders are focused upon the no frills proposition. There is the development of one original innovative idea, after which the focus is upon alignment and organisational knowledge in the form of hard to imitate activity systems. Bingham and Eisenhardt (2008: 247) argue that position logic is appropriate to stable markets in which complex systems or processes have time to develop, and that the duration of the competitive advantage is often long term. Under position logic the emphasis is upon *alignment* through tightly knit systems and *leverage* of that alignment.

OPPORTUNITY LOGIC

Opportunity logic takes the ideas of Roberts and Eisenhardt (2003) and Eisenhardt and Martin (2000) that competitive advantage comes from repeated entrepreneurial action in capturing fleeting market opportunities. Cisco's acquisition process is one example given (Bingham and Eisenhardt 2008: 249), since during the late 1990s it acquired a series of technology-rich companies more quickly and effectively than its competitors. Today Apple's product innovation process would be another example. Opportunity logic depends upon entrepreneurial skills (a form of tacit knowledge) and organisational knowledge in the form of processes which facilitate those skills. Such processes are likely to be semi-structured rather than the tightly linked organisational processes associated with activity systems. Bingham and Eisenhardt (250) argue that opportunity logic is appropriate to high velocity markets and the duration of competitive advantage is unpredictable, often resulting in a series of temporary advantages. Opportunity logic suggests the leverage of dynamic capabilities (Wang and Ahmed 2007) through continuous development. The emphasis is on *leverage* and *development* through a rapidly *reshaping* stakeholder network.

As the above discussion demonstrates, it is the chosen strategy that dictates the mix of leverage, engagement, alignment and development through which management execute the new economy (LEADERS) business model and changes to the SKN. Leverage is a key factor in the success of all three strategic choices and, as a general rule, with increasing leverage comes increasing risk. The other key factor is the uniqueness of the *engagement* (choice 1), the commitment to *alignment* (choice 2) and continual *development* (choice 3). Thus as a consequence of the need to coordinate with the stakeholder network, the three strategic choices might be better named as engagement logic, alignment logic and development logic.

The chapter now looks at further examples of the interpretation of reshaping strategy and stakeholder propositions in terms of LEADERS, starting with a successful company that was introduced in Chapter 7, Halma.

The Reshaping Examples

HALMA

Leverage is most easily achieved with the conceptual company. A conceptual company is one which can expand volume without requiring further investment in fixed assets and working capital (Lev 2007). A quasi conceptual company is one which requires investment but is able to finance this from borrowings. Halma is a case of a (quasi) conceptual company. From 2005 to 2007 (see Table 7.5), fixed assets and working capital reduced from £105.8 m to £94 m whilst CUVI increased from £290 m to £416 m. Thus Halma was able to improve the performance of its intangibles without any additional investment in operating assets. Hence it performed during this period as a conceptual company. In 2008 and 2009 Halma increased its combined investment in fixed assets/working capital firstly to £144.8 m and then further to £190.9 m. However, these increases were accompanied by loans so that the net investment actually fell in 2008 to £79.4 m rising in 2009 to £111.3 m. In 2008 CUVI rose to £474 m and in 2009 it rose further to £498 m. In 2007 there was a change in policy so as to take out loans as opportunity capital for acquisitions. The result was that in 2008 Halma operated as a quasi-conceptual company, increasing CUVI whilst decreasing its net investment in FA/WC. However, in 2009, CUVI increased by 5.1 per cent whilst the net investment in FA/WC rose by 40.2 per cent. The implication is that Halma may have ceased in 2009 to operate as a conceptual or quasi conceptual company, with implications for its future leverage ability and hence for its 2009 GOV.

Halma is managing a diversified portfolio of innovations within the health and safety sector, embedded in 80 or so subsidiaries. It uses good governance to encourage subsidiaries to leverage their innovations; this governance, which includes management training, is a mix of autonomy, central support and incentive that is attractive (engaging) to the managers in the subsidiaries. Halma is also a development story: (1) in terms of acquiring new subsidiaries so as to leverage its governance skills; (2) through research and development expenditure; and (3) by bringing complementary resources together from more than one subsidiary in pursuit of new products.

Its strategy, therefore, is a powerful blend of: (1) leverage at both the level of subsidiary and head office; (2) engagement of subsidiary managers through good governance and of customers through leading-edge products; and (3) development through acquisition, R and D, management training and cooperation between subsidiaries, all within a long-term growth sector. It adopts leverage, positioning and entrepreneurship. The only cautionary note is the company's failure to operate as a (quasi) conceptual company in the recession-hit 2009. However it recovers well in 2010 and 2011.

J D WETHERSPOON (JDW) 2005

J D Wetherspoon's customer proposition, as it appears every year in its annual report is shown as Figure 9.1. This is JDW's original (single) good idea and the company moved swiftly to implement this idea through pubs in high streets across the UK. The company was greatly helped by the branch closure programmes of the banks which released many interesting sites for conversion. In the early years the key skill was the ability to roll out its concept across as many sites as possible as quickly as possible (leverage) since its customer proposition can be copied. At this stage JDW was functioning as a quasi-conceptual company, and its acquisition of good sites was a key entrepreneurial activity.

However, J D Wetherspoon is a typical retail concept company in that its concept has limits upon its ability to travel through time and space. Over time, its customer offering may be seen as less exciting and in terms of space, once it has filled every profitable site in the UK, then its customer concept may not travel well abroad. Typically the financial results of such a company start slowly

Wetherspoon owns and operates pubs throughout the UK. The company aims to provide customers with good-quality food and drink, served by well-trained and friendly staff, at reasonable prices. The pubs are individually designed, and the company aims to maintain them in excellent condition.

Figure 9.1   J D Wetherspoon's customer proposition

whilst the concept is tested, rise steeply through the roll-out programme and then plateau and taper off as the limits of the customer concept are felt. Thus the results follow a wave pattern and it is important in terms of judging the future that investors recognise the point on the wave that the company has reached.

A company like J D Wetherspoon leverages its customer concept by increasing like for like sales through existing outlets and by expanding the number of outlets. When a company increases its like for like sales (whilst maintaining margins) it is effectively leveraging both the original idea and the fixed assets: the performance of both its tangible and intangible assets improves. However, if the company is dependent upon new openings to leverage its idea, then the idea is being leveraged but its fixed assets may show lower rates of return if the new sites are not as profitable as the old. Relative and absolute returns come into conflict.

The following comments upon J D Wetherspoon are based upon the company's press release giving the highlights of the company's performance for the year ended 24 July 2005 and relate to that time. In 2005 the company is no longer riding the wave since turnover is static in real terms and profit is down. Notably, the leveraging of the original concept through the opening of new pubs has slowed to a crawl. The company is continuing to re-purchase shares and this may signal a lack of investment opportunities. The company has successfully leveraged its fixed asset premises by using them as a coffee bar as well as pub. However, like for like sales through the public houses are no longer increasing.

The company has leveraged its knowledge of the pub business by developing another pub concept in the shape of Loyds and it intends to leverage its reputation as a value brand through Wetherspoon Lodges. However, the financials do not indicate the significance of these activities to the business as a whole and they appear to be relatively small. All in all, in 2005 it is difficult to see growth and opportunity value in J D Wetherspoon.

However, by July 2009, the company is bucking the decline in the UK public house sector by once again opening new pubs, some being taken over from other companies, and increasing profits, even though its retail concept remains fundamentally the same. The story has changed to one of tight activity systems resulting in a strong alignment of stakeholders with the low cost, no frills product. It is these activity systems which are now being leveraged through both improved margins and new business at the expense of competitors, in a shrinking market. Whilst in the glory days J D Wetherspoon was leveraging its retail concept, by 2009 it is leveraging a different intangible, its activity systems. The strategic blend has shifted its emphasis from leverage of the engagement created by its innovative retail concept, to leverage of its disciplined alignment of stakeholders resulting from its activity systems. The source of leverage has changed as the market environment has changed.

GSK

GSK is one part a big systematic machine (tight activity systems) for the testing and bringing to market of drugs, and one part a creative and adaptive piece that finds new drugs and families of drugs (see Figure 9.2). GSK, like other big pharma companies, is a story of development through mutual leverage between systematic and creative knowledge; a coming together of complementary resources. The big machine needs new drugs and the drug discoveries need a big machine to reach the market.

GSK is also a story of development through engagement and alignment. At one time it was thought that new drugs could be found by 'big pharma' through the systematic testing of each possible compound. However, this was not very successful and has been scaled back in favour of a number of smaller, more nimble research units (DPUs or Discovery Performance Units) that can mimic the creative environment of biotech companies. Thus the control relationship with research employees shifted, from one suited to systematic behaviour, to one suited to creativity. Consequently, the top management of GSK has to be bicultural in the sense of being able to manage and bring together two quite different activities – the big machine and the creative units.

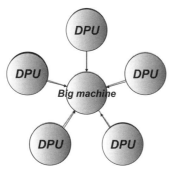

GSK is a big machine that takes drugs through the process of delivering
to the market AND a set of 38 creative units (DPUs) that discover the drugs.
Holistic management ensures that there is mutual leverage

Figure 9.2   The GSK network

GSK also have 'virtual' research units that do deals with outside biotechs,
smaller and mid-sized pharmaceutical companies and academic institutions.
It is possible to shape the proposition made to those engaged by the virtual
research unit along the lines of an option such that there are high rewards for
successful drug discovery but that costs are still met in the event of failure.
An 'option like' proposition redistributes the risks and rewards around the
stakeholder network, limiting the risk for the outside researcher and introducing
a reward contingent upon success. Such arrangements can of course be copied
for internal research teams.

Indeed the CEO of GSK, Andrew Witty, has suggested that innovative
propositioning should be used to reduce some of the difficulties experienced
by/with NICE (National Institute for Health and Clinical Excellence) who are
responsible for evaluating the cost efficiency of new drugs on behalf of the
National Health Service (NHS). The suggestion is that the price paid for the
drugs should reflect the NHS' experience of the success of the drugs. Initially
the drugs are taken at a low price so that the risk of failure in terms of the
drug being ineffective is born by the drugs company, whilst the rewards for the
drugs company are there if the drug proves successful, through higher prices
that reflect proven value.

Thus GSK are committed to innovative propositioning as a concept to
increase engagement and alignment for drug consuming as well as drug
creating activities. This innovation is based upon the retention of risk by GSK
and is not really innovative except for its use in this setting. For example, it was

used in the customer proposition famously adopted by Xerox when they leased their copiers at a low cost per copy and thereby retained the risk of failure of their 'value presumption'. The value presumption was that their new photo technology would lead to a revolution in copying habits towards far greater volumes.

REXAM 2004

The performance of Rexam, the packaging company, in the first half of 2004 is also a story of innovative propositioning in response to a challenging environment (Felsted 2004). Rexam reshaped its supplier and customer propositions in response to rising raw material and energy prices. In relation to rising aluminium prices in the US, Rexam agreed to its biggest customer, Coca Cola, buying aluminium directly from the aluminium suppliers and passing it to Rexam for processing into cans. Thus the customer was satisfied because it believed it had the superior purchasing expertise and clout. It was an engaging proposition for Coca Cola. In Europe Rexam determined its supply prices for three years ahead through hedging, allowing it to offer equivalent terms to its customers, who found the price certainty attractive. In relation to rising resin prices for its plastics packaging, Rexam entered into sales agreements that allowed it to pass on price rises to customers who therefore carried the price risk. This proposition served to align customers and suppliers on the price issue.

Overall, Rexam's first half results for 2004 showed slightly lower sales compared to 2003, but a 14 per cent increase in pre-tax profits. The increasing margins were a reflection of Rexam's initiative in re-shaping and re-aligning its supplier and customer propositions according to the stakeholders' individual needs. Whilst the packaging business itself is a highly systematic business with high levels of fixed assets (an old economy business), the threat of continuing price rises can be turned into an opportunity through innovative and adaptive management of stakeholders, putting the company's knowledge of those stakeholders and their needs and attitudes to good effect. It is of course always possible to increase profits by taking on higher risk. However, insofar as the revised propositions either hedged price risk or passed it on to customers, then it is reasonable to assume that management's initiative resulted in an increase in value as well as profit. The company leveraged its engagement and alignment through higher margins. On a different front, it should be noted that the company faced risks from environmental legislation and that these risks were increasing. This is another issue that requires an innovative response by the company.

Introducing the Development Pathway

Formula Hotels is a pedagogic case, though it is a derivative of several real cases and has elements typical of the development issues facing many retail concept companies. Formula's development pathway is given in Table 9.1 with the development tracked from the bottom up. The pathway shows how the chosen strategic business objectives were implemented through management actions which generated new knowledge for the stakeholder network (the learning pathway) from various sources. This new knowledge in turn generated new strategic choices (development options) for the company.

Table 9.1   Formula hotels development pathway

Business objective	Action	Learning pathway	Knowledge source	Development options
To leverage the holistic knowledge	Acquire overseas	Overseas market	Existing employees, employees acquired	Further acquisitions
To resolve tension between WE and Formula	Separate WE division	Holistic – how the two pieces work together	Board	Spin out WE as separate company or sell WE
To improve weekend occupancy	New weekend (WE) product	Leisure market expertise	Specialist employees	Extend WE agency to non-formula hotels
To provide finance	Franchise	Franchising expertise	Supplier (bank)	Take work in-house
To leverage the formula	New hotels	Site analysis	Specialist employees	Real estate speculation
To implement the formula	Began with three hotels	Operating formula	Company intangible asset	1. Sell services as hotel operator, 2. Roll out the formula

A crucial issue is which of the development options are actually taken up and why. The following three paragraphs hypothesise the main issue to emerge in the development story of Formula. In resolving this issue the 'mind set' of the Board is seen as critical. The idea is that the constituency of the Board in terms of prior experience and allegiance plays a major role.

Formula Hotels leveraged its 'value' hotel concept through a roll-out programme of new hotel build and franchises. The 'formula' was designed for business people who wanted a reliable, recognisable, modestly priced product wherever they were staying to do business. As a consequence of this business orientation Formula found that it had spare capacity at the weekend. Formula therefore diversified its product range, offering the traditional 'formula' for the business market Monday to Thursday, and a weekend experience (WE) for the leisure market. Promotion of the leisure market requires its own distinctive marketing skills and 'WE' was set up as an agency to match the experience offered by each hotel and its surroundings with WE's knowledge of the leisure customer.

Subsequently, WE's management put forward a proposal to offer its services to other, possibly rival, hotel chains. Similarly, under this proposal Formula would no longer be obliged to place all its weekend leisure business through WE. The problem from WE's point of view is that although both WE and Formula need to grow, WE, in order to keep ahead of its competition, needs to grow at a faster pace in terms of new hotels than it is possible for Formula to provide. This sets up a tension within the Formula main board between the Formula 'traditionalists' who believe that WE's role is to support Formula hotels (and vice versa), and the WE people who want to leverage their skills across as wide a network of hotels as possible, and so offer greater choice to a larger number of customers. One argument put forward by the WE people is that opening up their business enables both WE and Formula hotels to operate as autonomous units and might lead in due course to the spin out of WE as a separate independent company providing value for Formula's shareholders (for now this is a real option). Formula managers in particular would need to be trained in the skill of negotiating prices for weekend occupancy in order to align with their new autonomy.

Since the main board is dominated by Formula 'traditionalists', it is they who win the day and WE are not allowed to deal on behalf of other hotels. This, however, puts WE at a competitive disadvantage, demotivating WE managers, and the WE venture fails. WE were overtaken by marketing operations that were not limited to one hotel chain and formula. The key message is that the Formula board got it wrong because they employed 'old' economy thinking. Consequently, the board persisted with the wrong proposition to WE management. The board wanted the 'WE idea' to help leverage Formula's fixed asset investment in hotels. They did not see WE as an idea worthy of leverage in its own right. New economy thinking would see the role of the hotels as leveraging the WE idea, not the other way around.

Introducing the Financial Pathway

The case of J Sainsbury prior to 2003 is used to illustrate a development path for a real company and to introduce the parallel idea of a financial pathway.

J SAINSBURY 2003

Table 9.2 represents the development pathway of retailing company J Sainsbury, up to 2003. The pathway starts at the bottom of Table 9.2 with the original shopping proposition and proceeds upwards, finishing at the disposal of Homebase. The disposal of Homebase is billed as a financing transaction. Until the funds are reinvested, the transaction is negative in terms of the development and leverage of J Sainsbury's intangibles. The pathway is only approximate, having been put together on the basis of the information contained in the 2003 financial statements and Operating and Financial Review and this does not give the chronology.

The development path gives the major strategic initiatives of the company (columns 1 and 2), the need for complementary knowledge/resources (column 3), the source of that knowledge (column 4), further development options resulting from that new knowledge (column 5) and the impact of the strategic initiative upon the profits for 2003 relative to 2002 (column 6: the financial pathway). Although J Sainsbury was performing poorly in 2003, its Annual Report did contain sufficient information to allow a meaningful stab at piecing together the financial pathway. However, since the publicly available financial reports do not in many cases allocate fixed assets/working capital or indeed interest expenditure, to the various steps in the development pathway, it is not possible to calculate the impact on residual income but only, and even then on a limited basis, upon profit.

Table 9.2   The J Sainsbury development path

1 Business objectives	2 Action	3 The learning pathway	4 Source of knowledge	5 Development options	6 Financial pathway – 2003 increase in profit/ (loss)
To release funds for the core businesses	Dispose of Homebase	DIY market knowledge (loss of)	Transferred to purchaser		£61 m
To increase the loyalty card's versatility and attraction	Introduce Nectar with other partners - a new customer proposition	Knowledge of wider customer set and managing the partnership	Nectar partners	Extend the partnership Merge with credit card	NI*
To diversify retail channels	Sainsburys to You (on line)	Knowledge of e-commerce	Specialist employees and suppliers	E-banking	£ 21 m
To leverage retail knowledge	Acquisition of Shaws (US)	Knowledge of US retailing	Incoming Shaws employees	Further acquisitions	Nil
To diversify product offering	Sainsbury's Bank	Banking expertise	Partner – HBOS	Additional financial services	Nil
To cut cost base/improve delivery	Transformation program	New fixed assets/new IT systems	Suppliers – IT outsourced	Share logistics/ systems	£25 m
To leverage retail knowledge	Develop Homebase (DIY store)	DIY market knowledge	Specialist employees and suppliers	Other retail markets	N/A**
To leverage real estate knowledge	JS Developments	Real estate knowledge	Own specialists and suppliers	Property investment company	(£3) m including property sales
To leverage shopping formula	New stores and logistics	Site analysis, logistics capability	Specialist employees	Real estate development, share logistics	(£4) m

*NI: No information given in the annual report and accounts
**N/A: Not applicable due to sale of Homebase

Nevertheless, what is shown is interesting. It is found that profit momentum in 2003 is almost all dependent upon: (1) the disposal of Homebase; (2) the transformation programme, being a substantial investment to correct deficiencies in the distribution and IT systems; and (3) Sainsburys to You, the on-line shopping activity. There is no separate information concerning the attempt to engage customers through the loyalty card. However, most significantly there is no momentum coming from leverage through expansion of its traditional supermarket customer proposition, the major part of its business. The conclusion is that such a financial pathway, if it were to be included (as part of a company's development pathway) in the Annual Report, would allow the investor to read across from the incremental knowledge (developments) in the learning pathway to the impact of the leverage of this knowledge upon profit. J Sainsbury's development path displays many of the available options for company development including, acquisition (Shaws), accessing complementary resources through a joint venture (with HBOS), implementing stronger systems as part of the transformation programme, innovative propositioning for customers (a versatile loyalty card) and a branch roll-out programme. However, few of these developments were proving their worth in the hands of the management at that time.

Growth and Opportunity Value: the Rolls Royce Case

The reason for addressing the connectivity between strategic choice, market conditions and financial outcome is that an understanding of that connectivity is vital to an ability to predict future financial performance. 4S reporting requires an assessment of Growth and Opportunity Value (GOV) based upon a prediction of future financials and this has to be done at present on the basis of the information available through the current mode of business reporting. Rolls Royce is used as an indication of the issues involved in doing this. The discussion starts by placing the analyst back in time to 2008.

Table 9.3   Rolls Royce 4S comprehensive balance sheet

2,007 £m	Year	2008 £m	2007 £m		2008 £m
2,975	FA/WC/other investments	3,623	2,029	Loans	2,667
1,314	CUVI	2,464	555	NVP	2,572
139	Precautionary cash	643	9,937	Market Cap	6,187
1258	Opportunity cash	1,218			
6,835	GOV	3,478			
12,521		11,426	12,521		11,426

Table 9.3 gives the comprehensive balance sheet of Rolls Royce in 2008 at the height of the financial crisis. The GOV (excluding opportunity cash) shown in the comprehensive balance sheet is the growth and opportunity value implied by the year end market capitalisation. This has declined substantially from £6,835 m to £3,478 m. Between 2007 and 2008, CUVI improves substantially and yet GOV declines substantially. Thus a first reading of the 4S accounts would suggest that, in 2008, Rolls is substantially undervalued.

However, it could also be that Rolls was overvalued in 2007 on the back of a bullish stock market prior to the financial crisis. The key issue for the analyst is to test the credibility of the 2008 GOV and hence to test the credibility of the 2008 share price. The question is whether the closing GOV is justified by the likely reshaping of the business through future leverage, alignments, engagements and development. The following credibility test is based on what the directors themselves say about the future in the 2008 Annual Report. The Report does not give a detailed future pathway showing leverage and development but, according to the directors, profits in 2009 are expected to stay at 2008 levels whilst by 2018 the company is expected to double in size through organic growth alone. This implies an 8 per cent growth rate from 2010 onwards. These estimates of future profit provide growth and opportunity value of £1,367 m (Table 9.4) on the basis of a discount rate of 12 per cent and a conservative effective tax rate of 30 per cent. The discount rate has been held at 12 per cent in spite of the future uncertainties regarding airline finances and carbon legislation. This accepts that the risks facing the business are mitigated by Rolls' continuing diversification through the increasing proportion of revenue: (1) from the aftermarket; (2) from emerging economies in Asia; and (3) from the three divisions other than civil aviation. The company also has a very substantial order book.

In addition, the directors expect a redundancy programme to yield annual savings of £100 m from 2010. These savings, assuming they are achieved and do not result in a loss of capability, have a value of £521 m ({70 / 0.12} / 1.12). Finally, it might be assumed that the pound recovers against the dollar coming back from exceptionally low 2008 year end rate of $1.438 towards the average rate of $1.72 in the outstanding foreign exchange contracts. If we expect the exchange rate to come back fully to $1.72, then the loss in value of the exchange contracts might be expected to reverse. If the loss in value on the exchange contracts is taken to be £2577 m (Table 8.12), then the reversal gives a one off benefit net of tax of £1,804 m (0.7*2577). On the basis of these future values the credibility test suggests a GOV of £3,478 m is not unreasonable, being broadly comparable to £3,692 m, the sum of £1,367 m, £521 m and £1,804 m.

Table 9.4   Rolls Royce value of projected residual income

Year	Residual Income £m	Discounted to 2008 (12%) £m
2009	295.7	264.0
2010	319.4 (8% growth)	254.6
2011	344.9	245.4
2012	372.5	236.7
2013	402.3	228.3
2014	434.5	220.1
2015	469.2	212.2
2016	506.8	204.6
2017	547.3	187.5
2018	591.1 (c 2*295.7)	190.4
2019 onwards	591.1	<u>1,586.8</u>
		3,830.6 net present value
		<u>2,464.0</u> included in CUVI
		1,366.6 GOV

Some conservatism has been built into the estimate of net present value. Most significant is the fact that Table 9.4 assumes Rolls to be a proportionate company, that is, if sales double then assets double and so on. In reality it is likely that Rolls, having substantial intangibles, might operate in part as a conceptual or quasi conceptual company so that when sales double, profits more than double. Furthermore, the calculation of GOV assumes no growth after 2018. Finally, if the redundancy programme reflects a new and more efficient alignment then the cost savings have the potential to double if the company doubles in size, and no allowance has been made for this.

The largest item in the valuation of GOV is the reversal of the losses on the foreign exchange contracts demonstrating the importance in valuation of judgments about future macroeconomic conditions. Reversal depends upon the recovery of sterling and since the crisis the best sterling has managed is around $1.6. In this regard the calculation of GOV was optimistic.

LOOKING BACK WITH HINDSIGHT

Table 9.5 gives the 4S balance sheets for 2009 and 2010. It is seen that by 2009 there has been a substantial increase from the CUVI of 2008. It has risen by £4,477 m from £2,464 m to £6,941 m, an increase well in excess of the 2008 GOV of £3,478 m. In this time the share price has risen from 332 p to 638 p. The first reading of the 4S 2007/2008 accounts was right – 2008 would have been a good time to buy. A first reading of the 2009/2010 4S accounts might suggest that 2010 was a good time to sell. These show a modest decline in CUVI but a substantial (388 per cent) increase in GOV. However, the share price has continued to increase in 2011 though there are signs in 2011 that the growth in CUVI is slowing down and has been more dependent on growth in margins. Nevertheless since 2011 the company has continued to do exceptionally (unexpectedly) well in terms of sales of engines for civil airliners based upon the demand for more fuel efficient engines.

Table 9.5 shows that Rolls had substantial opportunity cash and in 2012 this has been used to the tune of £1,500 m (£1.5 billion) to purchase (jointly with Daimler) German industrial engine maker, Tognum. This is a strategic acquisition to create opportunities for Rolls' marine and energy businesses. It might require the analyst to consider Rolls' prospects anew! Strategic acquisition is the subject of the next section.

Table 9.5   Rolls Royce 4S balance sheets 2009 and 2010

2010 £m		2009 £m	2010 £m		2009 £m
3,906	FA/WC/other investments	3,724	3,123	Loans	3,058
6,116	CUVI	6,941	1,807	NVP	1,626
452	Precautionary cash	406	11,501	Market Cap	9,355
1,667	Opportunity cash	1,864			
4,290	GOV	1,104			
16,431		14,039	16,431		14,039

Strategic Acquisition: Croda and Uniqema 2006

Strategic acquisitions are a popular choice for the development of a company and can have the effect of transforming the stakeholder network through the inclusion of a new range of stakeholders and stakeholder knowledge. On 1 September 2006, speciality chemical company Croda purchased Uniqema from ICI. As the 2006 Annual Report of Croda stated (Croda 2007: 2) '*the acquisition of Uniqema is a transforming move for Croda*'. Uniqema had total assets of £591.2 m relative to Croda's consumer care division with £174 m and Croda's industrial specialities division with £84 m. Thus Uniqema was more than twice as big as Croda in terms of assets but its operating profits were substantially lower being of the order of £12.9 m against Croda's £48 m for consumer care and £9.2 m for industrial specialities. Thus Croda's profits were more than four times as big as Uniqema. Uniqema was an old economy company with a commodity product, high fixed assets, high turnover and low margins whereas Croda's dominant consumer care division in particular was a new economy operation with low fixed assets, high profits and high margins. The new/old economy divide is shown in Table 9.6 by Croda's 2005 CUVI of £190 m and Uniqema's CUVI of negative £151 m.

Table 9.6   Accounting for the Uniqema acquisition

	1 Croda 2005 £m	2 Uniqema £m	3 Finance effects £m	4 Other movements £m	5 Croda 2006 £m
ESTA	175.0	296.0	(321.2)	(33.7)	116.1
CUVI	190.0	(151.0)	65.9	86.0	190.9
NVP	(100.9)	(98.8)	Nil	18.8	(180.9)
GOV	363.9	335.6	(65.9)	60.3	693.9
	628.0	381.8	(321.2)	131.4	820.0
Loans		321.2	321.2		
Equity		60.6			
Acquisition cost		381.8			

Table 9.6 shows the impact of the Uniqema acquisition upon the four slices of equity and thus permits an analysis of the financial impact of this major strategic development for Croda. Required rates of return on tangibles and intangibles are taken to be 8 per cent and 10 per cent respectively for 2005

rising to 9 per cent and 11 per cent in 2006 as a result of the risk attaching to the acquisition. Croda paid £381.8 m, funded £321.2 m by new debt and £60.6 m by new equity. This purchase price valued Uniqema's GOV, having revalued its assets and liabilities, at £335.6 m. The acquisition of Uniqema brought not only the CUVI of negative £151m and GOV of £335.6 m, but also traditional assets of £296 m and NVP of negative £98.8 m. Outside of the takeover, Croda's original business did well, improving CUVI by £86 m (a rise of 45 per cent) and GOV by £60.3 m (a rise of 16.6 per cent). It did this whilst reducing the equity stake in fixed assets and working capital by £33.7 m, thus confirming its status as a conceptual, intangibles-based company.

Table 9.6 (column 3) shows separately the effects on the four slices of equity of funding the acquisition with new debt of £321.2 m. First of all ESTA is reduced by this amount. Secondly, CUVI is increased by £65.9 m and consequently GOV is reduced by the same amount. This increase in CUVI is the net effect of two countervailing consequences of the substantial debt issue. Firstly, as a result of debt replacing book equity, CUVI benefits through residual profit being net of interest on debt rather than being charged with the slightly higher required rate of return on ESTA. On the other hand, CUVI declines since the required rates of return on both ESTA and intangibles increase slightly, following the substantial increase in Croda's gearing as a result of the new debt issue. This increase in gearing is assumed to result in an increase in risk and the required rates of return.

The acquisition of Uniqema transforms Croda from a highly successful, new economy company with low debt to a significantly indebted company with a major old economy operation to manage. On the face of it this does not sound an attractive move, though it should be recognised that Croda's industrial chemicals division had much in common with Uniqema and performed better. The acquisition could therefore be seen to leverage Croda's management expertise in industrial chemicals. Indeed by 2008 the now combined industrial specialities segment had indeed improved profits by a few million on reduced assets. However, over the same time, the consumer care segment had increased operating profits from £48m in 2006 to £89.9 m in 2008. Set against this performance, the acquisition of Uniqema was surely a distraction for Croda management requiring substantial and expensive reorganisation, and the management of disposals. Indeed it appears that industrial chemicals may be the riskier of the two segments being exposed to sectors that have suffered in the recession, with customer care remaining resilient. One small illustration of the extra management effort and change in thinking required by the acquisition is the need to reconsider the basis of Croda's health, safety and environmental targets. The 2006 Annual Report (Croda 2007: 16) reports:

The acquisition of Uniqema in September 2006 has had a marked effect on many aspects of the Croda group. Although there are many products and processes in common there are also significant differences, such as the addition of commodity fatty acid manufacture to the product profile.

As a result, the manufactured tonnage has increased more than tenfold. Since all Croda targets are normalised to the manufactured tonnage this has had a large effect on the performance target statistics.

A rather different question to whether the acquisition made strategic sense is whether Croda overpaid. The total consideration was £381.8 m resulting in goodwill of £177.7 m. The company claims (Croda 2007: 67) that the goodwill is justified by: (1) the acquisition of a skilled workforce; (2) the fact that Uniqema's product portfolio complements and enhances Croda's existing product offering; (3) further expected growth as a result of rationalising and improving Uniqema's distribution network; and (4) cost saving synergies as a result of bringing the business within Croda's existing structure. 4S accounting, however, does not look at the price paid for goodwill but at the price paid for GOV and at £335.6 m this could only be justified by an increase in profits which would have to be of the order of £30 m plus for the industrial chemicals division. This is an increase which by 2009 continued to seem totally out of reach. At the time of the acquisition the combined profits of the Croda industrial chemicals division and Uniqema were £22.1 m and the reported operating profits of this segment in 2009 were £17.9 m. However, remarkably, in 2010 the profits of industrial chemicals increased more than threefold to £62.1 m. Table 9.7 illustrates the impact on the 4S figures. At last the benefits of the acquisition were being felt as the industrial chemicals rebounded strongly from the recession. However, the main factor appears to have been a strategy to focus on high value speciality industrial chemicals and the consequent disposals since the Uniqema acquisition of commodity activities which had previously dominated industrial chemicals. The difficulty for shareholders was that this strategy was not clearly articulated at the time of the acquisition; not, for example, in terms of the justification for goodwill outlined above. The good news is that Croda is back on track as a high value adding speciality chemical company. The results for 2010 provided generous bonuses for the executives based upon the growth in earnings per share and in total shareholder returns over a three year period to 2010. However, the improvements had to a substantial extent already been paid for once by the shareholders when they bought the GOV in Uniqema? This underlines the importance of the historical perspective provided by a development and financial pathway so that accountability for past decisions is not lost. The historical perspective needs to last longer than three years.

Table 9.7   Croda's spectacular 2010

	2010 £m	2009 £m	2006 £m
ESTA	223.5	174.4	116.1
CUVI	870.8	448.0	190.9
NVP	(153.9)	(219.9)	(180.9)
GOV	1,321.2	717.1	693.9
MC	2,261.6	1,119.6	820.0

It should be noted that the Croda/Uniqema case demonstrates how 4S accounting provides the natural vehicle for the financial reporting and evaluation of acquisitions.

Conclusion

The purpose of this chapter has been to explore and illustrate with both real and pedagogic examples, the connectivity between strategic choice, the stakeholder network of propositions and the financial outcome. Strategic choice flows as both a response to competitive market opportunities and challenges (the outside-in approach) and as a response to the opportunities and challenges of knowledge development through the stakeholder network (the inside-out approach). The Formula Hotels case is designed to illustrate that the attitudes and (limited) experience of the Board are factors in making the strategic choice sometimes with negative effects. The notion of development, learning and financial pathways is introduced, using the J Sainsbury example, as a tool for representing strategic choice in the context of the opportunities and challenges facing the company. In most cases there is insufficient information in company reports to produce these pathways from outside of the company. However, they may represent one way ahead for the integration of business and financial reporting. Pathways segment according to strategic choices rather than business units. An important contribution of the pathway is that it does not lose sight of the current financial impact of strategic choices made in past years and hence continues to provide accountability for those choices. According to Kay, the stakeholder network is a product of social and commercial values. These values develop throughout the history of an organisation and cannot be easily created or changed (Kay 1993). The development pathway is essentially a strategic pathway.

The reason for addressing the connectivity between strategic choice, market conditions and financial outcome is that an understanding of that connectivity is vital to an ability to predict future financial performance. 4S reporting requires an assessment of Growth and Opportunity Value (GOV) based upon a prediction of future financials and this has to be done at present on the basis of the information available through the current mode of business reporting. The Rolls Royce case gives an indication of how this might be done. It segments the business into three strategic choices (leverage of knowledge, currency hedging and cost control initiatives) and predicts the financial future of these. However much remains unpredictable.

The case examples given in the chapter cover most of the strategic choices available to a company. In particular, acquisition is a strategic choice that is both popular and at the same time difficult to fit into conventional reporting frameworks. 4S accounting, however, is ideally placed to capture the impact of acquisition on the financial value structure of the company and provides an appropriate platform for future evaluation of the acquisition. The Croda/Uniqema case has been chosen as a suitable vehicle to highlight these points.

The connectivity of strategic choice and the Stakeholder Knowledge Network comes through the LEADERS approach to the strategic management of the stakeholder network. The LEADERS framework has been mapped to the strategic logics of Bingham and Eisenhardt. The connectivity between financial outcome and the stakeholder network comes from the 4S accounting where the four slices of equity are aligned with the dimensions of the network. Thus it is the Stakeholder Knowledge Network that integrates strategic choice and financial outcome and in this sense provides the key to the future of business reporting.

10

Financialisation

Financialisation is taken to occur when speculative capital grows at a faster rate than productive capital. This chapter looks at financialisation at the corporate level through the lens of 4S comprehensive income. In 4S comprehensive income the four slices of equity, two representing speculative capital and two representing productive capital, are treated as four separate funds and the analysis provides an explanation of value changes in each fund including fund transfers and distributions. 4S therefore can provide both a measure of financialisation and an understanding of its origination. The chapter starts with a pedagogic example of the ability of 4S to highlight and analyse financialisation in a non-financial company. The chapter proceeds to a discussion of the relevance of the analysis to the financial sector, in particular banking. It is suggested that only gains in productive capital should be considered eligible for distribution as dividend, bonus or taxation, and that speculative gains should instead, when realised, be invested in productive activity. Productive activity is directly associated with the production of currently consumable product or service. This conservative approach to distribution is in response to the lessons provided by the 2008 financial crisis and the difficulties experienced in rebalancing the economy. It is an approach of particular significance for banking and other financial sector activities. Performance measurement too can take a conservative approach with a focus upon the growth in productive capital, whilst speculative capital growth suggests an opportunity for future investment in productive capital. Such performance measures when embedded in executive compensation schemes serve to align the interests of management with the interests of long-term shareholders and the rebalancing of the economy toward productive capital.

A Pedagogic Example of 4S Comprehensive Income

The following example is used, adapted from an example originally contributed by UBS (2007: 37–8) and introduced in Chapter 8. For simplification, a discount rate of 5 per cent is used for both the spot rate market and the fixed price contract. It can of course be argued that the spot price market is riskier than the fixed price contract in which case a required rate of return in excess of 5 per cent should be used to calculate CUVI, but this adjustment is not made in the example. 5 per cent becomes, for convenience, the required rate of return on both tangibles (ESTA) and intangibles (CUVI). Details of the example are as follows:

At the end of the accounting year a company has four years left on a five-year contract to supply a commodity of 100 units each year at a price of £10. The spot price of the commodity at the start and finish of the accounting year was £8 and £8.5, respectively. The spot price rise was not anticipated at the beginning of the year. The cost of producing the commodity is £3 per unit. The current accounting profit is £700 (revenue of £1000 less costs of £300). Dividends of £500 are paid. The value of the contract at the beginning of the year is calculated as £865.9 being £200 (the 'excess' profits) for each of five years at a 5 per cent discount rate. At the end of the year the value of the contract based upon the higher spot price is £531.9 being £150 for four years at a 5 per cent discount rate. Thus the contract loses £334 of value during the year moving from £865.9 to £531.9.

At the beginning of the year the expectation is that the spot price will rise to £9 at the end of the contract (beginning of year 6) and then stabilise and this expectation is unchanged at the end of the year even though the spot price has unexpectedly risen to £8.5.

The company has £9,000 invested in fixed assets and working capital (there are no loans) throughout the year. It remains constant since cash from depreciation is reinvested in fixed assets.

Table 10.1 illustrates the price patterns which are driving the value of the contract (NVP) and the value (MC) of the business. The full value of the company is £12,554.5 being the value shown in Figure 10.1 (£12,354.5) plus the cash retained of £200 (£700 cash profits less £500 dividends paid).

Table 10.2 sets out the movements that combine to give 4S comprehensive income in respect of the example. Table 10.2 explains the flow of value generated during the year by the interaction of: (1) the past strategic agreement to share risk and reward with the customer; and (2) the change in market conditions in respect of price. In Table 10.2 the £9,000 investment in the traditional assets of fixed assets and working capital (ESTA) is increased during the year by the 5 per cent yield of £450 but this is paid as dividends so that at the end of the year the (ESTA) fund remains at £9,000.

Table 10.1   Price patterns driving contract and company value

	At time 0, expected spot prices and company value based on spot prices £	At time 1 expected spot prices and company value based on spot prices £	At time 0 expected unit price and company value based on contract £	At time 1 expected unit price and company value based on contract £
Year 1	8.00		10.00	
Year 2–5	8.00	8.50	10.00	10.00
Year 6 plus	9.00	9.00	9.00	9.00
Value of company (MC)	11,567.0	11,822.6	12,432.9	12,354.5
			11,567.0	11,822.6
Value of contract (NVP)			865.9	531.9

Table 10.2   Statement of comprehensive income

	ESTA	CUVI	NVP	GOV	MC
Opening balance	9,000.0	1,000.0	865.9	1,567.0	12,432.9
Yield (5%)	450.0	50.0	43.3	78.3	621.6
Fund transfer			(200.0)	200.0	Nil
Change in spot price		177.3	(177.3)		Nil
Change in spot price		822.7		(822.7)	Nil
Dividends	(450.0)	(50.0)			(500.0)
Comprehensive income	Nil	1000.0	(334.0)	(544.4)	121.6
Closing balance	9,000.0	2,000.0	531.9	1,022.6	12,554.5

The current contribution of the intangible assets through sustainable residual income (CUVI) is the capital value of residual income assuming current business conditions persist. The existence of the contract with a price well in excess of the spot price indicates that the accounting profit of £700 is not sustainable beyond the period of the contract. To calculate sustainable profit on which CUVI is calculated the benefit of the contract should be removed from current accounting profit. This benefit is £200 per annum based upon the opening spot price, declining to £150 based upon the closing spot price. Opening CUVI is based upon a sustainable residual income of £50 (700 – 200 – 450) which at a multiple of 20 (equivalent to 5 per cent) gives a CUVI of £1,000. The required return or normal profit on the £9,000 invested in fixed assets and working capital (ESTA) is £450. Similarly, closing CUVI is based upon a sustainable residual income of £100 (being 700 – 150 – 450) giving a CUVI of £2,000, an increase of £1,000 during the year. The 5 per cent yield on the opening CUVI is both earned and distributed during the year.

The NVP column shows that, as in Chapter 8, the £334 loss in the value of the contract can be explained as follows (UBS 2007: 38):

1.   an increase of £43.3 (5 per cent of £865.9) as a result of the passing of the year (the yield from the contract);

2.   a reduction of £200 due to the realisation of the benefits of the contract (£100*2) during the current year;

3.   a fall in the value of the remaining years of the contract (£177.3) due to the reducing benefits of the contract following the rise in the spot price (£50 for four years at 5 per cent discount rate).

The change in the value of the contract is the result of yield, realisation and change in spot prices. The £200 cash from the realisation of benefits is transferred to GOV (a fund transfer: see Table 10.2) and becomes opportunity cash that can facilitate new or further investment. The loss of £177.3 recognises the fall in the value of the contract as a result of the spot price rise but it is offset by the impact of the spot price rise on CUVI (a rise in CUVI of £1,000) less the impact on GOV (a fall in GOV of £822.7). Thus in this example the change in the spot price has an overall effect on market capitalisation of zero. This is because the current change in the spot price has not affected the anticipated spot price outside the 'price protected' contract period.

Current business conditions are unlikely to persist and so growth and opportunity value (GOV) therefore exists based upon expectations of the future. In the example it is assumed that: (1) at the beginning of the year the expectation is that the spot price will rise to 9 at the end of the contract and then stabilise; and (2) that this expectation is unchanged at the end of the year even though the spot price has unexpectedly risen to £8.50. Opening GOV brings into account the impact of the rise in spot price to £9 in five years time at a value of £1,567 being £2,000 (the additional profit of £100 at a multiple of 20) discounted for five years at 5 per cent. At the end of the year GOV shows as £822.6 being £1000 (the additional profit of £50 at a multiple of 20) discounted for four years at 5 per cent. The decrease in GOV during the year is £1567 – £822.6 = £744.4 but this is reduced by the fund transfer of £200 to give an overall reduction of £544.

INTRODUCING CURRENTLY CONSUMABLE PRODUCT (CCP)

In Table 10.2 the total comprehensive income of £121.6 is the total yield of £621.6 less the dividends paid of £500. The reconciliation of comprehensive income and accounting profit is shown in Table 10.3. It is necessary to consider the value of the company's production at current market value (£800) over and above resources consumed (£300). The result of £500 is the value of the addition to gross domestic product (GDP) from the year's activity and represents currently consumable product (line 3 of Table 10.3). The accounting profit of £700 is in fact this production value (CCP) plus a wealth transfer of £200 from the company's customers as a consequence of the fixed price contract. The yield of £450 on productive tangible assets and £50 on productive intangibles, totalling £500 is also the CCP since the yields on NVP (£43.3) and on GOV (£78.3) do not provide consumable production. Thus, as shown in Table 10.3, the accounting profit of £700 and the total yield of £621 reconcile through the CCP of £500.

Table 10.3   Reconciling accounting profit (AP) and 4S comprehensive income (CI)

	Accounting profit (AP) £	4S comprehensive income (CI) £
Yield on traditional assets	450	450.0
Yield on intangibles	<u>50</u>	<u>50.0</u>
Currently consumable profit/product (CCP)	500	500.0
Yield on NPV (contract)		43.3
Yield on GOV		<u>78.3</u>
Comprehensive income		621.6
Wealth transfer re contract	<u>200</u>	
Accounting profit	700	
Dividend	<u>500</u>	<u>500.0</u>
AC/CI after dividend	200	121.6

In this example the company has restricted the dividend to the CCP added through the productive activities with the transfer generated by the fixed price contract and (unrealised) yields on non-productive (speculative) assets being highlighted separately. Dividends have only been paid from yields on productive assets. This conservative dividend policy reflects the fact that the wealth transfer is not sustainable beyond the period of the contract. It is of course possible to pay the realised wealth transfer as a special dividend highlighting its 'limited period' character. The customer who is the counterparty to the contract will be showing accounting profit 200 lower than its currently consumable product generated so that the payment of a special dividend should not, from a macroeconomic viewpoint, result in distributions in excess of currently consumable product. However, the reporting of wealth transfers as distributable profit for the company and loss for the counterparty would likely distort the flow of capital and other resources toward the more 'profitable' company. From a resource allocation perspective therefore it becomes important that the wealth transfer is highlighted separately and not confused with sustainable (distributable) profit.

For contracts that increase in value without a counterparty loss, then any treatment of the capital gain as distributable profit would, from a macroeconomic viewpoint, result in distributions in excess of CCP. This can result in economic imbalances that might contribute towards general inflation, specific asset price bubbles or balance of payments deficits in the economy as a whole. Of course, restricting dividends and other distributions to the yield on productive assets, does not of itself ensure that consumption and production in the economy are in balance since there are many other factors at work especially in determining consumption. However, the inclusion of speculative gains in performance measures and bonus schemes provides an incentive to executives to seek speculative gains and this may not be consistent with the well-being of the economy. It is likely to be a significant contributory factor in generating imbalance.

THE CONTRACT AS A RISK MANAGEMENT PRODUCT

It is seen from Table 10.2 that in the example neither the change in the spot price nor the realisation of benefits under the contract (the funds transfer) impact upon the market capitalisation, which increases only as a result of the passage of time (yield) on the four funds. The change in the spot price impacts upon, and generates transfers between, CUVI, NVP and GOV but not upon overall market capitalisation. Thus in the example the contract eliminates risk to the MC in relation to the spot price for the next four years though not in relation to the individual slices of equity. The role of the contract as a risk management product is to reduce uncertainty and to justify therefore a lower required rate of return, resulting in higher capital values. In this way risk management operates upon capital values but does not generate currently consumable product.

Financialisation

Krippner (2005: 174) has written of financialisation as a 'pattern of accumulation in which profit making occurs increasingly through financial channels rather than through trade and commodity production'. It is accompanied by the growth in power and influence of those in the financial sector (Elliott and Atkinson 2008: 16–17). In terms of 4S accounting it is ESTA and CUVI which are grounded in the profitability of current production (production capital) and NVP and GOV which are open to assessment by the financial markets (speculative capital: speculative in the sense that value is a function of expectations of the future). A strategy directed by financialisation will attempt to impress the stock markets through the sophistication of its contracting and the consequent strength of its growth 'story' in order to maximise its speculative capital. Enron was an extreme example. In 4S, financialisation is revealed by the growth in speculative (non-productive) assets/wealth (NVP plus GOV) being in excess of the growth of productive assets/wealth (ESTA plus CUVI) and/or the growth in distributions from NVP and GOV being in excess of the growth in distributions from ESTA and CUVI. Investors need to look hard at whether a growth in the speculative assets in excess of growth in the productive assets is believable and justifiable. In the case of the financial sector and banks in particular, financialisation is of concern not just to investors but to everyone with a stake in the economy.

THE 2008 FINANCIAL CRISIS

In essence, the financial crisis arose because of a number of interrelated and mismanaged macroeconomic factors. Consumption was, for the US and UK at least, persistently in excess of domestic production. Consumption was underpinned by both borrowing on historically low interest rates and by the consequently high asset prices which created security for borrowings and a feeling of affluence. The increase in debt and low interest rates were underpinned by an Asian, most notably Chinese, willingness to save and lend at low interest rates. The international macroeconomic condition was thus a key issue (Turner 2009, Elliott and Atkinson 2008) though this underlying condition was supported by many contributory factors. These include belief in globalisation irrespective of the mercantilism of trading partners (Greenspan 2007), stakeholder greed and materialist lifestyles, a policy of inflation control that focused upon the price of consumable product rather than capital values, poor regulation and governance that did not recognise financialisation, and innovative financial products which provided the opportunity for highly leveraged growth and a plausible explanation for high profits. Domestic consumption in excess of domestic production was associated with increased debt facilitated by banks eager to leverage their business networks. In the run up to the crisis, global trading imbalances and bank balance sheets both grew at a spectacular rate (Turner 2009). The financial sector's increasing profits and balance sheets did not represent a corresponding increase in the wealth of the non-financial economy or in GDP. It seems the financial sector organised a substantial wealth transfer in favour of itself. Financialisation is the term given to this process through which, arguably, the non-financial sector serves the financial sector rather than the other way around (Heilpern, Haslam and Andersson 2009). The thesis is that financialisation results from bank activities that are neither associated with currently consumable product nor with increased longer term saving. In a sense, financialisation represents a departure at the macroeconomic level from the basic rule of double entry bookkeeping that productive assets should be in equilibrium with their funding/ financing.

The growth of the banks was facilitated by rapidly increasing capital values, especially in property markets and by the ability to create new capital without any corresponding increase in long-term saving. When a bank lends money it flows back to the banking system in the borrower's current account and again into the recipient's current account when it is spent by the borrower. If it is spent in China it may be lent back to the UK, firstly to the Treasury and then into the banking system. Thus lending reappears in the banking system as cash available for further lending and, subject to the fractional reserve required by regulation to be retained as cash, there is little requirement for further lending to be constrained by the need to find new savers. There may be a rather limited requirement to find new equity as a consequence of (Basel) regulation but, nevertheless, expansion is relatively unrestrained. The growing use of derivatives was a further source of unrestrained expansion.

The one banking activity which creates currently consumable product is lending to companies that create consumable product. This is the mirror image of borrowing by non-financial, productive companies to invest in fixed assets that leverage their intangibles. Just as it was assumed that performing non-financial companies will repay loans with new loans so it is assumed that the bank will replace its loans to performing non-financial companies with new loans. For the banks such lending is a sustainable business that benefits the economy. However, banks are engaged in a wide range of other lending activities that are not directly associated with the creation of currently consumable product and include lending to individuals for consumption, to private equity, hedge funds and property developers for speculation (capital gains) and to facilitate distributions from speculative gains. They are also involved in meeting risk management needs through derivatives and in the securitisation and repackaging of debt, the latter activity in respect of mortgages being a highly proximate cause of the 2008 crisis. Banks will charge fees for their arrangement and financial support of deals. Thus banks transform or help transform capital positions in respect of nature, size, duration, liquidity and risk, but much of this transformational activity is, in terms of the phases of profit introduced in Chapter 1, 'phase 3' and is not associated with the creation of 'currently consumable product'. The concept of 'phase 3' can be illustrated by a simple example using shares as a speculative security investment. Suppose at the beginning of the year the investee's profits are running at 5 and the shares are valued at 50, but at the end of the year profits are running at 10 and the shares are valued at 100. The investor makes a capital gain of 50 but these are 'phase 3' gains and if distributed and spent will not be matched by added production represented by the 'phase 1' profits of 10. Recognising phase 3 gains as distributable profit is likely to cause economic imbalance between production and consumption. The banking sector might talk of capital as a product and the transformation of capital as a production process, but it is not the creation of a currently consumable product.

It is not the case that innovation in financial services is of itself a bad thing. Innovative propositions can encourage saving and give greater access to capital whilst innovative transformation within and between banks enables such capital to be adapted to the needs of borrowers. However, the bottom line is that both the regulator and, given the regulatory risk, shareholders, must understand how the 'real' economy is being served. In a non-financialised economy the role of the financial sector is to provide the capital for the non-financial sector. The motive for finding innovative ways of transforming or raising capital should be to increase investment in the non-financial sector.

This requirement for a non-financialised economy constitutes a major challenge to the accounting profession in relation to the presentation of banks' financial statements. To meet this challenge, 4S accounting for banks should treat the lending to companies that create currently consumable product (CCP businesses) as being the banks' sustainable and productive business. ESTA becomes the equity stake in lending to CCP businesses and net interest on such lending is the distributable revenue profit. It is this profit that underpins both ESTA and CUVI. The bank's portfolio of all other financial contracts are treated as promises and valued at fair value net of precautionary cash (NVP). The regulator might specify the NVP to be kept in precautionary cash and this is likely to depend in part upon volatility. GOV is a function of both expected changes in the sustainable business (CUVI) and expected future fair value changes in the other financial positions. The debate between the incurred loss model and the expected loss model could be settled by charging incurred losses on business loans to ESTA, on individual loans to NVP and all expected future losses and impairments to GOV. Net interest on, and fees in connection with, the 'other' financial contracts, are retained within the NVP 'fund'. Distributions should not be made from the NVP fund but rather realised gains that are not retained in the NVP fund for precautionary purposes should be invested in loans to CCP businesses. The realised funds are a fund transfer to GOV in anticipation of the new loans and thence to ESTA once the loans to CCP businesses are made.

As illustrated in the pedagogic example, the 4S statement of comprehensive income can demonstrate how value flows or transfers between the four slices of equity. It should therefore reveal the extent to which value is flowing from NVP to the sustainable 'productive' business (ESTA and CUVI). Non-financialisation requires that value flows in this direction. In effect distributions should be made from the NVP 'fund' to expand the lending to CCP business and should not be made directly as distributions in the form of bonuses, taxation or dividends all of which might well be destined to finance consumption that is not currently backed by consumable product. What is needed is not so much a ring-fence around the bank's productive capital but a one way valve that allows capital flows from speculative capital to productive capital but not in the reverse direction. The universal banking model is one in which a bank supplies corporate customers both lending and other products such as derivatives that allow the bank to share risk and reward with its corporate customers and to bind its network of customers more closely. However, the challenge is to show that (see whether) this results in a more successful non-financial sector alongside the benefits to the bank. The universal banking model needs to be non-financialising.

Conclusion

Financialisation occurs where bank (and other financial sector) balance sheets and profits grow at a faster rate than in the productive sector that financial services are designed to support. Such financialisation has been closely identified with persistent trading imbalances and ultimately with financial crisis. The conclusion is that regulation of the financial sector should be focused upon financialisation and that 4S accounting can alert stakeholders to this issue provided ESTA and CUVI are only based upon profits from lending to support customer activities that directly result in currently consumable product. In the case of banking there may be a case for regulations to restrict or prohibit the making of distributions to stakeholders directly from NVP or GOV. The motive behind innovative financial instruments should be to raise capital directly or indirectly to invest in the productive sector. Thus realised gains in the NVP fund should not be distributed as dividends, bonuses or taxation, but should be transferred to ESTA or CUVI through investment of the gains in productive tangible or intangible assets. It is the yield on ESTA and CUVI that supports distributions. These arrangements should have the effect of dampening the excesses of the bonus culture. They should motivate investment in and lending to support productive activity. They should also remind governments that their consumption activities should not be financed by the taxation of capital gains.

Post-2008 crisis and the write offs which banks have suffered, there has been a requirement for banks to rebuild their balance sheets and so financialisation has re-emerged albeit from a much lower base. Bank balance sheets are growing faster than the productive economy since the rebuilding of the balance sheets has not concentrated on lending to productive business. Thus financialisation at the level of the economy is matched by financialisation within the banks' own balance sheets. At the end of the day, confidence in both the economy and the banking system stems from investment in and lending to support profitable productive activity. It is the degree to which a bank's assets are supporting, and supported by, productive activity which drives the need for precautionary cash (liquidity) and restrictions on financial gearing. Less liquidity and capital are required when the bank assets are well supported by profitable production in the economy. Bank regulation must be designed to incentivise lending to productive businesses. If it does not then it is by definition counterproductive.

11

The Significance for Financial Reporting

4S accounting has many implications for, and highlights problems with, current accounting standards and this chapter identifies 12 of these implications. Since 4S accounting coordinates with the stakeholder knowledge network which in turn coordinates with strategy to generate the LEADERS business model, 4S should also play a prominent role in the business review section of the annual report. It is possible to structure the business review around four sections, each linking movements in a slice of equity to changes in the stakeholder propositions and tracking these changes to both environmental change and strategy. This chapter reviews the significance of 4S for financial reporting in terms of both the accounting and the business review section in the annual report.

Implications for Accounting

The twelve comments upon existing accounting standards are as follows:

(1) THE STATEMENT OF COMPREHENSIVE INCOME

Penman (2007a: 36–7) identifies two accounting models in current usage. The first computes accounting profit as the difference between the value of outputs sold and the cost of inputs necessary to create the products sold (the matching concept). The second takes the fair value of assets (less liabilities) at the beginning of the period away from the fair value at the end of the period. Following the four slices methodology, the first is used to place a value on activities that transform inputs into outputs to generate currently consumable product (ESTA and CUVI) and the second for promises and other speculative activities where value is based upon (changing) future expectations (NVP and GOV).

In 4S accounting, ESTA, CUVI, NVP and GOV are separate funds each with its own equity matched by assets, and with movements in each fund separately identified. In current accounting there is only one fund of assets/ equity represented by the balance sheet. In general, this does not include intangibles (CUVI) or growth and opportunity value (GOV), but does include traditional assets at cost (ESTA) and most contractual promises at fair value (NVP). This is a mixture of Penman's two accounting models and therefore already starts to lack clarity. The picture is further confused by the fact that some intangibles are included in the fund represented by the balance sheet. Intangibles purchased, for example in an acquisition, are included. In current accounting, movements in the fund that is the balance sheet are split into profit for the year and other comprehensive income (OCI). Profit includes the returns on both tangible assets (ESTA) and intangible assets (CUVI) but these returns are not separately identified. Other comprehensive income covers many, but not all, of the movements in the fair value of contractual promises (NVP). Some of these movements in NVP, notably in respect of derivatives, are included in profit, whilst other comprehensive income currently handles changes in the pension deficit, changes in the value of available for sale assets, certain changes due to the impact of currency translation and changes in the value of a limited range of derivatives. There does not appear to be a clear conceptual basis for the split between profit and OCI.

Thus current accounting's statement of comprehensive income provides a very messy (unclean) analysis when it comes to understanding the relationship between accounts and much of modern business, given the role of both intangibles and complex contracts in determining current and expected future performance. Current accounting's statement of total comprehensive income has developed piecemeal over time in response to emerging problems with accounting. Unlike the 4S statement of comprehensive income, it has little in the way of a conceptual basis.

The statement of comprehensive income in current usage combines accounting profit with value changes for certain legacy promises. It is unclear what this combination explains. Hence although the components of comprehensive income may be of significance to investors, the total comprehensive income is unlikely to be so. The 4S statement of comprehensive income explains changes in market capitalisation. 4S comprehensive income has four sections corresponding to changes in ESTA, CUVI, NVP and GOV.

(2) THE TREATMENT OF IMPAIRMENTS

Impairments are one offs that accelerate and represent the capital value of expected future losses. The focus of the 4S methodology on sustainable accounting profits suggests that impairments should not be charged in arriving at accounting profit. Currently, accounting combines the profit from current transformational activity with capitalised future losses and is once again mixing apples and pears. Impairments should be dealt with instead in the (4S) statement of comprehensive income as part of the movement in GOV.

(3) A ROLE FOR REPLACEMENT COST ACCOUNTING

The emphasis of the 4S methodology upon sustainability suggests a role for replacement cost accounting, at least in regard to companies with significant fixed assets or fixed interest loans. Maintaining the productive capability of the company is an implied commitment/promise of sustainable profit. Insofar as a company is going to expand, reduce or change its business in future, then this is handled through GOV. If a company has ageing fixed assets or its fixed assets have risen in replacement value, then backlog depreciation should be included in the balance sheet as a legacy promise and replacement cost depreciation charged in arriving at sustainable profit. In similar vein, a company which experiences a change in its credit rating should charge interest on fixed rate term loans at the rate that would be charged for the new credit rating with the number of years of interest savings or extra cost valued and treated as a promise (asset or liability) in the balance sheet. The change in the value of the loan should not go through accounting profit but through the promises section of comprehensive income.

(4) LEASES

At present, accounting standards require the capitalisation of finance leases and there are moves afoot to extend this requirement to operational leases. However, requiring new economy companies to capitalise leases may be pointless insofar as the desire to capitalise leases is to allow comparability of return on asset ratios between companies that own assets and companies that lease assets. Return on (recorded) assets is not a meaningful performance measure in the new economy company where many intangibles are not capitalised.

(5) ACQUISITION ACCOUNTING

At present, accounting standards require the purchase price of an acquisition to be analysed into: (1) net fixed assets (and working capital) at fair value; (2) identifiable intangibles; and (3) goodwill. However, under 4S accounting, the purchase price would be analysed into the four slices of equity in the acquired company, to be identified in the comprehensive income statement as additions to ESTA, CUVI, NVP and GOV resulting from acquisition rather than continued activities. An acquisition is financialising when the proportionate increase in NVP/GOV is greater than that of ESTA/CUVI. Insofar as the four slices form a universally applicable analysis of value for any equity holding, then proportionate consolidation of ESTA, CUVI, NVP and GOV becomes appropriate for all equity holdings irrespective of whether or not they create ownership or control of the investee. In 4S the focus is upon access to knowledge and resources through a network of stakeholders rather than ownership and control. This is more appropriate to the new economy and has significance not just for the consolidation of subsidiaries but for joint ventures, associates and any equity investment.

(6) CASH FLOW STATEMENTS

At the present time cash flow statements reflect the traditional accountant's business model by identifying transactions with cash consequences as financing/investing or operational. 4S accounting suggests a new style of cash flow statement that reflects the three motives for holding cash (and other realisable non-operating assets) being for working capital, precautionary and opportunity purposes. The first section of this cash statement would include the opening cash held for working capital, the cash flow from transformational activities (operating cash flow) and the closing cash required for working capital, with any balances transferred to/from precautionary cash. The second section includes the opening cash held for precautionary purposes, the cash flow from the liquidation of legacy promises, transfers to/from working capital and the required closing cash for precautionary purposes with the balance transferred to opportunity cash. The third section deals with opportunity cash, including the opening balance, and the funding of opportunities including fixed assets purchase and research and development. The adequacy of the closing balance would be assessed by management. The new cash statement is more appropriately described as a cash management statement.

(7) NET DEBT

The above perspective suggests that the reporting of net debt, which sets debt against all cash balances whether held as working, precautionary or opportunity capital, should be dropped. Precautionary and opportunity cash balances are required for their own purposes and should not be offset against debt unless they are surplus to requirements.

(8) EARNINGS PER SHARE

A price to earnings multiple is a crude basis for valuing a company and effectively replaced by 4S accounting where the sustainable residual income is capitalised using a multiple based on the required rate of return on intangibles and the promises are recognised as already being a capital value. In response to any dilution and capital flows, however, it might be helpful to disclose the performance of a holding of say 100 shares at the beginning of the year as being the total return of dividends plus the increase in value of the shareholding, including any bonus shares or rights issues, net of the purchase price.

(9) RATES OF RETURN

Companies should report their assessment of the required return on equity invested in tangible assets and the required return on equity invested in intangibles linking these assessments to risk. Other things being equal, risk may be expected to increase with greater leverage whether that be financial or in terms of higher volumes.

(10) FIVE YEAR RETURNS

Companies should include a five year review of their 4S comprehensive accounts to facilitate an understanding of how the four funds relate one to another and so provide an understanding not only of where value lies but where and how it is developing.

(11) INCOME RECOGNITION

Banks should report separately their profit from lending to productive companies, from profits and fair value movements in their other contracts and financial positions. Profit from lending to production companies supports the bank's ESTA and CUVI whilst other (speculative) gains form part of NVP and

GOV. In similar vein, it is arguable that companies that make capital goods should spread the profit on sales over the time for which the capital goods will produce currently consumable profit in the hands of the customer. Deferred profit would form part of the NVP fund. Following this line of thought, there would be no recognition of profit during long-term construction projects until the project was generating service. Hedging contracts should be considered speculative rather than productive and allocated to the NVP or GOV fund that contains the underlying asset to be hedged. Under 4S the issue is not so much when income should be recognised but in which of the four funds it should be recognised.

(12)SEGMENTATION

At present, segmentation follows the internal reporting structures of the company. This could be changed in favour of a development/financial pathway where the segments follow key strategic initiatives.

The Business Review

4S comprehensive accounting is part of a wider proposal to view the company as a continually reshaping set of stakeholder propositions. As previously discussed, this reshaping is in terms of a LEADERS business model, in which management action is to leverage the network, secure an effective network through engagement and alignment and develop the network. In terms of Figure 1.1, the role of the business review is to coordinate business as strategy with business as value, value being represented by the four slices of equity. The first part of the business review should outline the company's strategy in terms of leverage, engagement, alignment and development of the network of stakeholders. This is followed by a four part evaluation of where value lies and how it is developing, with each part corresponding to one of the four funds (slices of equity) under management. The evaluation includes consideration of the principal business risks. The first three slices of equity (ESTA, CUVI and NVP) provide an evaluation of the success of the business model to date based on the past shaping of stakeholder propositions. The fourth slice of equity (GOV) stands as a value of the company's positioning for the future based upon both past and the potential future (re)shaping of stakeholder propositions. The credibility of the growth and opportunity value implied by the stock market price provides a judgment on the stock price.

Conclusion

This chapter has outlined the potential of 4S accounting ideas to challenge a conventional accounting in line with current accounting standards and practices. Twelve substantive challenges are identified and they cover major issues. Moreover, these accounting recommendations are made as a consequence of the coordination of business as value, business as a stakeholder network and business as strategy. It follows that 4S accounting lends itself as a four part framework for the business review. The LEADERS/4S framework provides the ideal structure for any business review whether conducted by management, by the investment manager, or by the auditor (Hatherly 2003).

12

Illustration of 4S Accounts

This chapter uses the SMD case first introduced in Chapter 2 to show how 4S accounts are constructed from the traditional accounts to provide the required feedback on how business value responds to strategy and stakeholders. The chapter analyses the movements for the year both within and between the four slices of equity. These movements provide the framework for the (4S) business review. The chapter is in three sections. Section 1 repeats the traditional accounts discussed in Chapter 2. Section 2 develops and discusses the 4S accounts. Section 3 provides a business review based upon the four slices of equity.

Section 1: The traditional Accounts

Systems Maximise Delivery (SMD plc) is a supplier to builders' merchants. At the end of year 1 the market capitalisation is £119.58 m and at the end of year 2 it is £133.52 m. Its conventional balance sheets at the beginning and end of year 2 are as shown in Table 12.1.

Table 12.1   SMD traditional balance sheet

	Year(X+)1 £m	Year (X+)2 £m
Fixed assets	60	70
Cumulative depreciation	(30)	(34)
Intangibles	12	10
Cash	25	33.94
Other current assets	18	20
Loans	(20)	(25)
Promises	(16)	(22)
Equity (book value)	49	52.94

The profit statements and movements in equity for years 1 and 2 are given as Table 12.2.

Table 12.2   SMD profit statement and movement in equity

	Year 1 £m	Year 2 £m
Sales	200	230
Cost of sales	(160)	(180)
Administration	(20)	(25)
Interest	(1.4)	(1.75)
One offs*		5
Research and development	(4)	(7)
Profit before tax	14.6	21.25
Tax (25%)	3.65	5.31
Net profit	10.95	15.94
Dividends	5	8
To equity	5.95	7.94
Opening equity		49
Retained profit for year		7.94
Revaluation of promises		(4)
Closing equity		52.94

* profit on disposal of £7 m less impairment of intangibles of £2 m

Table 12.3 gives the movement in the LTRP promise and Table 12.4 gives the movement in net fixed assets. These figures expand upon the movements shown in Table 12.1 (the balance sheet). Table 12.5 provides the reconciliation between the net profit before interest and the cash flow for year 2.

Table 12.3   The movement in promises

	Year 2 £m
Opening balance	16
Promises met by payment	(2)
New promises charged to cost of sales	4
Revaluation of legacy promises	4
Closing balance	22

Table 12.4   The movement of fixed assets

	Year 2 £m
Opening balance (cost)	60
Opening balance (cumulative depreciation)	(30)
Opening Net book value	30
Additions	15
Depreciation charge for year	(6)
Cost of disposal	(5)
Cumulative depreciation on disposal	2
Closing balance (cost)	70
Closing balance (cumulative depreciation)	(34)
Closing Net Book Balance	36

Table 12.5   The reconciliation of profit and cash flow

	£m
Net profit for year before interest	17.69
Depreciation charged	6
Profit on disposal	(7)
Cash from disposal	10
Movements in other current assets	(2)
Promises charged this year	4
Promises paid this year	(2)
Impairments charged on intangibles	2
Cash from operations	28.69
Additions to fixed assets (investing activity)	(15)
Increase in loans	5
Dividends and interest (financing activity)	(9.75)
Increase in cash (cash flow)	8.94

Section 2: The 4S Accounts

A preliminary to the calculation of the four slices is the analysis of the SMD cash balance across ESTA (working cash), NVP (precautionary cash) and GOV (opportunity cash). This assessment needs to be done by management along with a cash management statement. SMD management's assessment of the demand for cash at the beginning and at the end of the year is incorporated in the opening and closing balances of the cash management statement of Table 12.6.

The statement shows that at the end of the year the company is holding £12 m of working cash, equivalent to 6.7 per cent (around 24 days) of cost of sales. This is much the same as the opening position of around 23 days. Precautionary cash at the end of the year (£11 m) is 50 per cent of the balance promised for the LTRP (£22 m) and is the same percentage as at the beginning of the year. The closing opportunity cash represents 1.56 times the annual R and D expenditure compared to 1.75 times at the beginning.

Table 12.6 analyses total cash at the end and the beginning of the year across working cash, precautionary cash and opportunity cash and it also shows the movement in each category over the year. Total cash flow (row 2 of Table 12.6) increases by £8.94 m over the year (as per Table 12.5) and of this £2 m was paid in respect of promises and belongs as a reduction of precautionary cash. The remaining £10.94 m are payments or receipts that impact traditional assets and liabilities, and therefore belong in working cash. The transfer (row 3) of £8.94 m reflects the fact that only £12 m is considered necessary by management as the year end balance on working cash and the surplus is transferred to precautionary cash. Similarly, the transfer (row 4) of £3.94 m reflects the fact that £11 m is considered adequate as precautionary cash and the surplus is transferred to opportunity cash. Management should assess the level of opportunity cash in the context of growth and opportunity value as part of the business review. The question is, does the company have the cash necessary to support the investments on which GOV is based?

Table 12.6   SMD cash management statement for year 2

	Working cash £m	Precautionary cash £m	Opportunity cash £m	Total £m
1 Opening balance	10	8	7	25
2 Cash flow	10.94	(2)*		8.94
3 Transfer	(8.94)	8.94		
4 Transfer		(3.94)	3.94	
5 Closing balance	12	11	10.94	33.94

* the promises paid of £2 m

If SMD investments in new fixed assets and R and D are regarded as opportunity taking rather than maintaining the status quo, then the cash management statement can be revised to reflect this as shown in Table 12.7.

Table 12.7   4S cash management showing opportunity taking

	Working cash £m	Precautionary cash £m	Opportunity cash £m	Total £m
Opening balance	10	8	7	25
Cash flow excluding opportunity taking	17.94	(2)		15.94
Fixed asset purchase			(15)	(15)
Disposal proceeds			10	10
New loans			5	5
R and D			(7)	(7)
Transfer	(15.94)	15.94		
Transfer		(10.94)	10.94	
Closing balance	12	11	10.94	33.94

The total cash flow in Table 12.6 of £8.94 m is split into cash paid for fixed assets, disposal proceeds, new loans, R and D and the remaining cash flow of £15.94 m. Thus the cash flows associated with what might be termed 'opportunity taking' are separated out and shown as movements in the opportunity cash column. In this particular case no opportunity cash has been used to fund the new fixed assets which have been funded by new loans and disposal proceeds. The size of the transfers between working cash, precautionary cash and opportunity cash is adjusted to leave the same closing balances for working and precautionary cash as before.

THE CALCULATION OF ESTA AND CUVI

The calculations of ESTA and CUVI are given in Tables 12.8 and 12.9 respectively. These calculations follow the methods introduced in Chapter 5. In Chapter 5, in order to simplify the calculations, required returns have been applied to closing balances rather than average balances. It should be noted that in Table 12.8 only the working cash is included in ESTA, precautionary cash is included in NVP and opportunity cash in GOV.

Table 12.8   The calculation of ESTA

	Year 1 £m	Year 2 £m
Fixed assets	60	70
Depreciation	(30)	(34)
Working cash	10	12
Other current assets	18	20
Loans	(20)	(25)
ESTA	38	43

Table 12.9   The calculation of CUVI

	Year 1 £m	Year 2 £m
Profit before tax	14.6	21.25
Adjust for 'one offs'		5
Sustainable		16.25
Tax (25%)	3.65	4.06
After tax	10.95	12.19
Return to ESTA (10%)	3.8	4.3
Residual income	7.15	7.89
CUVI (at 12% return)	59.58	65.75

THE 4 S COMPREHENSIVE ACCOUNTS

The 4S accounts of SMD are exhibited in Table 12.10. In Table 12.10, growth and opportunity value (GOV) is calculated as MC + NVP − ESTA − CUVI, giving for year 2, an opening balance of £30 m and a closing balance of £35.77 m. NVP has an opening balance of £8 m, being promises of £16 m less the precautionary cash of £8 m. Similarly, the closing balance is £11 m, being £22 m less the precautionary cash of £11 m.

Table 12.10   SMD 4S comprehensive accounts for year 2

	ESTA £m	CUVI £m	NVP £m	GOV £m	TOTAL £m
Opening balance	38	59.58	(8)	30	119.58
(1) Yield	4.3	7.89			12.19
(2) Transfer	7.89	(7.89)			
(3) Dividends	(8)				(8)
(4) One offs less tax	3.75				3.75
(5) Impairment	2			(2)	
(6) Promises charged	4		(4)		
(7) Revaluation			(4)		(4)
(8) Transfer		6.17		(6.17)	
(9) New expectations				10	10
(10) R and D	7			(7)	
(11) Cash transfer	(15.94)		5	10.94	
Closing balance	43	65.75	(11)	35.77	133.52

It should be noted that since SMD's fixed asset additions were not financed from equity they do not feature in Table 12.10 which shows changes in the value of equity. The additions do however appear in the cash management statement and they are discussed in the business review. It is instructive to go through the movements in each of the four slices since such an analysis forms the basis of the (4S) business review. The analysis for each of the slices is by reference to the rows, numbered (1) to (11) of Table 12.10.

For ESTA

(1) The opening balance is increased by the required return on the fund (the yield of £4.3 m, taken to be 10 per cent on the closing balance of £43 m).

(2) and (3) The yield on CUVI (£7.89 m) is transferred to ESTA and together the yields on the productive funds (ESTA and CUVI) cover the distributed dividend of £8 m.

(4) ESTA is increased by the 'one offs' less tax at 25 per cent. This comes to £3.75 m, being the profit on disposal of £7 m less the impairment of £2

m less tax of £1.25 m (being 25 per cent of 5). The 'one offs' less tax (£3.75 m) bring the yield (£4.3 m + £7.89 m) up to the reported net profit in Table 12.2 of £15.94 m.

(5) and (6) The impairment of £2 m and promises of £4 m, both of which have been charged in arriving at the net profit of £15.94 m (Table 12.2), are not a charge against ESTA but against GOV and NVP respectively, and accordingly are transferred out of ESTA to the funds in which they belong. It should be noted that tax effects have been dealt with through ESTA.

(10) Following the idea that R and D represents the expenditure of opportunity cash, then R and D is not a charge to ESTA but is an internal transfer within GOV. The opportunity cash within GOV is reduced by £7 m but the non-opportunity cash element within the fund, based upon prospects, benefits from the market's assessment of the future impact. Accordingly, the R and D expense is transferred out of ESTA to GOV. If only some of the R and D is regarded as opportunity taking (and the rest is maintaining the current competitive position) then this transfer would be restricted accordingly to the opportunity taking element. For example, it is plausible that the increase in R and D of £3 m would be regarded as opportunity taking.

(11) The cash in the ESTA fund at the end of the year which is not required as working cash is transferred out of ESTA to precautionary cash (£5 m) and opportunity cash (£10.94 m) as per Table 12.7, the cash management statement.

For CUVI

(1)The opening balance of £59.58 m is increased by the required return (£7.89 m) on the fund (the yield taken to be 12 per cent on the closing balance of £65.75 m).

(2) The yield is transferred to ESTA since all (retained) profit whether originating from traditional assets or intangibles ends up being invested in ESTA (the traditional assets). This is because accounting recognises the profits coming from unrecorded intangibles but not the intangibles themselves.

(8) The transfer of £6.17 m from GOV to CUVI represents the increase in CUVI during year 2 (Table 12.9). It is assumed that at the beginning of year 2, this prospective increase in CUVI was anticipated and formed part of end of year 1 GOV. Now that the prospective increase has been 'realised', it is transferred from GOV to CUVI. Explaining the increase in CUVI in terms of change in sales, margins and traditional assets is a key part of the business review.

For NVP

(6) and (7) The opening promise of £8 m is increased by the promises charged during the year (£4 m) and by the revaluation upwards (£4 m) of the legacy promises made in previous years. The revaluation of promises increases the promises balance but since it is charged directly to equity in the traditional accounts there is no adjustment of net profit in the ESTA column.

(11) There is an inward cash transfer of £5 m in order to achieve the level of precautionary cash considered necessary at the year end.

It should be noted that the promises payment of £2 m during year 2 is an internal transfer within the NVP fund. Precautionary cash is reduced but so are the outstanding promises within the NVP fund. Accordingly, the payment does not appear in the 4S accounts except in the accompanying cash management statement.

For GOV

(5) The impairment charge of £2 m is a charge to GOV since it relates to the (inadequacy of) future expected cash flows and is part of the assessment of the future.

(8) GOV is the capitalised value of expected future increases in residual income and £6.17 m is the capitalised value of the £0.74 m increase in residual income in year 2 from £7.15 m to £7.89 m (Table 12.9). It is assumed this increase was (correctly) anticipated at the beginning of year 2 and was therefore already recognised in the opening GOV.

(9) The increase of £10 m in GOV relates to new GOV, being the capital value of future increases in residual income which are recognised (for the

first time) at the end of year 2 and were not recognised at the beginning of the year. Assessing the new GOV in terms of the prospects for the business is a key part of the business review.

(10) The reduction of £7 m is the expenditure of opportunity cash on R and D.

(11) The increase of £10.94 m is the transfer in of opportunity cash from both ESTA and NVP where it is not considered to be required for working or precautionary purposes.

Section 3: The Business Review (Management Commentary)

The following paragraphs are a suggested wording for SMD management's business review for year 2. It is based upon the framework of the 4S accounts.

BUSINESS MODEL: STRATEGY AND STAKEHOLDER PROPOSITIONS

The product is specified to our customers in terms of delivery times, availability and range. On all of these criteria we aim to be the best in the market whilst remaining competitive on price. The strategy is one of operational excellence which we seek through expansion to benefit as many customers as possible. To achieve operational excellence all our stakeholders are engaged and aligned with the customer proposition. This is facilitated by our IT systems which support our costing, logistics and pricing models. These models are being constantly developed and improved. We develop our own IT systems wherever we consider that it is part of our competitive advantage. The four slices of equity are used in the performance evaluation stage of our business model to evaluate the performance of our strategy and its impact upon business value.

EQUITY STAKE IN TRADITIONAL ASSETS (ESTA)

This fund accounts for 32.2 per cent (31.8 per cent) of the total equity value of £133.52 m. It has increased by 13.2 per cent from £38 m to £43 m as a result of new investment and gives a yield of 10 per cent on its closing value of £43 m.

Since our traditional assets are largely in saleable stock and realisable depot sites, and we enjoy high levels of cover for our returns, we believe ESTA to be a low risk fund. Loans currently stand at 69.4 per cent of fixed assets, up slightly from 66.7 per cent last year. The yield on equity invested in traditional assets is 10 per cent compared to our average loan interest rate of 7.8 per cent. This gives a spread of 2.2 per cent in respect of the additional risk. The cover for the loan interest is approximately 10.3 times (excluding 'one off' income), indicating very little risk. The cover for the return on ESTA is 2.84 (12.19/4.3), comparable to the cover required by the market for 10 per cent loans.

The dividend of £8 m has increased by 60 per cent from last year and is well covered by the combined yields on ESTA and CUVI of £12.19 m.

We have invested £15 m in a new depot in Scotland in order to improve our geographical reach. At the same time a number of smaller depots in England have been shut and sold for proceeds of £10 m. This has given us a handsome profit on sale of £7 m since several of the sites were sought after by developers. The proceeds plus the increase in loans have funded the fixed asset additions.

As regards working capital, working cash increased by 20 per cent from £10 m to £12 m whilst sales only rose by 15 per cent. Management consider that the higher level of working cash is necessary to ensure that we meet our payments to suppliers on schedule (protecting supplier relationships). In particular, many of the builders' merchants who are our traditional 'customers' are now also delivering to our on-line customers on our behalf: to this extent, traditional customers are also operating as suppliers and become eligible for our supplier bonus based upon delivery performance. Cash needs to be held to meet these bonuses as they fall due. Current assets other than working cash have only increased by 11.1 per cent compared to sales at 15 per cent. Stock and debtors are under control for the moment. In respect of stock there has been a small but discernable change in the sales mix towards high turnover products.

CURRENT USE VALUE OF INTANGIBLES (CUVI)

This fund accounts for 49.2 per cent (49.8 per cent) of the total equity value. It has increased by 10.4 per cent to £65.75 m and gives a yield of 12 per cent on this closing value. The increase in CUVI based upon increasing sales and margins is evidence of our business model's success in leveraging intangibles. We have shown our ability to increase market share in a difficult market and believe that this points to a lower risk for our CUVI relative to the building supplies market as a whole.

The yield on equity invested in intangibles is 12 per cent, giving a 2 per cent spread over the yield on traditional assets in respect of the additional risk. Construction is a volatile market but we have shown ourselves to be resilient in the downturn due to the strength of our stakeholder propositions. We have a number of contracts that do present a risk in the event that our sales decline. Ten per cent of our purchases are on long-term supply contracts that protect us on price but expose us in the event of a drop in sales. It should be noted that we are committed to fixed interest payments on loans and that a drop in profit would also disproportionately impact on residual income since the return on ESTA must be met first.

The key intangible is our ability to deliver operational excellence on a consistent basis. The constituents of this capability are: (1) the engagement of customers through an attractive and clear customer proposition; (2) a set of stakeholders who are aligned and engaged with the customer proposition; and (3) computer systems that provide the necessary support. In addition to competitive prices, the attraction of the customer proposition rests upon prompt and reliable delivery. This in turn is facilitated by our systems and by our suppliers with whom we negotiate a performance bonus based upon delivery that is responsive to our needs. Committed and flexible employees are also essential and to demonstrate our commitment to them, after each five years of service, we pay an additional lump sum to the employee based upon the five year increase in CUVI.

We have approximately 23 per cent of the overall UK market and there are two other major suppliers with approximately the same share of the market as ourselves. The overall market is not growing due to the continuing recession in construction, but the three large players have continued to grow at the expense of smaller operators. What is remarkable about our performance is that we have been able to increase margins. Whilst sales have grown by 15 per cent, the cost of sales has only grown by 12.5 per cent. This is largely the result of the opening of a new web site – build direct – that sells directly to the public. This has been successful in attracting business, and, though we use our existing network of customers (builders' merchants) to deliver, we do make a bigger margin on web sales. This new line of business has in part been responsible for the increase in administration costs from £20 m to £25 m. Administration cost increases also reflect the increase in the bonuses of senior management resulting from this year's performance.

NET VALUE OF PROMISES (NVP)

This fund is negative and accounts for negative 8.2 per cent (6.7 per cent) of the total equity value. It has increased from a net liability of £8 m to a net liability of £11 m and relates to the promises made to employees in respect of the long-term rewards sharing plan. Since the plan is based upon long-term increases in CUVI, the plan does not open up equity to new risks and the increase in the liability reflects the success of our business.

After each five years of service an employee receives a bonus calculated on the basis of the increase in the CUVI fund during the five years. The service cost of this plan during the year was calculated as £4 m. In addition, previous service accumulated under the plan was revalued upwards by £4 m due to a lowering of expectations of staff turnover and increasing expectations regarding the growth of CUVI. Payments under the plan during the year were £2 m. The year end obligations under the plan increased by £6 m to £22 m against which the company holds £11 m of precautionary cash. In effect, the remaining liability (negative equity) of £11 m is invested in the business on behalf of the employees.

GROWTH AND OPPORTUNITY VALUE (GOV)

This fund accounts for 26.8 per cent (25 per cent) of total equity value. It has increased by 19.2 per cent to £35.77 m and is 54.4 per cent of CUVI. The fund includes £10.94 m of 'opportunity' cash and we consider that to be at an appropriate level. It is 1.56 times our annual R and D spend. At the year end, and prior to publication of the accounts, market capitalisation has increased by 11.7 per cent from £119.58 m to £133.52 m whilst the percentage distribution of this value across the four funds has remained substantially the same at 32.2/49.2/(8.2)/26.8 (last year 31.8/49.8/(6.7)/25). This reflects the consistency of both the business model and changes in market outlook.

Prior to release of the accounts, the market at the year end recognised new expectations with a value of £10 m, reflecting an improving outlook for the company. There is a reduction in GOV due to the increase in CUVI this year of £6.17 m. There is a further reduction of £2 m due to an impairment charge on goodwill. This relates to depots in the north east of England which has been particularly hit by the recession and for which little improvement is foreseen. We acquired them as part of our past acquisition of NE Building Supplies (see the development and financial pathway on page xx). We intend to hold these depots for now since we need national coverage but some rationalisation may be possible.

We believe our computer systems are already amongst the best in the business, not just in terms of ensuring delivery but in allowing us to cost and price products. We are now seeking to gain an even greater edge on our competitors by improving the service to customers still further, in particular that provided through our build direct platform. We have therefore spent £7 m on IT research and development, increasing expenditure on development and testing from 2 per cent to 3 per cent of turnover. No opportunity cash has been used to increase the capability of our fixed assets.

Cash of £10.94 m has been transferred into the fund from the ESTA and NVP funds and provides a year end opportunity cash balance of £10.94 m. We believe this balance is more than adequate to cover planned R and D expenditure whilst there is no planned expansion of fixed assets. We do not anticipate making any acquisitions.

Management consider that the total market in building supplies in the UK is unlikely to increase substantially in the near future but that there should not be any further fall. Future increases in residual income depend upon the three major players continuing to take market share from the smaller operators and upon the continuing growth in the direct sales market. There is little attraction in acquiring smaller UK competitors. There is little scope for acquisition overseas as we would have to acquire a major overseas operator to achieve the necessary scale and delivery capability in another country. However, it might be possible to sell IT expertise to our counterparts overseas and with this in mind we are planning to create a distinct IT division. For the moment, our target is to grow to one-third of the UK market based upon our current customer proposition and in particular the growth of on-line sales. This would represent an increase of 50 per cent in our business with modest need to invest in further capacity.

We are confident in our prediction that the UK market will not shrink further and that we can achieve our targets for growth.

Conclusion

This chapter has taken the reader through the process of preparing the 4S accounts from the traditional financial statements introduced in Chapter 2. The pedagogic case company, Systems Maximise Delivery (SMD), is somewhat more straightforward than many but covers the principal accounting entries involved. The chapter also presents a business review for SMD. The review starts with a brief discussion of strategy and stakeholders and then proceeds to discuss the impact on each of the four slices of equity in turn.

For ESTA the review provides discussion of:

1. The closing balance in relation to market capitalisation and in relation to the opening ESTA;

2. A discussion of yield (the required rate of return on ESTA), in relation to the risk profile of the fund including the fund's financial gearing;

3. The dividend;

4. The movement in fixed assets and loans along with the impact of the disposal;

5. The levels of working capital and working cash.

For CUVI the review provides discussion of:

1. The closing balance in relation to market capitalisation and in relation to the opening CUVI;

2. The yield in the context of the risk profile of the fund, including the fund's financial gearing;

3. The key intangibles and the role of the stakeholder propositions giving access to those intangibles;

4. The leverage of intangibles through increasing sales and margins, and new distribution channels, including an assessment of the market and market share;

5. The leverage of administration and other costs.

For NVP the review provides discussion of:

1.   The closing balance in relation to market capitalisation and in relation to the opening NVP, split between the promises and the precautionary cash;

2.   The risks inherent in the fund;

3.   The reasons for movement in the fund including: a) movements which impact on profit; and b) movements which impact on cash.

For GOV the review provides discussion of:

1.   The opening and closing balances in relation to the other slices of equity and market capitalisation;

2.   The new expectations and reasons therefore, together with the impact on GOV of changes in this year's CUVI;

3.   Expenditure of opportunity cash on opportunity taking through: (a) R and D; and (b) expanding the capabilities of fixed assets;

4.   Transfers into opportunity cash of cash not required by the other funds;

5.   The adequacy of closing opportunity cash to meet the company's future plans;

6.   An assessment of the closing GOV balance in the context of the future market and market share, including risks. This includes the status of the company as a conceptual company and the potential for further leverage of the intangibles.

13

Summary

This book provides a new accounting (4S accounting) based upon an understanding of business and accounting that comes from the coordination of three different representations of business – business as strategy, business as a stakeholder network and business as value. A second but important source of understanding that shapes the new accounting is the coordination of company accounts and the macro economy.

4S is Rooted in Networks

To achieve coordination between strategy and the business as a network, strategy is represented in terms of the leverage, engagement, alignment and development of the company's stakeholder network. The network is itself represented as a set of stakeholder propositions. To achieve coordination between the network and business value, the stakeholder propositions are in turn mapped onto equity value represented by four funds (or slices) of equity. The four slices of equity provide a new comprehensive balance sheet whilst movements within and between the four slices give the new comprehensive income. Accounting tells us where value lies whilst the coordination with strategy through the medium of the stakeholder network tells how that value is created. For accounting to play its feedback role effectively, then it must coordinate with both strategy and the stakeholder network.

The evaluation of the business provided by the accounting does not sit outside the business model but is integral to it and leads to the reshaping of the stakeholder network and possibly the strategy itself. Overall, the business model, being the articulation of how business is carried out, is represented by the mnemonic LEADERS. LEADERS stands for *leverage*, *engage*, *align*, *develop* (the strategic dimensions of the model), *evaluate* (the accounting dimension of the model) and on the basis of the evaluation, (re)shape (the stakeholder network). Thus the business model is not static but learns from experience.

Leverage of the network is achieved through increasing volumes and/ or margins. A particular focus is on the leverage of intangibles being both the knowledge and relationships within the network. Knowledge is defined broadly to include not only formal knowledge but skills, experience and capability. Stakeholder propositions are designed to achieve engagement and alignment and they include risk and reward sharing agreements that help to engage the stakeholders and bind the network together. Such agreements play an important role in the new economy where risks tend to be higher than in the old economy. Engagement is necessary to secure access to knowledge and capability; whilst alignment avoids inefficiency and ineffectiveness. Development of the network can take the form of new stakeholders giving access to new knowledge and/or building on the platform of knowledge already accessible to the network through existing stakeholders. The company makes available its fixed assets in order to provide productive capability to the network. It is therefore a stakeholder in its own network.

Management of the network is a key management skill. The selection, engagement and alignment of stakeholders depends upon: (1) the specification of the product to be provided; (2) the price and volume of the product; (3) the stakeholder knowledge and capabilities required; (4) the nature of the relationship with the stakeholder; (5) the contractual promises made to the stakeholder; and (6) prospects for the entity and its business model (based on non-contractual expectations). These same six dimensions apply to each stakeholder proposition although the importance of each dimension will vary depending upon the type and circumstances of the stakeholder. Accordingly, the six dimensions form the columns of the network as a whole, expressed as a grid whilst the rows of the grid represent the different stakeholders. Leverage and development of the network need to be in balance with engagement and alignment. If leverage and/or development are pushed too hard then there is a stakeholder risk of disengagement and misalignment.

4S and Traditional Accounts

Conventional accounting starts with definitions for assets and for liabilities and records them whenever they can be reliably measured. In practice, this excludes internally generated intangibles which are difficult to measure and consequently performance analysis based upon recorded assets (ROTA) or on recorded equity (ROE) is difficult to use in the new economy. Conventional accounting consists of a single fund of equity/assets – the balance sheet – but within this balance sheet some funded assets (and liabilities) are measured at cost and others at fair value (a mixed measurement approach). Effectively therefore, the balance sheet is a single fund but containing two sub funds corresponding to two measurement approaches. The movement in the single fund's equity is currently captured in a statement of comprehensive income which is subdivided into profit and other comprehensive income (OCI). However, this subdivision does not correspond to the two sub-funds within the balance sheet. For example the movement in un-hedged derivatives, which are accounted for at fair value in the balance sheet, are included in profit along with movements in the fund of assets measured at cost. This lack of correspondence, along with the absence of many intangible assets from the balance sheet, can make conventional accounts difficult to relate to any business model.

For 4S accounting the starting point is not the recognition of individual assets and liabilities but, in order to be comprehensive, the market capitalisation of the business as a whole. Market capitalisation is taken to be a surrogate for the value to the shareholders of their interest in the company's stakeholder network. It is the value of the promise made by the company to its shareholders and it is the combined value to shareholders of all the resources to which the network gives access. This value is inclusive of network assets irrespective of whether they are tangible or intangible, and irrespective of whether they are based upon current production or expected future performance. 4S accounting analyses or allocates the market capitalisation (equity) across four funds (the four slices of equity) representing: (1) traditional assets (fixed assets and working capital); (2) intangibles (valued in terms of their current contribution to profit); (3) promises; and (4) growth and opportunity value (future prospects). The four funds are referred to as ESTA, CUVI, NVP and GOV. Whilst ESTA and CUVI are rooted in the profitability of current production and therefore considered production capital, NVP and GOV derive their value from future expectations and are considered speculative capital.

To achieve coordination between the 4S accounting and the stakeholder network, the six dimensions of the stakeholder network are mapped onto the four slices of equity (the four funds). Price and volume drive an accounting profit which matches inputs with outputs. This accounting profit, if sustainable, underpins both the traditional assets (ESTA) and the value of the current contribution of intangibles to profit (CUVI). Promises, including the value of risk and reward sharing agreements, map onto the fund known as NVP whilst prospects map onto GOV.

The Four Slices of Equity

Each of the four funds represents a slice of equity backed by a particular asset type. ESTA is equity backed by traditional assets, CUVI by intangibles, NVP by contractual promises and GOV by the discounted value of future growth. More specifically:

> *ESTA* – the equity stake in traditional assets – is that slice of equity invested in the assets traditionally recognised in accounts (fixed assets plus working capital) in order to help provide the productive capability that facilitates the leverage of intangibles through the translation of knowledge into product. It is calculated as fixed assets plus working capital less loans used to finance the traditional assets. It does not include leased assets since leased assets do not require an equity stake. Leases are a commitment and the expected value of that commitment should be included in the value of contractual promises, which is a separate fund. Working capital and hence ESTA includes an element of cash (working cash) to meet the day-to-day operational cash requirements. The inclusion of ESTA as a separate fund in 4S accounting allows 4S to reconcile with traditional accounting which recognises the distinctive attributes of traditional tangible (and monetary) assets in terms of reliable measurement.

> *CUVI* – the current use value of intangibles – is that slice of equity invested in intangibles valued on the basis of their current contribution to (accounting) profit. The current contribution of intangibles to profit is residual income. The calculation of residual income requires a figure for the required rate of return on equity invested in traditional assets (ESTA). Residual profit (income) is what remains after subtracting from profit a return for ESTA. Tangible and intangible assets operating together generate profit. The return for ESTA is the contribution to profit of the traditional assets and hence the residual is taken to be the contribution to profit of the intangibles. This residual income is valued as a flow in perpetuity on the basis that current business conditions are sustainable and will persist. This capitalisation uses a required rate of return on equity invested in intangibles. It would be helpful if companies were

required to publish what they considered their required rates of return to be and to explain their thinking on this. Investors could then compare them with their own requirements.

NVP – the net value of promises – is the slice of equity invested in legacy promises valued at fair value net of cash or other assets set aside to meet the commitment. The defined benefit pension is a good illustration. At the time of the promise the expected value of the promise is charged as an expense since it is part of the cost of achieving engagement. However, the promise is a legacy and as expectations, for example, on longevity and asset returns change, then the legacy assumes a value which is the pension surplus or deficit. The value of the legacy (promise) is included in the NVP fund. It is included at the current expected value of the promises net of the current value of the assets set aside to meet the commitment. Promises are contracts and commitments and, as well as pensions, include warranties, deferred tax, fixed price contracts, stock options and other derivatives. Thus the NVP fund can be divided into a number of sub-funds corresponding to the different stakeholder promises. If the company directly indulges in speculation then the fair value of the speculative assets can be included as an additional sub-fund. Defined benefit pensions are rather different to most promises since in most other cases there is no *formal requirement* to set aside cash or assets to meet the promise when it falls due. Nevertheless, management will need to keep an element of cash or other liquid assets within the NVP fund to meet its promises. A value for each of the promises is, for the most part, available from the (fair) values reported in the conventional balance sheet.

GOV – growth and opportunity value – is the slice of equity represented by the value which the market, on the basis of market capitalisation, ascribes to growth and opportunities. CUVI is the value of intangibles assuming constant business conditions. Of course, business conditions are not constant and the market will value expected future changes in terms of the impact of future change on CUVI. Although it might also include expected changes in the value of NVP, in essence, GOV is the discounted value of the expected growth (or decline) in CUVI. It is calculated as a capital residual, being market capitalisation less the other three slices of equity (the value of the other three funds). In 4S accounting, impairments for traditional assets are not subtracted from ESTA but are dealt with as an adjustment within GOV. This is because both impairments and GOV are based upon an assessment of the future and therefore correspond to the same asset type. They belong in the same fund. Unlike conventional accounting this avoids the asymmetrical treatment of good news and bad news. The GOV fund should include an element of cash necessary to respond quickly to the opportunities that are expected.

Reducing the Disconnect Between Accounting and the Economy

The need to balance and rebalance the economy has come to the fore as a consequence of the 2008 financial crisis. The imbalance between consumption and production was a feature of the build up to the crisis and whilst the need to rebalance the economy post-crisis is well recognised, its achievement is proving difficult. 4S has been designed on the assumption that gains that follow production should be reported separately from gains that follow speculation and that only gains which follow production should be available for distribution as dividends, bonuses, excessive remuneration or indeed taxation. In other words, speculative gains should not be available for consumption but should be reinvested in production. In this way, the amounts which the company distributes for consumption are matched by the amounts the company has contributed to production.

ESTA and CUVI are considered production capital since they are underpinned by the profitability of current production. The yields on ESTA and on CUVI are available for distribution. NVP and GOV, however, are not grounded in current performance but in current expectations. NVP represents the impact of current expectations upon legacy promises, whilst GOV represents expected future changes in CUVI and promises. Being based upon expectations, NVP and GOV are considered speculative capital. When realised, gains in NVP and GOV are available for investment in productive assets.

Distribution of speculative gains has been a particular problem in relation to financial institutions, notably banks. A bank's productive capital only exists in respect of banking products, such as loans to business, which contribute to the productive economy. From a macroeconomic perspective, distribution of speculative gains can lead to consumption running ahead of production and cause the economy to become unbalanced. A financial institution can make profit in a number of ways. It can lend to productive businesses or to individuals for consumption. It can monetise or securitise such lending and take the capital value to the balance sheet and profit statement as did Enron. It can reassess the capital value and take the reassessment to profit as Enron also did, and it can earn fees in connection with capital creation and transformation. Only the lending to productive business is a productive activity. Lending to individuals for consumption can lead to an imbalanced economy and needs to be appropriately constrained. Monetisation/securitisation accelerates future profits and does not generate current production. Revaluation does much the same. The revaluation of a contract with a counterparty is a capital gain to one party and a capital loss to the other. The result is wealth transfer rather than wealth creation. Fees in connection with capital transactions do not contribute to any currently consumable product. They could be written off against distributable profit by the payer but that would be inappropriate as such fees would be a capital expense.

Single fund performance measures such as return on equity, return on capital employed and earnings per share based upon traditional accounts struggle to cope in an environment where intangibles and promises play an important role. Indeed, performance measures based upon return on capital are liable to push an economy towards services and, whilst services do constitute production, they may be more difficult to export in volume than physical products, potentially leading to balance of payments issues. Performance is judged by 4S not in terms of returns but in terms of capital growth with the growth in productive capital and speculative capital separately identified. If one is growing much faster than the other as was the case in the run up to the crisis, then that is a warning signal. Consequently, under 4S there is an incentive for companies, even those specialising in intangibles, to do their own physical production providing it earns a profit, even if the returns from physical production are lower than the returns achieved on intangibles such as research, design and marketing. These profits from physical production might be seen as part of the leverage of its intangibles and a logical extension of a strategy based upon leverage. The company may still have an incentive to perform its own production in a cheaper economy. This is not a problem provided that exchange rates, living standards and regulatory requirements adjust to maintain global trade in balance. However, these sources of adjustment may not be adequate to maintain global trade in balance if different economies are fixed on different performance measures. Arguably, an economy where companies and investors are fixed on maximising returns will lose out to an economy that focuses on maximising productive capital. There has been too little attention given to the role of accounting and accounting-based performance measures in the performance and management of the economy both at a global and national level. This remains an area for further thought.

So what should the new financial reporting look like?

Chapter 12 gave a straight forward illustration. Comprehensive accounts are divided into four sections showing movements within and between the four slices of equity. Impairments are charged through the 'prospects' section and legacy movements in promises through the 'promises' section. The business review connects the four funds and their (relative) movements to both strategy and the stakeholder network. Traditional 'one fund' performance measures such as return on capital and earnings per share are irrelevant. A cash management statement replaces the traditional cash flow statement.

The cash management statement reflects the three motives for holding cash (and other realisable non-operating assets). These motives are for working capital (ESTA), precautionary capital (NVP) and opportunity capital (GOV). Management hold cash as liquidity for each of these funds. The first section of the new cash management statement includes the opening cash held for working capital, the cash flow from operations and the closing cash required for working capital, with any balances transferred to/from precautionary cash. The second section includes the opening cash held for precautionary purposes, the cash flow from the liquidation of legacy promises, transfers to/from working capital and the required closing cash for precautionary purposes with the balance transferred to opportunity cash. The third section deals with opportunity cash, including the opening balance, transfers in, loans received and repaid and the funding of opportunities including fixed assets purchase and research and development. The business review assesses the adequacy of the cash balances.

There are other substantial implications for current accounting standards and practices, notably in respect of accounting for business combinations and leases. With regard to an acquisition, the user needs to see how much of the change in each of the four funds has been purchased as a result of the acquisition. Upon an acquisition, the price paid should be distributed across the four funds acquired and these funds proportionally consolidated with the existing equivalent funds of the acquirer. There is no goodwill, no impairment testing of goodwill and no minority interest. It might be possible to treat all equity investments in a similar manner since 4S is concerned with where the value lies (that is, in which type of fund) and is not directly concerned with control or ownership. The implication of 4S for leases is that they need not be capitalised since there is no equity funding of leased assets and what is needed is to account for the equity stake in the network. Nevertheless, leases like loans and long-term fixed price commitments are an important part of the analysis of risk in the business review.

Overall, the potential impact of 4S on current accounting is considerable whilst 4S gives the business review a new direction.

Learning from Enron and the 2008 Crisis

Nearly every major challenge that accounting faces today can be seen in the 2001 Enron saga. Enron and its management were widely lauded as having transformed an old economy utility company dominated by plant and equipment, into a market-maker resembling a Wall Street bank; so much so that the demise of Enron should have signalled concerns for the future of Wall Street itself! The deficiencies in accounting highlighted by Enron include: (1) a lack of focus on the performance of intangibles; (2) no coupling of performance in the form of accounting profit with risk; (3) no clear reporting of the impact of legacy promises; and (4) no clear demarcation between current performance and future potential. Removing these deficiencies forms an important part of the challenge which 4S accounting is designed to meet. It is argued that conventional accounting has learned little from the Enron case or from the 2008 crisis. A step change in the profession's thinking is needed.

4S – A Step Change

For the profession of accounting, 4S accounting challenges much of conventional accounting and current accounting standards, including the treatment of leases, acquisitions, intangibles, impairments, derivatives, hedging and earnings per share through to the principles of profit recognition and the presentation of cash flow, profit, comprehensive income and segmental performance. In 4S a single fund (the balance sheet) is replaced by four separate funds that analyse market capitalisation. 4S embraces fair value accounting but through a separate fund from the equity stake in the traditional assets (being fixed assets and working capital).

For the analyst, 4S challenges a traditional accounting-based analysis of performance through return on equity, return on capital employed, financial (old economy) gearing and the leverage of fixed assets together with the use of liquidity ratios. These are replaced with an assessment of: (1) the leverage of intangibles; (2) financialisation; and (3) liquidity, through an analysis of movements within and between each of the four funds corresponding to the four slices of equity. The leverage of intangibles is associated with the relationship between ESTA and CUVI (new economy gearing). Although ESTA and NVP can play a part, financialisation is associated with the relationship between CUVI and GOV (future economy gearing). The focus of 4S financial analysis is on both the change in size and the change in composition (value profile) of the market capitalisation.

For the fund manager, 4S accounting allows the manager to manage the value profile (ESTA/CUVI/NVP/GOV) of an equity portfolio so as to match the requirements of the fund in terms of productive and speculative capital.

For the business manager, 4S sees business as a reshaping set of stakeholder propositions that form the network, giving access to stakeholder knowledge. Knowledge is defined broadly to include formal knowledge, skills, experience and capability. The company itself is one such stakeholder. Risk and reward sharing promises to stakeholders are included in the stakeholder propositions in order to bind and align the network. Strategy relates to the leverage and development of the network. Under this approach, strategy co-develops with 4S accounting so that the four funds coordinate with the rest of the business model.

For the financial sector, 4S accounting highlights the financialisation that occurred prior to the 2008 financial crisis due to the failure of accounting to distinguish between gains that were in the nature of speculative gains and gains from the yield on productive capital that could be justified as the basis for distribution. Financialisation caused the reported profits and balance sheets of banks to rise faster than the real economy which banks are there to serve through the provision of capital. This proved unsustainable. A lesson from the crisis for both accounting and economic management is the need to restrict distribution for consumption to the realities of the productive economy.

For the auditor, the four funds corresponding to the four slices of equity have different risk and 'auditability' characteristics from each other. At one end of the scale ESTA is relatively risk free and auditable, whilst GOV is at the other end of the scale. This sets up the possibility of a four part audit report in which the auditor takes a different level of responsibility for each of the funds. 4S also lends itself to business risk auditing since business risk can be understood through the coordination of business risk: (1) as strategic risk; (2) as stakeholder (network) risk; and (3) as the risk attaching to business value. Thus the understanding of business risk mirrors the understanding of the business itself which comes through the coordination of strategy, the stakeholder network and value as represented by the 4S accounts.

For the economy, the distinction between productive gains and speculative gains, with absolute productive gains providing the basis of a new performance measure, gives the incentives and motivation for both the rebalancing and growth of the economy. Traditional 'one fund' measures of performance such as return on capital and earnings per share are redundant. It should be recognised that when an economy, such as the one in the UK, consistently fails to provide growth and production it is necessary to look carefully at the incentives, such as management remuneration plans, that motivate the system. Performance measures are not neutral but in fact influence the type of economy that is created. 4S provides the basis of new thinking on the importance and design of performance measures in the economic system.

To conclude, the proposed accounting model – four slice (4S) accounting – through the coordination of accounting, strategy and stakeholders allows managers and shareholders to analyse the effectiveness of the business model and therefore for management to be held to account. The proposal prevents the misreporting of speculative gains as distributable income and therefore allows capital to be better allocated towards productive enterprise. This helps to both avoid and respond to financial crises such as that in 2008. Since the generation of equity value between production and speculation is clearly signalled, 4S provides the basis for new thinking on performance measures that coordinate the motivation of company management (the management proposition) with the well-being of the economy. Accounting and the economy are mutually dependent on each other. Without effective accounting, economic resources will be misdirected. Without appropriate economic management, interest and asset prices will be misleading and accounting will be unreliable.

Bibliography

Alfredson, K. 2001. Accounting for identifiable intangibles – an unfinished standard-setting task. *Australian Accounting Review*, 11(2), 12–22.

Armitage, S. and Marston, C. 2008. Corporate disclosure, cost of capital and reputation: evidence from finance directors. *British Accounting Review*, 40(4), 314–36.

Beattie, E. 2009. Don't blame the accountants. *Accountancy*, 143(1390), 38–9.

Bingham, C.B. and Eisenhardt, K.M. 2008. Position, leverage and opportunity: a typology of strategic logics linking resources with competitive advantage. *Managerial and Decision Economics*, 29, 241–56.

Caglio, C. and Ditillo, A. 2008. A review and discussion of management control in inter-firm relationships: achievements and future directions. *Accounting, Organizations and Society*, 33(7–8), 865–98.

Callon, M. 2008. Economic markets and the rise of interactive agencements: from prosthetic agencies to habilitated agencies, in *Living in a Material World*, edited by Pinch, T. and R. Swedberg, Cambridge, Mass: MIT Press, 29–56.

Collis, D.J. and Montgomery, C.A. 1995. Competing on resources. *Harvard Business Review*, 73(4), 118–28.

Croda, 2007. *Annual Report & Accounts 2006*. Goole, East Yorkshire: Croda International.

Dahmash, F.N., Durand, R.B. and Watson, J. 2009. The value relevance and reliability of reported goodwill and identifiable intangible assets. *British Accounting Review*, 41(2), 120–137.

DMGT, 2006. *Annual Report and Accounts 1st October 2006*. London: DMGT.

Doz, Y.L. and Hamel, G. 1998. *Alliance Advantage: The Art of creating Value through Partnering*. Boston: Harvard Business School Press.

Edvinsson, L. and Malone, M.S. 1997. *Intellectual Capital*. New York: Harper Business.

Eisenhardt, K.M. and Martin, J.A. 2000. Dynamic capabilities: what are they? *Strategic Management Journal*, 21(10–11), 1105–21.

Elliott, L. and Atkinson, D. 2008. *The Gods that Failed: How Blind Faith in Markets Cost us our Future*. London: The Bodley Head.

Enron, 1999. *Enron Annual Report 1999*. [Online]. Available at: http://picker.uchicago.edu/Enron/EnronAnnualReport1999.pdf [accessed: 12 August 2012].

Felsted, A. 2004. Canny hedging gives Rexam 14% profits rise. *The Financial Times*, 26 August 2004, 22.

FKI, 2007. *FKI plc Annual report 2007*, Loughborough: FKI.

Goold, M., Campbell, A. and Alexander, M. 1994. *Corporate Level Strategy: Creating Value in the Multi-business Company*. New York: Wiley.

Greenspan, A. 2007. *The Age of Turbulence*. London: Penguin.

Fusaro, P.C. and Miller, R.M. 2002. *What Went Wrong at Enron: Everyone's Guide to the Largest Bankruptcy in US History*. Hoboken, New Jersey: Wiley.

Hall, J. 2011. Tesco radically overhauls top executive pay. *The Daily Telegraph*, 1 June 2011, B3.

Halma, 2007. *Annual Report and Accounts 2007*. Amersham: Halma.

Hamilton, S. and Francis, I. 2003. *The Enron Collapse*, European case clearing house: Case no IMD-1-0195.

Hansen, M.H., Perry, L.T. and Reese, C.S. 2004. A Bayesian operationalization of the resource-based view. *Strategic Management Journal*, 25, 1279–95.

Hatherly, D. 2003. Auditing after Enron: reshaping the investor information value chain. *The General Journal of Management*, 28(3), 29–42.

Hatherly, D. and Kretzschmar, G. 2011. Capital and income financialization: Accounting for the 2008 financial crisis. *Accounting Forum*, 35(4), 209–16.

Heilpern, E., Haslam, C. and Andersson, T. 2009. When it comes to the crunch: What are the drivers of the current banking crisis? *Accounting Forum*, 33(2), 99–113.

Hicks, J.R. 1946. *Value and Capital: An Inquiry into some Fundamental Principles of Economic Theory*. Oxford: Clarendon.

Holland, J. 2004. *Corporate Intangibles, Value Relevance and Disclosure Content*. Edinburgh: The Institute of Chartered Accountants of Scotland.

Holland, J. 2006. *A Model of Corporate Financial Communications*. Edinburgh: Institute of Chartered Accountants of Scotland.

Hope, J. and Hope, T. 1997. *Competing in the Third Wave: The Ten Key Management Issues of the Information Age*. Boston: Harvard Business School Press.

Hutchins, E. 1995. *Cognition in the Wild*. Boston: MIT Press.

Jack, A. 2008. Industry's prescription changes in the search for value. *The Financial Times*, 22 April 2008, 26

Kaplan, R.S. and Norton, D.P. 1992. The Balanced Scorecard. *Harvard Business Review*, 70(1), 71–9.

Kaplan, R.S. and Norton, D.P. 2004. Measuring the strategic readiness of intangibles. *Harvard Business Review*, February, 52–63.

Kay, J. 1993. *Foundations of Corporate Success: How Business Strategies Add Value.* Oxford: Oxford University Press

Krippner, G.R. (2005). The financialization of the American economy. *Socio-Economic Review*, 3(2), 173–208.

Lafond, R. and Watts, R.L. 2008. The information role of conservatism. *The Accounting Review*, 83(2), 447–78.

Latour, B. 1995. Cogito ergo sumus! Or psychology swept inside out by the fresh air of the upper deck … A Review of Ed Hutchins Cognition in the Wild. *Mind, Culture and Activity: An International Journal*, 3(1), 54–63.

Lev, B. 2001. *Intangibles, Management, Measurement and Reporting.* Washington DC: The Brookings Institute.

Lev, B., 2007. *The Conceptual Company Risks and Rewards.* Unpublished presentation.

Lev, B., Nissim, D. and Thomas, J. 2007. On the informational usefulness of R&D capitalization and amortization, in *Visualising Intangibles*, edited by S. Zambon and G. Marzo, Farnham: Ashgate, 97–128.

Lev, B., Radhakrishnan, S. and Zhang, W. 2009. Organization Capital. *Abacus: A Journal of Accounting, Finance and Business Studies*, 45(3), 275–98.

Levinthal, D.A. and March, J.G. 1993. The myopia of learning. *Strategic Management Journal*, 14, 95–112.

Macintosh, N.B. 1994. *Management Accounting and Control Systems.* Chichester: Wiley.

Melrose, 2010. *Melrose plc Annual Report 2009.* London: Melrose.

Miller,P., Kurunmaki, L. and O'Leary, T. 2008. Accounting, hybrids and the management of risk. *Accounting, Organizations and Society*, 33(7–8), 942–67.

Mouritsen, J., Hansen, A. and Hansen, C. 2001. Inter-organizational controls and organizational competencies: episodes around target cost management/ functional analysis and open book accounting. *Management Accounting Research*, 12, 221–44.

Neely, A., Adams, C. and Kennerley, M. 2002. *The Performance Prism: The Scorecard for Measuring and Managing Business Success.* London: FT Prentice Hall.

Ohlson, J. 1995. Earnings, Book Values and Dividends in Equity Valuation. *Contemporary Accounting Research*, 11(2), 661–87.

Penman, S.H. 2004. *Financial Statement Analysis and Security Valuation*, 2nd Edition. New York: McGraw-Hill.

Penman, S.H. 2007a. Financial reporting quality: is fair value a plus or a minus? *Accounting and Business Research, International Accounting Policy Forum*, 37 (Supp 1), 33–44.

Penman, S.H. 2007b. *Financial Statement Analysis and Security Valuation.* 3rd Edition. New York: McGraw-Hill.

Pfeffer, J. and Salancik, G.R. 1978. *The External Control of Organizations: A Resource Dependence Perspective.* New York: Harper and Row.

Porter, M.E. 1996. What is strategy? *Harvard Business Review*, 74(6), 61–78.

Prahalad, C.K. and Hamel, G. 1990. The core competence of the corporation. *Harvard Business Review*, May–June, 79–90.

Rivkin, J.W. 2000. Imitation of complex strategies. *Management Science*, 46, 824–44.

Roberts, P.W. and Eisenhardt, K.M. 2003. Austrian insights on strategic organization: from market insights to implications for firms. *Strategic Organization*, 1(3), 345–52.

Rolls Royce, 2008. *2007 Preliminary Results Press Release.* [Online]. Available at: http://www.rolls-royce.com/Images/prelim07pr_tcm92-5654.pdf [accessed: 4 June 2012].

Siggelkow, N. 2002. Evolution toward fit. *Administrative Science Quarterly*, 47, 125–59.

Simons, R. 1995. *Levers of Control: How Managers Use Innovative Control Systems to Drive Strategic Renewal.* Boston: Harvard Business School Press.

Skinner, D.J. 2008. Accounting for intangibles – a critical review of policy recommendations. *Accounting and Business Research, International Accounting Policy Forum*, 38(3), 191–204.

Stewart, T.A. 2001. *The Wealth of Knowledge.* London: Nicholas Brearley.

Stiukova, L., Unerman, J. and Guthrie, J. 2008. Corporate reporting of intellectual capital: evidence from UK companies. *British Accounting Review*, 40(4), 297–313.

Sveiby, K.E. 1997. *The New Organisational Wealth – Managing and Measuring Knowledge-based Assets*, San Francisco: Berrett-Koehler.

Taleb, N.N. 2008. *The Black Swan: The Impact of the Highly Improbable.* London: Penguin.

Treacy, M. and Wiersema, F., 1996. *Discipline of Market Leaders: Choose your Customers, Narrow your Focus, Dominate your Market.* London: HarperCollins.

Turner, 2009. *The Turner Review: A Regulatory Response to the Global Banking Crisis* (Lord Adair Turner, Chair). London: Financial Services Authority.

Tushman, M.L. and O'Reilly III, C.A. 2002. *Winning Through Innovation: A Practical Guide to Leading Organizational Change and Renewal.* Boston: Harvard Business School Press.

UBS, 2007. *Financial Reporting for Investors*. UBS Valuation and Accounting. London: UBS, 16 April, 2007.

Viedma Marti, J.M. 2001. ICBS Intellectual benchmarking system. *Journal of Intellectual Capital*, 2(2), 148–64.

Viedma Marti, J.M. 2007. In search of intellectual capital comprehensive theory. *Electronic Journal of Knowledge Management*, 5(2), 245–56.

Volberda, H.W. and Baden-Fuller, C. 2003. Strategy renewal processes in multi-unit firms: generic journeys of change, in *Strategy Process: Shaping the contours of the field*, edited by B. Chakravarthy et al., Blackwell, 208–32.

Wang, C.L. and Ahmed, P.K. 2007. Dynamic capabilities: a review and research agenda. *International Journal of Management Reviews*, 9(1), 31–51.

Widener, S.K. 2007. An empirical analysis of the levers of control framework. *Accounting, Organizations and Society*, 32(7–8), 757–88.

Zeghal, D. and Maaloul, A. 2011. The accounting treatment of intangibles: A critical view of the literature. *Accounting Forum*, 35(4), 262–74.

Index

If you have found this book useful you may be interested in other titles from Gower

Inside Accounting:
The Sociology of Financial Reporting and Auditing
David Leung
Hardback: 978-1-4094-2049-1
e-book: 978-1-4094-2050-7

The Rise and Fall of Management:
A Brief History of Practice, Theory and Context
Gordon Pearson
Hardback: 978-0-566-08976-3
Paperback: 978-1-4094-4829-7
e-book: 978-0-566-08977-0

Integral Economics:
Releasing the Economic Genius of Your Society
Ronnie Lessem and Alexander Schieffer
Hardback: 978-0-566-09247-3
e-book: 978-0-566-09248-0

GOWER

**The Road to Co-operation:
Escaping the Bottom Line**
Gordon Pearson
Hardback: 978-1-4094-3202-9
Paperback: 978-1-4094-4830-3
e-book: 978-1-4094-3203-6

**A Social Critique of Corporate Reporting:
Semiotics and Web-based Integrated Reporting**
David Crowther
Hardback: 978-1-4094-4188-5
e-book: 978-1-4094-4189-2

**Territories of Social Responsibility:
Opening the Research and Policy Agenda**
Edited by
Patricia Almeida Ashley and David Crowther
Hardback: 978-1-4094-4852-5
e-book: 978-1-4094-4853-2

Visit **www.gowerpublishing.com** and

- search the entire catalogue of Gower books in print
- order titles online at 10% discount
- take advantage of special offers
- sign up for our monthly e-mail update service
- download free sample chapters from all recent titles
- download or order our catalogue